I'M A JOKE *AND SO ARE YOU*

'Clever, funny, kind and interesting – just like Robin.'

Sara Pascoe – comedian and author of *Animal*

'Profound, compassionate, eye-wateringly funny and immensely human. Robin investigates the big questions of the human condition with the razor-sharp insights and sensibilities of one of our very best stand-up comedians.'

Alan Moore – author of *V for Vendetta*

About the Author

Robin Ince is co-presenter of the award-winning BBC Radio 4 show, *The Infinite Monkey Cage*. He has won the *Time Out* Award for Outstanding Achievement in Comedy, was nominated for a British Comedy Award for Best Live show, and has won three Chortle Awards. He has toured his stand up across the world from Oslo to LA to Sydney, both solo and with his radio double act partner, Professor Brian Cox. He is the radio critic for the *Big Issue* and appears weekly on Steve Lamacq's show on BBC Radio 6 Music.

I'M A JOKE
AND SO ARE YOU

A Comedian's Take on What
Makes Us Human

Robin Ince

Atlantic Books
London

First published in hardback and airside trade paperback in Great Britain
in 2018 by Atlantic Books, an imprint of Atlantic Books Ltd.

1 2 3 4 5 6 7 8 9

A CIP catalogue record for this book is available from the British Library.

Internal illustrations © Sophie Richardson (www.studiosophie.co.uk)
Photograph on page 43 courtesy MRC London Institute of Medical Sciences
Photograph on page 85 copyright © David M. Bennett/Getty Images Europe

Trade Paperback ISBN: 978 1 78649 259 3
EBook ISBN: 978 1 78649 260 9
Hardback ISBN: 978 1 78649 258 6

Printed and bound by CPI Group (UK) Ltd, Croydon, CR0 4YY
Atlantic Books
An Imprint of Atlantic Books Ltd
Ormond House
26–27 Boswell Street
London
WC1N 3JZ

www.atlantic-books.co.uk

To Nicki and Archie,
who, in the words of Guy N Smith, have to 'put up with it all'
and to Barry Crimmins, an inspiration who used his voice
to make sure so many others were heard.

Contents

The moment a man questions the meaning and value of his life, he is sick . . . By asking this question one is merely admitting to a store of unsatisfied libido to which something else must have happened, a kind of fermentation leading to sadness and depression.

Sigmund Freud

The problem with Freud is that he never had to play the Glasgow Empire.

Ken Dodd

All Mimophants Now!

I n the otherwise thoroughly well-observed television drama series about 1950s American stand-up, *The Marvellous Mrs Maisel*, the titular character's first three spots, which wow jaded late night audiences at the Gaslight Café, are all the result of her turning up drunk and angry and impulsively storming the stage to riff in perfectly constructed sentences about the domestic injustices currently tormenting her.

The series contrives to give the impression that great stand-up routines are conceived on the hoof, in a booze or drugs haze, rather then as a result of endless hours of soul-searching, honing phrases and reaching for just the right word. I am sure lots of stand-ups have found themselves the worse for wear at least once at some late-night club gig where they improvised in the moment a bit that went on to redefine the direction their work was taking. (Mine was at The Classic in Auckland, New Zealand at about 4 a.m. in April 2005.) But a real-life Mrs Maisel would not have flounced into the world fully formed. We all know this, and so does Robin Ince.

I have, I suddenly realize, known Robin Ince for three fifths of my life, and most of the time I have spent talking to him was backstage, in bars near venues, or on shared rides ferrying us between underpaid 1990s gigs in far-flung locations. Nearly thirty years ago now, as we crossed the storm-tossed Severn Bridge in the small hours in a spluttering Austin Maxi, the delightful older comic driving us explained to me the that the weather conditions did not bother her as she was being looked after by her Native American spirit guide, who was sitting between us on the front seat.

I looked into the rear-view mirror and saw Robin raise a quizzical eyebrow as we tightened out seatbelts and settled in for the ride of a lifetime. I knew that both of us were thinking the same thing: what qualifications has a nineteenth-century nomad, perhaps only familiar with horse travel, that enable him to supervise late twentieth-century motor transport? And wouldn't you, if you were the ghost survivor of a genocidally exterminated indigenous culture, use the car as a weapon to take out as many of your oppressors' people as possible? It's moments like this that seal bonds that last a lifetime.

Ince's subtly significant influence on the trajectory of the better parts of British stand-up over the last few decades has been taken for granted. The resolutely anti-mainstream stand-up salons he began to run at the turn of the century gave a generation of left-field acts, me included, a safe space to experiment, and the connections he made in large-scale shows between comedy and the worlds of politics, philosophy and science went on to be commercially exploited by less scrupulous talents who declined to credit him for his innovations. Remove the jenga brick of Robin Ince from the foundations of the tower of the last few decades of British live comedy and it suddenly would start to look a bit wobbly. *I'm A Joke And So Are You* bequeaths us all the benefit of his experience.

This deceptively deep book is an invaluable and inspiring effort, worthy to sit on a shelf alongside other classics of stand-up comedy analysis, such as Stewart Lee's *How I Escaped My Certain Fate*, or *If Your Prefer A Milder Comedian Please Ask For One*, by Stewart Lee, or Syd Little's *Little By Little*. But it is also much more than that.

Taking the way stand-up comedy routines are crafted and the mindsets of the people who make them as his starting point, Ince swiftly swoops out into wider consciousness, attempting to analyse and anatomize the very essence of how imagination works, where creative ideas come from, and what conscious and subconscious processes the human mind engages in when it chooses to try to surprise itself with notions it never knew it was capable of.

Truth seekers from all walks of life will find it inspiring and illuminating, even if they are not stand-up aficionados already aware of the works of Sofie Hagen, Paul Chowdhry, Josie Long, Nina Conti, Noel Fielding, Jason Cook, Lenny Henry and Felicity Ward, who are all interviewed within, alongside a host of scientists, psychologists, cultural commentators and an astral-projecting occultist who worships a snake god.

A few years ago, I seem to remember, Robin Ince interviewed me at length for this book. And yet none of my comments appear in it. There is, however, a lengthy section of quotes from an interview with Ricky Gervais, a man whose stand-up is essentially a copy of mine, stripped of nuance, and performed by a comic who doesn't really understand it, and yet is paid literally tens of millions of dollars more than me for his ersatz version of my act, by a network which describes me as 'too parochial'.

I discovered Robin Ince had declined to use any of our interview in his book when he asked me to read it in advance of publication, with a view to furnishing him with an introduction. I have now completed this introduction despite being in dreadful agony due to a repetitive strain injury caused by the angle at which I have been gripping the mic stand with my tension-racked left hand for two and a half hours a night over two hundred and fifty dates of my recently completed eighteen-month tour.

Even as I type this sentence I am aware that merely raising my left hand to the keyboard causes terrible endless spasms of pain to shoot down my left side, numbing my shoulder and neck. Robin Ince has suffered for his art, and so have his audiences, and today I am suffering for Robin Ince's art too. Now, gentle reader, it's your turn.

Stewart Lee, writer/clown, Stoke Newington/Camden, June 2018

PS: Ince's book also includes, amongst a list of abandoned notes on scraps of paper he never developed into routines, the phrase 'All Mimophants Now!', surely a title Mark E. Smith of The Fall would have got around to using, had he lived long enough to see the publication of this book.

Shouting at Strangers for Money

I'm an insect who dreamt he was a man and loved it. But
now the dream is over . . . and the insect is awake.

The Fly by Seth Brundle

efore I began this book I thought I should 'check my privilege'. Then I thought, 'Why am I checking my *own* privilege? Why hasn't the publisher employed someone to do it
for me?'

The weight of my privilege requires excess baggage allowance.

I am a straight, white, middle-class male who has never had
to fight in a war, is not trusted to repair anything that is electrical or might splinter, and has never had to manhandle a plough
or turn the handle on a mangle. I am in a very small minority of
world citizens.

My childhood lacked severe beatings, and the smacked bottoms
I did receive were lacklustre, my parents having tired themselves

out on my far naughtier older sisters. I was also the youngest of three and the only boy, so I was considered best, which is of course true. In this book I will occasionally write about my misguided miserabilism and slumping into the doldrums, but be aware that I am neither seeking your pity nor worthy of it. If you find yourself thinking: I believe this writer is trying to engender a sense of 'pity me', then I am probably attempting to say, *I was an idiot* or *I am an idiot* or *I will be an idiot again.*

I am aware of my absurdity. I am a fool, on- and offstage. I think it is a pity that the entire human race has not been able to accept how silly it is and has not then got on with living ridiculously, but also more kindly and helpfully. It is dangerous to take yourself seriously. Only a few changes in your gene sequence and you are sitting in a tyre, hurling poo at a tourist. And perhaps for some it may not even require that change in gene sequence . . .

Our desperation to feel a sense of superiority over others means that we often don't notice the big strip of toilet paper stuck to the sole of our shoe as we walk across the room. It is when we take ourselves too seriously that the cracks begin to widen. For this reason, there is nothing I enjoy more than seeing a dictator slipping in dog shit. Sadly, dictators usually have the means to erase all evidence that they did so, by shooting the dog, destroying the shoe and murdering all the spectators. The colonel who innocently commented on there being 'a bit of a funny smell in the war room' is later found shot seventeen times in the head after having overzealously committed suicide.

To be self-conscious is to be aware of the perpetual possibility of being ridiculous. If you are not ridiculous right at this moment, then don't worry – you'll be ridiculous when you turn that corner and collide with a lamp post. So it's human nature to do all that is possible to avoid public derision and lamp posts. Who wants to have hiccups in the 'quiet carriage' of the train, or accidentally slip and fall into the open grave at their aunt's funeral? Though those who have called their teacher 'Mummy' are many, it does not lighten the sting of the blush. Many of the psychological problems of our existence come from our fear of being seen to be ridiculous. The effort of keeping ourselves together is often what pulls us apart.

There is one group of people who go out of their way to highlight their own absurdities, weaknesses and ridiculousness, and then shout about it for profit and in the name of art. Those people are comedians.

This is why comedians can be seen as so peculiar; it's as if they are deliberately going out of their way to potentially embarrass themselves. And yet revealing your stupidity for all the world to see could be said to be an intrinsic part of what it means to be a complete and psychologically healthy human being. This is why I love Laurel and Hardy, and I am more likely to trust people who love them, too. You can read academic psychology books on what it is to be human, or you can watch Stan and Ollie in *The Music Box*. I think all of us should spend more time trying to deliver pianos up steep hills and stairs. The trouble with Camus's *The Myth of Sisyphus* is that there's just not enough slapstick. The question of whether to live or die is written all over Ollie's face as that piano lands on his toe again.

I am fortunate in that I have had just enough peculiar thoughts to be able to fashion them into a career as a comedian, but not so many that I have had to be incarcerated. I have always thought of myself as a weirdo. In most rooms, train carriages and municipal parks I always imagine that anyone who notices me is thinking: Sheesh, that guy is a bit of a freak.

Perhaps because of this, even my wife has remarked on my ability to look out of place in all public situations. And perhaps that is why I became a comedian. With that level of paranoia, standing up in front of strangers and emptying out the contents of my head, for them to pick over and laugh at, was the obvious choice of career.

Comedy had been a childhood obsession. Robin Williams, The Goodies, Rik Mayall, Laurel and Hardy – these were the people who made life worth living for me. Aged nine, I would crouch next to the television, holding a tape recorder beside the speaker, capturing the sounds of my favourite comedy shows, but mainly gathering the noise of my own high-pitched, zealous giggling.

Aged fourteen, I started keeping secret notebooks with ideas for jokes. Aged eighteen, I did my first gig. Aged twenty-three, stand-up comedy became my full-time job. I have been professionally absurd for a quarter of a century. I have taken being an idiot very seriously.

I have been fascinated too by both the onstage and offstage personas of comedians. I have loved reading about their real-life tribulations, depressions and doldrums almost as much as I have liked watching their work.

Being a comedian meant that, with scant permission from a room full (or not so full) of people, I could scream and gurn and roll around on the floor, twist myself into unseemly shapes and mime legal and illegal acts. Then I would be given money

– sometimes coins on the night and sometimes a cheque twelve months later, once the booking agent had accrued enough interest to keep himself flush in silver cigar-cutters and nasal fancies. Sometimes I would be rewarded handsomely, sometimes scarcely – and sometimes I would be asked to do all these things for free. What could be better than having permission to be ridiculous, yet appreciated? What could be worse than being ridiculous, only to be ignored or scorned? That was the now-nightly gamble I took. Triumphant, shameful or mediocre – what would it be this time?

What *did* seem clear to me, though, was that I had become part of a mythical group that I had been obsessing about relentlessly. Comedians were not like the others. Comedians do not think or live like 'you'. The comedian is better than you, because he is in a long line of alcoholic, tearful misanthropes, who shine brightly in the spotlight and then lurk silently in the darkness, cursing the very audience they have come to please. Finally I could be privately miserable for professional reasons.

I was pretty certain on what I thought I knew about comedians – I'd read the biographies and seen the documentaries. Typically, the comedian's childhood is confused, laced with a lack of love or an oversupply of death. They can give love to a crowd, but they fail to share it with an individual for any meaningful period of time. When they get drunk, it's not like your stupid, pointless boozing on a Friday night because the weekend is here. Comedians drink because of the terrible poetry in their minds that must be silenced. They are sometimes drunk on a Tuesday, and when people see them in their dusty coats – hunched, snoring and dribbling onto their shoes as the train carriage runs over the points – they think: What a very noble figure of a human. That drool shines with a depth of meaning and melancholy. Tragically, they will almost certainly die before you, and before their time; Peter Sellers, John Candy, Peter Cook, John Belushi, Rik Mayall, Chris Farley, Mitch Hedberg, to name just a few.

But when all is said and done, don't you know people who are often drunk, have a predilection for feeling down in the dumps shortly after being boisterous and joyous, might have seen divorce or death close up as a child and yet live their life as a postman or computer programmer? Spike Milligan, who suffered from mental breakdowns throughout his comedy career, did not think comedians were more likely to be depressives – he just thought that depressive episodes show up more in a comedian, like a black ink stain on a white shirt or an archbishop on a tricycle. If all the people who could tick two of the categories of 'what makes a comedian special' became comedians, there would be no one left to form the audience. The world would reverberate to the phrase 'Have you heard the one about . . .', but no one would be listening. But as Penn Jillette of the revelatory conjuring duo Penn & Teller says:

> The same pain, the same suffering . . . the same tortures, the same doubts, the same misery are all there. In *show* business you show what you're feeling. So yes, they show the angst, but they're showing the angst of humanity. The angst that we all share. If you had a comic that truly had experiences that were outside the realm of the general humanity, no one would go see them.[1]

So perhaps in the end the only difference between comedians and other, quieter human beings is that comedians like to shout about their fury, unhappiness, delight and frustration, while the rest keep a lid on such feelings and experiences, sharing them only with their nearest and dearest – or, as it all crumbles around them, with their therapist. And could this reserve be a useful trait? For perhaps it is only by noticing and drawing on the absurdist and surreal that we can see the conflicts, incidents and coincidences that make all human beings such a curious and special species?

So I decided that I wanted to see whether the world could learn anything from comedians – their lives, their performances – by looking at why they do what they do, but also by asking whether all the clichés about comedians are really just that, clichés, and whether science and psychology can prove that comedians are, in the end, just like anybody else.

This book is my attempt to answer those questions, with each chapter looking broadly at a different aspect of how being a stand-up intersects with the psychology of life, and hopefully drawing out what we all can learn from comedy and comedians. I've talked to a lot of other comedians about what makes them tick, and to a lot of psychologists and scientists about how their study of humour, laughter, madness and sanity – their understanding of what it is to be human – can help us all as we navigate our way through life. Despite appearances, this has not merely been driven by the urge to get free sessions with psychotherapists, under the guise of writing a book.

What I also hope may come from this book is the realization that far more of us are madder than we thought. In fact so many of us are secretly mad that it may turn out that we're sane, and it's just that sanity is wonkier than we thought it was meant to be. Once we can be aware of that, then perhaps we can live with our hidden eccentricities, safe in the knowledge that many other minds contain absurd trains of thought. Imagine a world where we were so fearless that when someone said, 'Hey, what you thinking?', you had the confidence to say exactly what that was. 'I was just imagining what would happen if I licked all the statues in the National Gallery.'

Alternatively, I might discover that rather than Broadway, my career goal should have been Broadmoor after all.

CHAPTER 1

Tell Me About Your Childhood

When we were growing up, we were so poor that we couldn't afford any clothes, so we had to stay in the house. But my dad saved up and saved up, and finally, on my fifth birthday, he bought me a hat, so at least I could look out of the window.

Les Dawson

I was worried about becoming a parent. As someone who ruminates too much, the potential to get it wrong seemed daunting, and the number of ways of getting it wrong seemed myriad. I would lie in bed at night, wondering if it was best that I died in my sleep and my child never knew me. If my heart gave out from an undiagnosed inherited fault, it might save everyone a lot of bother and hopelessness. The child would be brought up with a memory and rumour of me that would be more satisfactory than the clumsy living reality.

These thoughts vanished from the moment my son mewled into the world. Within the first month of his life, the weight of responsibility for trying to turn him into a good human transformed into a jagged stormcloud of abject horror. A question reared up in my head, 'What would be my one mistake in bringing him up that would turn him into a mass-murdering serial killer?'

I imagined that day in the police cells, after he'd been arrested for killing, cooking and eating thirty different strangers from Bruges.

'Oh, Son, why did you kill, cook and eat all of those people?' I'd ask.

He would look at me and say, 'Don't you remember, Father?'

And I'd shake my head.

'It was that day on the beach. Chesil Beach, I think. There was a sudden gust of wind and I dropped my Strawberry Mivvi and it landed in the shingle. And you shouted at me, even though it was not my fault . . . And from that point onwards, I KNEW I'D KILL!'

In the last hundred years there has been a great deal of research in neuroscience, psychology and genetics into why we are the people and personalities that we are. Such research, which shines a light on both the intrinsic make-up of our brains and bodies and on our childhood experiences, can be incredibly valuable in understanding why we end up doing the things we do – whether it's working as a hairdresser, killing Belgians or becoming a stand-up comedian.

*

Fortunately, I was unhappy as a child. This has made it a lot easier to make the transition to stand-up comedy. I am sure I wasn't unhappy all the time, but the romantic memories of sitting alone, the outsider, in a graveyard, thinking about poetry have usurped the delightful nostalgic memories of larking about in woods and playing Horror Top Trumps.

If I think hard, there definitely are some good moments I can recall, such as the time I poured fruit punch into the hair of Tom Simpson, a boy who had made my life unpleasant at the school bus stop. The sugary punch attracted insects to his scalp, and it ended up becoming an unbearably itchy entomological menagerie. Happy days!

The biographical details of childhood can rarely be ignored these days, and it's the rise of psychotherapy and neuroscience that has made our childhood inescapable. We've all been given an alibi for our lousy behaviour.

'Don't blame me – my parents fed me my pet rabbit when I was four. They left the ears sticking out of the pie, that's why I've smashed all your collectible Beatrix Potter figurines with my hammer.'

We've read the childcare books and the memoirs, and we know that somewhere there is a childhood event that has doomed us.

It would be easiest to identify what such an event was, if it was one nice and neat, tumultuous emotional catastrophe that led in a direct line to a desperate need for public acclaim or just acceptance. Has your whole life turned out this way because of the day you wet yourself in art class and had to wear a pair of replacement pink frilly pants? And sometimes there really is just one such event. Alexei Sayle told me about the old saying, 'Show me a comedian and I'll show you someone who lost their father when they were eleven.'

Amongst contemporary comedians the most well-known example of bereavement being linked to creativity is Eddie Izzard. Eddie's mother died from cancer when he was just six years old. He believes that everything in his life has been about getting over that; it is where his comedy comes from. His analysis of his situation is that his audience acts as a surrogate affection-machine to replace his mother. Izzard has repeatedly spoken about the effect of the sudden loss of all the affection his mother provided, and his belief that it is linked to his desire to perform and achieve. 'I know why I'm doing this. Everything I do in life is trying to get her back. I think if I do enough things . . . then maybe she will come back.'[1] His drive to do twenty-seven marathons in twenty-seven days, to learn to do his stand-up shows in fluent French, German and Russian, his political ambitions – for Eddie, all this has been a direct result of losing love so young. I think it is a convincing theory.

Comedian Paul Chowdhry, who – like Eddie – has built himself up to arena comedian without using the regular mass-media route, lost his mother when he was five years old. 'You don't quite understand it when you're five, the only things you see are superheroes who have lost a parent and become a superhero. But that doesn't help a child. When you're five, you don't get it, you think they'll come back.'[2]

Comedy guru Barry Cryer lost his father in the war. Over a pint, he once told me that he never knew his father nor anything about him. With post-war stoicism and the muffling of grief, his mother never spoke of him. The only conversation he ever had with anyone about his father was at a Freemasons' event that he'd been hired to talk at many years later. A Mason asked if Barry was one of the brotherhood and Barry was then regaled with stories of his father's time in the Masons. I wanted to ask him how much he felt the loss of his father may have contributed to his desire to perform, but then I thought, 'He's got to eighty years old and without spending too long on the psychiatrist's couch. Why ruin it all now?' We had another beer instead. Eric Idle's father survived the war. But on his way home, with all the trains full, he hitch-hiked instead. He was killed in a car accident on Christmas Eve. Eric's brilliantly vicious festive song 'Fuck Christmas' is a far more haunting melody since I read this story.

Death and childhood bereavement aren't the only life experiences that a psychoanalyst would have a field day with, when examining what it is that may make a comedian tick. Neither of Richard Pryor's parents died at war, but he had an unusual upbringing nonetheless. His father was a pimp who was prone to violence, and Richard lived in the brothel where his mother worked and which his grandmother, his primary carer, ran. His mother was nearly beaten to death by his father and she left Pryor when he was five years old.

Lenny Bruce's parents divorced when he was five and he was shunted around different relatives during his childhood. Alexei Sayle mentions itinerancy as a possible springboard to showing off. He says that a sizeable proportion of the comedians he worked with at The Comic Strip were 'army brats'. Jennifer Saunders, Adrian Edmondson, Rik Mayall, Keith Allen, Dawn French and Rowland Rivron all had parents with some service-based itinerancy. Peter Cook saw little of his father, as he was away in Africa for the Colonial Service. Cook recalled that his father used to receive the news six months after it was published. 'It went to Africa by boat, then up the river. He'd then open up *The Times* and exclaim, "Good God! Worcester are seventy-eight for six!!"'[3]

Certainly, if you are moving school and location with frequency, then 'Ta-dah' – you have to keep making an impression on your new classmates in a desperate attempt to make new friends, so jokes and larks it has to be.

I only changed school once between the ages of five and thirteen, but that was bad enough. I was having a lovely time at the local village school, but when I was eight I was upgraded to a fee-paying preparatory school, to be moulded and prepared for a lifetime's sense of superiority. That's when it went downhill rapidly. I didn't even know I was odd until then. I automatically turned from being a normal boy with a normal group of friends into someone who seemed to be carrying a contagious disease, as, it appeared, were all of the other late entries. The playground was a contamination pit. You could get 'Calvert disease', 'Hagyard disease' or 'Ince disease'. Newcomers were outsiders, treated in much the same way that white blood cells would treat new bacteria. A few other rejected boys had been there longer and were no longer highly infectious, merely kept at a distance, as one was overweight and the other ran in a 'funny manner'. But was this enough of a traumatic experience to set me off on a completely different course from the one I would otherwise have pursued? I don't think so.

*

'Attachment theory' developed out of the horrors of the Second World War, when psychologists in the US and Western Europe began to study those people who had suffered loss or trauma in their very early childhood. Psychoanalyst John Bowlby, who had himself suffered an absent father during the First World War, was one of the leading proponents of the theory – one of the main tenets of which was that, in early infancy and child-hood, in order to build a strong and stable personality, a child must have had at least one committed, stable and loving primary caregiver. Recent studies by psychologist Sue Gerhardt seem to suggest that even what takes place during the first few hours and days of a child's life can have an adverse affect on their attach-ment profile.

Adoption can occur in very different circumstances, but can lead to attachment issues and is often said to impact heavily on a child's understanding of the world and the people around him or her; indeed, therapists have to undergo special training even to speak to an adopted person, so complex are the potential issues involved. At least eight comedians that I have worked with were adopted, including Stewart Lee, Mark Steel, Robert Newman and Rhona Cameron.

Some of them found out they were adopted when they were quite young, while others didn't discover this until well into their teenage years. Some of them have gone on to use their experi-ences as an adopted child as material for their shows, whilst others have brushed over it, giving it little meaning at all.

Jo Brand believes, though, that there is a statistical over-representation of comedians who were adopted and of those who lost a parent when very young. She believes that 'those sort of huge, catastrophic incidents in your early life do not bode well for your future mental health'.[4]

Mark Steel was brought up in a working-class family in one of Kent's less impressive towns. In middle age he found out that his biological father was a card-playing companion of the notorious Lord Lucan and of gambling wildlife park entrepreneur John Aspinall. Steel has discussed adoption with other adopted comedians and has concluded that 'We've all come to live with it. I don't think any of us are in a state about it. I never felt like an outsider.'[5] His conclusion is that the experience of adoption and grief is not rare, and yet most people who experience these things early in life will not decide to become comedians. Equally, I'd say that there are many who do not experience such things and do become wildly successful comics.

Perhaps I needed to look elsewhere for the childhood comedic impetus? Kurt Vonnegut suggested that the youngest child in any family was always a joke-maker, 'because a joke is the only way he can enter into an adult conversation'.[6] Straw-polling a group of fourteen comedian compatriots, I found that eight were the youngest in the family, two were only children (which technically makes them the youngest), three were the oldest child and only one was the middle child. The middle child was Matt Parker, a stand-up mathematician, so I am sure he would tell me that such a small sampling risks being statistically irrelevant. One of the youngest was a twin and was only the youngest by an hour, but I reckon that still counts for my bias. In my unscientific trial, it seems there was an element of truth in Vonnegut's words. But looking at the work of the comedians polled, I am unable to draw any conclusions on how their family positioning affected their level of funniness or success. I have certainly laughed as much at one of the eldest-child comedians, Mark Thomas, as I have at most of the youngest. Thank heavens he doesn't have the extra privilege of being last from the womb or I would have found it even harder to follow him at the benefit night in the Red Rose Comedy Club.

And as I ponder these various childhood experiences that have stimulated or influenced comedic greatness, I wonder how – if at all – I fit into any of these groups? I am not adopted. I did not lose a parent in childhood. My parents weren't in the army and, as far as I know, my grandmother wasn't a pimp for my mum or for anyone else. But I am the youngest of three. Though I have grown up to be the biggest show-off of the three, I was the least outwardly confident in the family. I was highly strung, volatile, shy and likely to become visibly upset if I didn't win Pass the Parcel at my own birthday party. I was the babyish baby brother.

I do have a 'traumatic event' filed in my memory-card box, though, but even now I wonder if it was traumatic enough to count as trauma, and I feel a certain embarrassment at bringing it up at all.

It was late winter and dark. My sister had been riding a pony with her friend, and she and I were both in the back seat of the car, with my mum driving the short distance to our home. I was searching for my machine gun, my favourite toy, under the passenger seat. It had a handle on the side and it made a rat-a-tat-tat sound when you turned it.

I don't remember the moment of collision, but I presume there was a thud and a jolt. Everything stopped and was quiet, and then the sobbing started. I was two years old – though I was a grown-up three-year-old in my mind, as my birthday was only a week away. I know this because there was going to be a party, and Mum had planned the cake. It was my sister who was sobbing. Her head had struck the right-side passenger window and was bleeding. Another car had been on the wrong side of the road, hurrying to get home. His impatience changed everything.

Mum was motionless in the driving seat, head up, eyes shut.

I can still see it all clearly. Though I am aware my memory may have changed the details with each revisit, the stillness of her face is consistent.

I remember saying, 'Why's Mummy's eyes closed?'

My sister didn't say anything. She was seven. Time moves differently when you're two. It's much bigger then, and there is more room to play in it. Such long afternoons up trees. My mother's stillness dominated everything. Although I could still see her face clearly, I couldn't see the damage done.

The rest is collage and jumpcuts.

One woman ran from her car with a toilet roll, to stem the flow of blood from my sister's head. She was quite a big lady, who looked kind. My dad had been following us in his car and this was the one piece of good fortune in all the bad luck, as it undoubtedly saved my mother's life. He persuaded the ambulance driver that the local hospital did not have the facilities to deal with Mum's injuries and that she must be taken somewhere better equipped. Later on, the medical people would say it was this act of furious persuasion that saved her life.

We are all unreliable narrators of our past. My injured sister, Sarah, remembers it slightly differently. She saw more than me because she was sitting up rather than searching for a plastic gun. She saw the lights of the car coming straight at us. She believes she was too shocked to cry, as she noticed the stickiness of the blood in her hair. She remembers the police asking where our shoes were, because they had apparently come off our feet due to the force of the impact. She, too, remembers our mother's stillness. My eldest sister was home alone, waiting for *Top of the Pops* to begin, when the police arrived, so she never got to see Marc Bolan singing 'Telegram Sam'.

What I recall most viscerally is the knowledge that it was all my fault. This had happened because I was looking for my toy machine gun. Somehow, that had caused the crash. If I hadn't been squatting behind the passenger seat looking for that gun . . . ? I knew people would be very cross with me. I had caused a lot of trouble. I was taken in the second ambulance, then sat alone in a hospital corridor. Collected by the friends who owned the pony, I was put straight to bed until my other, undamaged sister explained that I had had no supper, and then I was brought downstairs again to eat soup or spaghetti shapes. Something red anyway.

When was I going to be told off? It never happened, but I didn't see my mother for some time. She was still in a coma on my birthday.

We had a party anyway, but the cake was bought from a shop.

During this period an older woman in tweed was employed to look after us. She was no Disney Mary Poppins, and she forced me to sit on a potty, even though I had a painful boil on my bottom. I cried and cried and cried. My sisters rebelled, as they would again and again, and fought against the beastliness that was being inflicted on their little brother, then ran away in protest with their anoraks and biscuits.

After the protest, a kinder woman in tweed replaced the anti-Poppins, and Mum eventually came home.

Her jaw was held together by screws, and she didn't know who that boy or his sisters were. She had woken up in a time before any of us existed. I have very few memories of those days when she first left hospital, and perhaps that's just as well. The cover-up of the situation was done very proficiently by the grown-ups. Eventually Mum's memory caught up with reality and then life went on, though not in the same way it would have done if someone hadn't been on the wrong side of the road at the wrong speed. Not a bad life, just a changed future.

That is my creation story. If I want to thank or blame one incident for why I am what I am, I choose that one. With time, its magnitude seems to have increased and its ability to explain many things has become greater. But I don't know how much importance it really has in the tale of an idiot's progress.

During that stage of a child's brain development, how much effect does blaming yourself for a traumatic car crash have? What does the confusion around a mother being in a coma do to the child? My 'make-do-and-mend' mentality, nurtured by watching Sunday-afternoon British war films on telly as a child, says, 'Forget it all, just keep moving on', but the boy in the library is filled with questions.

As I have grown distant from the event, it seems that I can see it more clearly for what it was and what it might be. I do not see what happened as an excuse for what I am, but I slice into it forensically, wondering what it did to me.

Like so many events in our lives, all the raking over will only lead to 'maybes' and vague ideas concerning the probability of outcomes. When I asked Essi Viding, Professor of Developmental Psychopathology at University College London, about the possible effects, she told me, 'Although we can say with confidence that any big trauma typically impacts the individual experiencing it, I think it would be difficult to say with certainty how precisely the event you describe would affect a child and shape his development.' She explained that the impact of such an event can vary enormously from one individual to the next, depending on their predisposition, as well as the life events that follow the trauma. Although Professor Viding thought that comedy may have been a critical outlet following trauma, she is also aware that cannot be said conclusively, for it perches in the category of 'reasonable hypothesis'.

Now middle-aged, I still try and pick apart the effect that event could have had on my young mind – the neural connections that were made that day, when I thought I had caused a terrible catastrophe, and then the confusing guilt-ridden years that followed.

As human beings as much as comedians, we all have a repertoire, a few core bits of material that become our regular anecdotal routines. As we retell them, how much further away do they get from the now-forgotten reality? The neuroscientist Dean Burnett explained that memories such as this could be described as a 'flashbulb memory'. The most important events in our life create more and more links in our brain, so that they become easier to retrieve. The flashbulb memory is attached to traumatic events. It is a survival strategy. The adrenaline released at the time of the event helps keep everything more vivid in the future, and hopefully it helps us avoid traumatic situations as well. You won't find me looking for my toy machine gun in the back seat of the car any more, I promise you. I learnt my lesson there.

The importance of schooldays frequently looms large among those comedians who turn to jokes as a form of defence or acceptance, such as those 'army brat' children, and then make those punchlines into a career.

You don't have to feel like an outsider to become a comedian, but it can help. It's easier to focus on being creative if you are not preoccupied with socializing with popular people. Sitting on the edge is a better spot from which to observe than being hugged in the middle.

I was fortunate in this respect. Firstly, I wore glasses. My prescription arrived just as Elvis Costello made his debut on *Top of the Pops*, so in addition to 'speccy four-eyes', a chorus of 'Oliver's Army' would frequently greet my entrances and exits into the classroom.

Secondly, I joined the school much later than most of the other pupils, hence my earlier mention of being an outsider and feeling as unwanted as an infectious disease.

Thirdly, I had the sort of dimpled chest that meant I looked as if I had small breasts. (I know you are wondering just how many advantages one child can have, when it comes to placing petals on the pathway to being a comedian?)

I was around eight years old when I experienced the dawning self-realization of the freakery of my flesh. This was presumptive of me, as neuroscientist Sarah-Jayne Blakemore, an expert on the teenage brain, believes that the acutely self-conscious phase really kicks in at eleven. I can content myself with the knowledge that I have always been ahead of the curve in such matters.

My fleshy chest caused me acute embarrassment in PE, when I was in the team that would be marked out by not wearing tops (skins). I would try and conceal my 'breasts' by keeping my arms crossed at all times, though this severely hindered dodging in dodgeball, and pretty much ruled out any activity that required a modicum of balance. If only I could have uncrossed my arms, I could have been a gold-medal gymnast.

This noxious horror remained with me long enough for it to be recycled, eighteen years later, into a five-minute stand-up routine involving my breasts, a macabre sex-change revenge story, and the punchline 'my sister's cock'. This was my most popular punchline when I went to entertain the troops in Bosnia. What had made my stomach ache with anxiety, for most of my school life, was now turned into a revenge drama in which I was victorious over those boys who had maximized the hellishness of existence. You just don't get as much material if schooldays are the happiest of your life.

At times I had tried to fit in, but – to my relief, in hindsight – I never managed to run with the pack. If I had, I most certainly would only have ended up with a stitch. As I was unable to fight my corner physically, the speed at which I could use words was my right jab. It wasn't a swollen eye they gave; it was the ability to bruise an ego, which would lead to you having a bruised eye, but also the vestiges of some sort of bloody-nosed dignity. Quite often I would say nothing, but never fear – I was scripting ripostes in my head, for a 'what might have been' universe.

Leaving my school for the final time on the bus, I had a horrific thought: 'What if schooldays really are the best days of your life?' Within weeks, would my memories have rewritten those years as relentless jolly japes? Fortunately, my rose-tinted spectacles fell into the toilet the last time my head was shoved in it, and I have never hankered for my mythical past. Being bullied at school is a mainstay in the 'shortcut to reasons people became comedians' list. But does bullying turn you into who you are or does it simply speed up the working-out of who you are? If you are quirky, offbeat, unusual or just different, then you may only come to realize that you have such a difference when you are thrown mercilessly into a crowd, and the tribe hostilely shows its suspicion for any such lack of conformity.

'Did you tell jokes as a way to deflect the bullying?'

'No, I think it was the jokes that started the bullying in the first place.'

What came first: the punchline or the head in the puddle?

Joking about your own ineptitude is an attempt to create some kind of control as you sit in a puddle surrounded by aggressors screaming furiously, 'You've just lost us the game.' A study from Keele University, though, suggests that joking at your own failure may not be helpful. It studied more than 1,200 children between eleven and thirteen years old and their ways of joking, and found that the so-called class clown can heighten his or her status with what is known as 'affiliative humour'. This is where a child who already feels they are of a lower status uses self-defeating humour that relies on mocking themselves. In an attempt to have some sense of control over the mockery, they show that they are quite aware of their own feebleness and so they may even instigate self-mockery, thus pre-empting the bullies. In stand-up, this is seen when a comedian hastily makes a mention of some idiosyncrasy concerning their appearance when they reach the microphone. If you have made a fat-joke about yourself, the heckler's shout of 'You fat bastard!' is made impotent. This won't stop a bullish or inattentive heckler, and should they continue shouting out about the comic's weight, they may find out that it is because every time the comic has sex with the heckler's mother, she gives him a biscuit. (I first heard the comedian Andre Vincent deal with a fattist heckler with this line, so I will credit him with its creation, but the patent of a heckle put-down is much-fought-over territory.)

Other types of humour that the Keele study described were 'aggressive', with the use of jokes to attack others; and 'self-enhancing', where jokes were seen as reducing anxiety by encouraging laughter at things that were in reality quite frightening. Dr Kate Fox stated that the study showed that humour plays an important role in how children interact with each other, but that using humour to make fun of yourself makes you prone to more bullying. In such situations children try to take control of the situation with self-mockery, which only increases their susceptibility to bullying. So as you up the self-mockery, the next thing you know, you are touring small-town art centres and appearing on radio panel shows. If I had kept to my earlier plan of punching people through the cheek with an ink pen, this would never have happened.

But despite being a highly strung child and being moved to a school where I discovered that I was both odd and infectious, by the time I was twelve I had still only stabbed two people – Adrian Chorley in the cheek with an ink pen, and Robert Boughton in the hand with a craft knife. I am quite sure both were accidents, and

I haven't stabbed anyone else since then. Were my short-tempered outbursts a result of having been in the car accident, being the youngest of three or some other forgotten minor trauma of my youth? Or was it just common-or-garden bloodlust? Was I simply on the path towards being a serial killer, as both my sisters used to taunt me – and way before it was fashionable?

When I asked the Jungian analyst Andrew Samuels what he thought of people using a single incident to justify or explain their ensuing life, he answered me brusquely. 'This is the kind of turgid rubbish that drives me nuts. Comedians are artists. You wouldn't talk about an artist like that . . . People's motivations just don't work like that . . . I would be more comfortable with a comedian who just said, "I haven't got a clue, it's just what I'm supposed to do, but I don't know why."'

One night in a bar I was with a group of comedians, digging through our miserable pasts in jocular fashion, when the youngest comic there suddenly became furious.

She was affronted. She had had a lovely childhood, no beatings, bereavement or bullying and she felt that, in a roundabout way, we were saying she couldn't be as funny as the rest of us. We explained that we were toying with ideas for drunken psychotherapy fun, and we were not suggesting that infantile melancholy was something to judge the quality of your jokes by. If it was, then every comedian would footnote each joke with 'And that punchline stems from the day I was pushed out of a treehouse by a Mother Superior', and then the audience would laugh even more, as they shrieked excitedly, 'It comes from her pain, it comes from her pain.' Equally, others might say, 'I went to see a comedian the other day; he seemed quite funny, but I had a nagging suspicion that he was happy, so that spoilt it a bit.'

The comedian's sad childhood may be a pleasing story for the public, but not all comedians fit the bill. The comedian, author and *I'm a Celebrity . . . Get Me Out of Here* survivor Jenny Eclair has said that it wasn't the misery of her childhood that made her a comedian, but the wonderfulness of it. She hoped that by making a career in nonsense and delight, she could rekindle the nonsense and delight of her youth. International surrealist Noel Fielding told me he had a childhood of joy and encouragement from hip young parents. His art was not an act of rebellion; he fell into art because his talent was encouraged. Meanwhile, when I asked international absurdist Ross Noble if he had anything to say on the matter, he explained that he had very little time for the inspection of doomed childhoods to find artistic inspiration. Ross just wanted to have fun, and he also comes from a happy family of encouragement.

But Eddie Pepitone fits the bill, if you want your analyst's couch to be dented by the expected level of neuroticism that a comedian should exhibit.

'I've screamed onstage for thirty years, it's hard for me to connect with anyone, but through comedy I've built a life,' says Eddie.[7] Pepitone is an actor and comedian, born in Brooklyn, but now based in Los Angeles. He is a comedian that all the other comics love watching. Watching Eddie perform, you know that he has to be onstage. It is a volatile and hilarious scream at and about his life, his insecurities and the injustices of the world, both personal and political.

He has a tempestuous relationship with his father. They share a similar volatility. For much of Eddie's childhood, his mother battled with mental health issues and was eventually diagnosed with manic depression, now called bipolar disorder. He remains furious over his relationship with his mother and her mental illness. Eddie felt his mother wasn't really there, and that is where much of his anger came from. He believes that the attention he missed from his mother is why he has spent so much of his life asking for attention onstage. When we talked, he told me, 'All of it just breaks my heart. And it's the reason I'm a comedian. Because, the only way to deal with that is either kill yourself or . . .'

He finds it amazing that he has been screaming onstage for so long. He says that he has only recently learnt that he doesn't need to scream. 'I've had all this pent-up rage in me, and comedy has been the way for me to express that rage through a socially acceptable manner – in my case, barely. In some parts of America, people aren't used to seeing such raw emotion.'

The surprise of greater age is the discovery that most of us don't become adults and ditch the fear of our parents' judgement. Eddie is amazed at how much fear and desire to please his father he still has left in him. Some days he wakes up and wonders why he hasn't called his father for a while, and then he realizes it is because he is scared that he will become antagonistic and will reawaken his father's disapproval. 'I'll say something, he's very sensitive to tone and he'll call me up on the tone of my voice and that will then trigger me.' Eddie realizes this is behaviour that was established when he was very small.

I understand his fear of judgement. It is easier to risk the judgement of strangers on a nightly basis than risk disappointing your parents just once. I didn't let my parents come and see any of my shows for the first fifteen years of my stand-up career. My dad getting Google Alerts was what began to make my elusiveness no longer an option.

Jerry Seinfeld describes that strange moment when a grown-up person quakes at being observed doing stand-up in front of their parents. 'I was so nervous that night because I was showing them this whole side of myself. It was like my little gay closet moment. I had to say, "Hey, Mom, Dad, I don't know how to tell you this – I'm a funny person and I don't want to be ashamed of it any more. I want to lead a funny lifestyle now."'[8]

It was while supporting Ricky Gervais at the London Palladium that I thought, 'If I can't let them see me play the Palladium, then when can I?'

My worry trebled, the night I knew they were in the audience for the first time. I scoured my set list for jokes that I should remove, ideas that I was happy to voice with strangers, but horrified to share with my parents. My dad's general judgement now on most of the things he has seen or heard on TV or radio involving me is that the show was terrible, but I was the least-bad thing on it. He prefers my later work.

Eddie Pepitone remains livid, though he is getting used to who he is. His stand-up is still an exorcism of all the rage absorbed from his father. There is a beautiful moment towards the end of his documentary, *The Bitter Buddha*: his dad hasn't seen him work in ten years, but Eddie is returning to New York to do a headline set, and his dad will be there. Despite only living a few miles from Manhattan, his father hasn't ventured into the city for seven years. Eddie is a ball of anxiety. The audience loves him, though, the show goes brilliantly and, after wrapping it up, with the crowd going wild, Eddie walks straight up to his dad. The pride is clearly visible in his dad's eyes. His son has killed – and on home turf, too. 'You had them eating out of your hand. Any fucking thing you said, they were rolling in the aisles.' It's as if everything has been building up to this moment, and all Eddie's work was for this instant.

So does the bullying that I was on the receiving end of, or the crash, or fear of judgement, or any other significant early event in my life explain my seeking the nightly approbation of strangers? Like Andrew Samuels, I can't see how, and yet if that is the case, perhaps my desire for such acclaim is just something I was born with? And so to that age-old question: nature or nurture? Is your destiny defined as you emerge screaming from the womb, or will it take a series of unfortunate events before the age of seven to turn you into the mess you are now?

For a while, scientists declared that we were born as a blank slate. Since then, the amount of information on that slate has been aggressively debated, though it is unlikely we will ever return to the idea of us having a totally clean slate from birth. Some of our ghastly foibles may be foretold in our genome, but does that leave us predestined, whatever the chaos or kindness in our life? When I first saw my toddler son swear, as the coloured bricks he played with refused to behave as he wished, I wondered if there was a gene for pointlessly swearing at inanimate objects that had been passed down from me, or if he had just eavesdropped on me punching a misbehaving printer or cupboard door.

Remove one event from my early life, and does that find me managing a shoe shop rather than pacing onstage? Would a new cut of brogue arriving in-store have brought me as much pleasure as a possible encore and the laughter of strangers?

Maybe none of my school experiences or toddler trauma played any part in my future career path, and perhaps instead it was destiny. It is in my genes. Some of our genetically inherited eccentricities are overtly on display. For instance, I have quite small thumbs – an object of great fascination to Ricky Gervais. Not really, really small thumbs. They are not the sort of thumbs P. T. Barnum would have made money from, but they are a bit stubby and blunt. Ricky would talk so loudly and publicly about them that I still get complete strangers approaching me in the street, asking to see them.*

Geneticist Adam Rutherford is the author of *A Brief History of Everyone Who Ever Lived*, presenter of Radio 4's *Inside Science* and sometime advisor on films about duplicitous, sexually attractive robots.[9] Like most scientists, he is keen to have a law named after him before his life comes to an end. So far, Rutherford's Law is 'If a headline states that "Scientists have discovered a gene for X", where X is a complex human trait, they haven't, because in actual fact that gene doesn't exist.' Since the human genome was sequenced, the popular press has been keen to declare that there is a gene for this or that, from

---

* My relationship with Ricky Gervais has led to the creation of many apocryphal tales that still haunt me to this day. There are people who believe that I drank milk directly from a cow's udder and that I was once made to sit on ham bare-arsed, as a supposed cure for worms. Not a week goes by without me being asked if these stories are true. When I deny them, this is seen as an admission that they must be true. 'Aha, why would you deny them unless they were true?' Ricky is a very persuasive man when it comes to making up myths about his friends.

sexuality to murderousness, but Rutherford explains that this is not the case. Fortunately, from a genetic perspective, we are not given an alibi for who we are, and we are not given an alibi that gets us off our responsibility for who or what our children become. Adam says, 'It doesn't matter whether we are talking about criminality, or psychological characteristics, or psychiatric disorders, or perfectly normal human behaviour like political bent, or susceptibility to alcohol, or being gay or anywhere on the spectrum of sexual preferences, the biology that is revealed by genetics are not causes, or triggers, or foundations. They are potential factors: probabilities.'

Many geneticists no longer see the fight of who we are, and what we become, as nature versus nurture. Your genes may change the odds, but they do not tell you who will win and who will lose. The culture around you, the environment, your diet, love – or the lack of it – will all go to shape you. Your story does not end with cutting the umbilical cord. Neither nature nor nurture reigns supreme.

Adam thinks of it all as 'messy and complex and in the middle', which is often how we all feel. He told me about a paper from Cambridge that quantified the genetic effect that people have on each other. (It is important to know here that, more often than not, when scientists say 'people', they mean 'mice'.) The research attempted to look at the genetic effect that other people have on those they interact with. It is all about genotypes and phenotypes. Your genotype is your code. Your phenotypes are the observable characteristics, such as small thumbs, that come from it. This paper was looking at how the code of your partner affects your observable characteristics.

I read it for the first time and thought, 'Sorry?' 'What?' says an almost exasperated Dr Rutherford. Then he gave some fairly trivial examples and it all seemed to make sense. If your partner is bipolar – a condition that has a genetic component to it – spending half your life with this person is going to have a phenotypic effect on you. 'What they tried to quantify in this paper is the genetic effect someone else has on you . . . the weight of the social genetic effect is greater than your own genetic effect for certain characteristics. That's bonkers.' And this means that what was already messy gets even messier. There is even greater complexity in the interaction between the environment and our genes. The reasons you are who you are are many and varied, and are sometimes impossible to calculate, unless you have been perpetually observed and chronicled. And if you were perpetually observed and chronicled, then this too would also have taken its toll.

There is one set of behaviours that, when grouped together, are often associated with comedians, and they are those that are suggested as the markers for someone being on the autistic spectrum. Those with an Autistic Spectrum Disorder (ASD) are characterized as having any number of a set of characteristics, such as obsessive behaviour, hyperactivity, tics, anxiety (particularly of the social kind), difficulties communicating in social situations and a general susceptibility to depression. The cause of ASD remains unclear, although a genetic component is suspected.

Whilst ASD is brought into conversations about what makes a comedian, the evidence that there is any greater representation of this condition in comedy than in any other walk of life seems scant. Most comedians whom people like to bracket as having ASD are simply the victims of conjecture, and in general it seems that the phrase 'I reckon he's a bit on the spectrum' comes from anyone who has decided it might be abnormal to put records in alphabetical order, or to like crosswords enough to do them twice a day, or to be able to work out who any member of the cast of *Downton Abbey* is from their silhouette. Being obsessed does not always need to lead to a diagnosis and, in my view, poor social skills are not always the signs of a clinical condition, either.

Comedians Dan Harmon and Dan Aykroyd have been diagnosed as being on the autistic spectrum, and Jerry Seinfeld has stated that he believes he is. But in terms of a statistically significant number of people on the autistic spectrum within one profession, mathematics and theoretical physics score far higher than comedy.

In the last few years there has been a rise in young comedians identifying with being on the autistic spectrum. In the UK, Robert White is an exuberant musical comedian who wrote a show about how what he intended as a vengeful practical joke against an ex-partner was misconstrued by the police and led to him going to prison for three months – a situation he puts down to his Asperger's. Before being a comedian, he had sixty-seven jobs in seven years, losing many predominantly due to his joking around. At one job there was no rule about not wearing a home-made Gareth Gates mask at work, so Robert wore one for three hours – and that was the end of that. Comedy has made his life easier. 'Onstage, I can make jokes in the context of making jokes. Saying the same things at work was perceived as a misunderstanding of the social situation and seen as inappropriate.'[10]

Ria Lina was diagnosed with Asperger's ten years into her career and went on to write a show about what is 'special' and what is 'normal'. She explained that being diagnosed had helped her understand why she saw the world in a certain way, perhaps giving her a unique comedic advantage, though she went on to say, 'Being labelled as autistic also made me feel like I'd lost some of the uniqueness that made me special.'[11]

The 2016 documentary *Asperger's Are Us* tells the story of four friends with Asperger's who bonded through a shared sense of humour at an Asperger's summer camp for teenagers, and then created a comedy troupe. One of the quartet, Jack Hanke, gets out a graduation photo and talks of how he was voted 'most outgoing' by the class, which seems ridiculous to him. He sees jokes as his way to communicate, and explains that jokes are how he learnt 'to cross the bridge between me and the rest of the world'.

While I was in Toronto for the annual *Generator* show I met Michael McCreary. Michael is the self-proclaimed 'aspie comic'. He was ostracized in elementary school, so his parents thought it would be good if he took some comedy classes to boost his spirits, and it worked, as well as helping him bond with others on the 'Stand Up for Mental Health' course. Michael believes an important part of his stand-up routine is to eradicate the stigma that surrounds mental illness. He loved performing from an early age, but he found acting in plays worrying, as he always knew his lines but was anxious about others who didn't. He needed complete control, and that is what solo stand-up gave him. Wondering about any advantage for comedy that may come from being diagnosed with Asperger's, Michael tells me, 'One of Asperger's' defining characteristics is that you tend to fixate on a handful of niche subjects. For me, one of those subjects is stand-up comedy, which enables me to attack it with all of my enthusiasm.'

This obsessiveness is something I have found to be common among the comedians with whom I work closely, whether diagnosed or not. Being on the autistic spectrum does not make a comedian, but as with all the other events and conditions discussed here, it appears that it can be usefully applied to stand-up, and stand-up can be a useful way of expressing what may otherwise be seen as socially problematic behaviours and attitudes.

Similarly, Attention Deficit Hyperactivity Disorder (ADHD) crops up as a bystander diagnosis of certain comedians. It has been suggested that I have ADHD, but I believe it is caused by stand-up rather than being a cause of it. I think I may appear to act as if I have ADHD when the adrenaline starts pumping under the lights, but not when I am sitting in the dark at home alone. I like talking about lots of things. I cram my mind with reading and experience, then I am given the chance to share it all for an hour, so the adrenaline and the desire to please and share create a very hectic performance. Should the bystander diagnosis be correct, I do not believe it would either improve or damage my existence, so I will happily remain in the hyperkinetic, occasionally spotlit dark.

This does not mean that having ADHD or being on the autistic spectrum cannot be something that can be turned into comedy. Rory Bremner, a comedian and impressionist who has been a television fixture since his early twenties, was not diagnosed with ADHD until he was in his fifties.

Rory sees a marked crossover between traits associated with ADHD and those that are part of a comedian's make-up: 'impulsivity, speed of thought, lack of inhibition, and so on'. He sees the similarity in the way comedians release from their mouth what many others may stop and filter. He told me that he thought being impulsive and irrepressible made him want to perform and show off; and then experience and peer reaction teach you how to show off properly, rather than just be an attention-seeking pain, which he believes he was at various stages of his childhood and adolescence. He sees his ADHD as his best friend and worst enemy – 'Enemy in that it's not fun being disorganized, not paying attention, forgetting things, messing up, but it makes me who I am in terms of the leaps of imagination, the random connections, the energy and the impulsivity.' Rory sees it as quite natural that people with ADHD will be drawn to the creative industries – a place in which to turn childhood disadvantages into career boons.

Would events such as the loss of your mother at six years old, as Eddie Izzard experienced, change the expectations about how active the genetic, or biological, component of personality might be? Is the diagnosis more important than the life events, or the other way round? Does one override the other? Adam Rutherford explains that there is no method for assessing such a scenario. He suggests taking 1,000 comedians, sequencing their genomes and then asking whether a geneticist would expect to find a pattern suggesting something unique to this group, and the answer would have to be 'no'.

I suggest attempting to set up an experiment. Say I discover an identical twin separated at birth, who has become a comedian. I then find her twin sister, who has become an accountant. Is there anything I could discover in this situation?

Adam tells me that even this fiendishly clever experiment would need 100 more examples to become statistically interesting and relevant. And I see it becoming a resource-hungry experiment, as well as an ethics-board nightmare.

So if I succeed in finding 200 identical twins, and half of them became stand-up comedians while none of their sisters and brothers did, what then?

'We could extract some meaningful data out of that, but I wouldn't draw any firm conclusions from it,' Adam says bleakly.

Is the scrutiny of our childhood any more use than a game, to justify why we are what we are? Does it make the slightest difference to my present life that I was in that traumatic car crash? Perhaps if my mother had died in the car accident, I'd have been a more successful comedian, in 20,000-seaters for ten nights rather than 200-seaters for one. But I prefer the destiny I had. Perhaps if that car hadn't been so eager to be on the wrong side of the road, I wouldn't have become a comedian at all. Perhaps.

Hopefully there is something satisfying, even beguiling, in knowing how murky and complicated our story is, rather than how straightforward, simple and linear. Perhaps we all have the possibility of being more than the sum of our worst experiences, or our best. Neither our nature nor our nurture has a singular control over what we become. When my son uses me in his defence, after being caught cooking and eating all those Belgians, and declares it was due to that bellowing over the broken ice-lolly, I will say, 'Your Honour, I think you'll find it's a bit more complicated than that.'

We are an amalgam. Your destiny is not written in stone, due to a single event or a strand of DNA. And I turn to Eddie Pepitone's inspiring and motivational words, which we can all draw on: 'The only things stopping me today are: genetics, lack of will, income, brain chemistry, and external events.'

CHAPTER 2

The Brain, Hardware and Chemistry

'Me' is just one of the things that my brain does.

Ken Campbell

When the obsessionally self-reflective author Karl Ove Knausgard asked the neurosurgeon Henry Marsh about the disappointment that arises if all of our perceptions and creativity are proved to come from nothing more than matter, Marsh replied, 'It upgrades matter, it doesn't downgrade thoughts and dreams.'[1] Somehow, this matter and the chemical and electrical interactions that take place within it are creative to a level that seems to us way beyond the necessity of pure survival. Our brains are so complicated, by the standards of most of the objects in our universe, that we are still only just getting to know them. Despite all the cauliflower-shaped neurone bundles bobbing in jars on museum shelves and secreted in dry storerooms, the contents of our skulls are still enigmatic and problematic.

Whilst I am not one to post online baby photographs, holiday snaps or images of my latest parsley-and-walnut risotto, I cannot stop myself sharing the 'selfies' that I have of my brain. *And here's my brain doing a word puzzle. Oh, that one is a bit blurry, but that's my brain thinking about Bob Hoskins. And here's my brain thinking about how to try to make an edible walnut-and-parsley risotto.*

After I had had my first fMRI, I couldn't resist projecting the resulting brain scan onto a screen during my shows. I had to tell the audience, 'Look, this is my brain.' I was proud, though also vaguely paranoid, fearful that a sharp-eyed surgeon in the crowd might corner me in the bar afterwards and tell me of an ominous shadow missed by the neuroscientist who had scanned me, before announcing my imminent death. Fortunately, the folds were in the correct place and the lobes were functioning without impediment.

I had been wanting to see my brain for a long time. I wanted to see the physical object that I could blame for my poor decisions, paranoia and misplaced desires. Then I met a man on a train from Tunbridge Wells and he made my dream come true. Finally I could check on my hippocampus, my amygdala and my medulla oblongata.

'I've heard your radio show, I think you should have a brain scan,' said the neuroscientist in my carriage.

I wasn't sure if this was an insult or if my presenting style hinted at faulty wiring, but I didn't care; this man had the equipment to show me my brain, and that was all that mattered. He asked if he could arrange the scan with 'my people'. I explained that I was 'my people' and gave him all my contact details.

He was surprised. 'Don't you want to check who I am, and what I do, first?'

I didn't.

My general rule is if a stranger approaches you and asks you if you'll take part in a scientific experiment, say, 'Yes'. At the very worst, you'll have an adventure and a story to tell about how you ended up having your left arm replaced with a vacuum-cleaner hose, or your mouth sewn onto someone else's anus, after overly trusting someone who appeared scientifically official.

So far, neither of these things has happened, but in being open to a scientific challenge, I have had magnetic pulses sent to the motor region of my brain to stop me being able to talk, a couple of EEGs, and I've communicated with a raven and talked with a starling. So my advice, to anyone who cares to listen, is to take these strange scientific opportunities as and when they arise.

On 18 July 2014 at 9.30 a.m. it was finally confirmed that I definitely had a brain. Its existence was no longer debatable. This is it. Admire the folds and lobes.

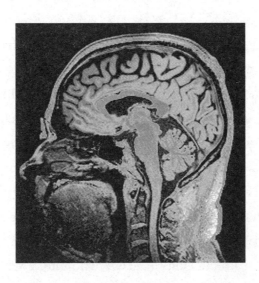

The scanners took me on a tour of my own brain, from right to left and through the middle. At one point Agnetha, who was in charge of the scan, said, 'It's too big, I'm not sure I can fit it all in,' and then blushed.

It was a rare *Carry On* moment in my life. Nothing about my outward physical appearance has ever made a woman blush, but I'm happy that my quite big occipital lobe finally achieved such an effect. It's what's inside that counts, especially if it is a great big occipital lobe or extra-curvy hippocampus. I am not bragging about the size of my brain because, within certain parameters of general averages, the size of your brain doesn't make much difference. Einstein had a smaller brain than me and, despite that, I still believe he had the intellectual edge.

I loved my time on the fMRI. Some people had told me it was claustrophobic and that the clanging of the magnets was annoying, but I am a solitary figure and enjoy listening to Lou Reed's much-derided cacophony *Metal Machine Music*, so I was quite content.

The scan was to aid the research of Peter Bloomfield, the neurologist and stranger on the train. He was researching a subset of brain cells that are the brain's equivalent of immune cells. My working memory and verbal recall were tested – certainly very necessary elements for creativity, though there was no test of creativity within this part of the research. My brain was also scanned in a state of rest, although this didn't go very well, as my brain wouldn't shut up and started running through a scene-by-scene replay of *The Long Good Friday*. I presume the peaks on their readings came during the scene where Bob Hoskins shouts, '"Nothing unusual" he says! Eric's been blown to smithereens,

Colin's been carved up, and I've got a bomb in me casino, and you say nothing unusual?' It's not a very restful scene, so I can see why Peter was confused by my rest-reading. Imagine where that reading would have been if I reached the speech that begins with 'Well, bon voyage then . . . I'll tell you something, I'm glad I found out in time just what a partnership with a pair of wankers like you would've been. A sleeping partner's one thing, but you're in a f***ing coma!'

I wondered how much he could tell about the me-ness of me, or anyone else, from a brain scan. Can we trace the secrets of how we act and feel in the world, by looking at the patches and shapes on the screen representation of our brains? Is any form of personality revealed by a scan, or is it only useful for identifying areas of the brain that are suffering from tumours or damage from disease? The fMRI demonstrates which areas of the brain require the most blood during tasks, so where more blood flows, there is more neuronal activity.

As Peter's tests involved working memory and verbal recall, much of the processing was in the frontal and parietal lobes. There was also more activity in the motor cortex in the rear of the frontal lobe, as the task involved pressing a button. By scanning many people, a regular pattern emerges that allows the neuroscientist to define the areas most used during specific forms of activity. Peter explained that by measuring behavioural responses alongside cortical responses in a patient group, neuroscientists can start to understand how different cognitive and psychiatric illnesses relate to behaviour and biology. So it seemed to me that actions can be directly connected to what is going on in the hardware, but can the person also be?

Peter explained that personality is very difficult to define. Fear and overwhelming emotional responses, such as happiness or sadness, are the easiest aspects of a personality to study using an fMRI, because they are such basic, powerful and primal emotions; but he said that you have to be careful and precise with what questions you ask and what answers you seek, as a result of using brain imaging. You couldn't ask of an fMRI study, 'Where in the brain is personality encoded?' as that is not really how the brain seems to function. You could try to identify a behavioural trait related to a personality type, and then probe that during the scan. Peter laid out a possible hypothesis of finding a group of people who were particularly sensitive to angry facial expressions. On showing them a set of pictures of angry faces, he could compare their physiological, emotional and cognitive responses and what was going on in their brains to those of another group who might feel calm about angry facial expressions. 'You might end up finding that the sensitive group have much more activity in places like the amygdala, which is the fear centre, compared to the control group. A crude example, but it gives the general idea,' he explained patiently.

An analysis of the brain's humour centre is not high on the necessary investigative uses for an fMRI, so despite my own brain scan, I left with little knowledge about the typical comedian's brain. As Peter laconically put it, 'Sadly, our level of understanding is dictated by the allocation of funding. I would imagine similar approaches and ideas could apply to humour, but a sense-of-humour failure is unlikely to result in medical treatment.'

How many more years of social-media outrage and days spent explaining 140-character ribaldry, before a sense-of-humour failure becomes an urgent medical issue?

Having a photo of my brain soon proved useful for me on social media. In the midst of some tiresome row about how climate change isn't happening, because giant polar bears have been seen running decathlons on expanded icebergs, an aggressive troll asked, 'Is there actually any evidence you even have a brain?'

I simply sent him a jpeg – and that was that. The conversation ended.

Having waited forty-five years for my first brain scan, it took only six months to find myself back in the machine again and, despite the lack of publicity or funding, this time the scientists didn't need just anybody's brain; they needed a comedian's brain, or at least those of people who ad-lib for a living in front of an audience. While they were at University College London (UCL), neuroscience students Joe Necus and Joseph Devlin decided they wanted to experiment on the minds of comedians. They wanted to find out if different areas of the brain are more or less active when the professionally eloquent are asked to make things up.

When I first met Joseph, he was pessimistic about the number of comedians' brains that he would get to scan and probe. I reassured him. The combination of self-obsession and curiosity that makes a comedian would have them queuing around the laboratory for a chance to have someone probe their brain. With the exception of two comedians who suffer from claustrophobia, and one who was too worried the scan would reveal that he had spiders hatching in his brain or similar, everyone I passed the invitation on to replied with a positively excited, 'Yes!'

Much of the research on human eloquence has been based on what happens in the brain when something goes wrong, such as when a stroke removes the ability to form sentences. Joseph wanted to focus on what happens when it goes right. He wanted to see what was operating, when the brain was working at its best in creating sentences and imaginative flourishes. He decided that a good model for the test would be solo-playing a version of the 'long-running panel show' *Just a Minute* inside the scanner. He would give the comedian in the scanner a topic to talk about, and they would have to attempt to soliloquize out loud on that topic without repetition of any word, without stumbling and without deviating too far from the subject.

For those who are unaware of *Just a Minute*, it's a BBC Radio 4 show that has run for more than fifty years. The rules are simple, but the game is fiendish. There are four contestants, usually comedians, writers and actors. The host, Nicholas Parsons, gives a contestant a subject as random as 'seaside postcards', 'the county of Rutland' or 'the number thirty-three bus route' (Fulwell Station to Hammersmith via Priory Lane). The player must then attempt to talk about that subject for a whole minute without deviation, hesitation or repetition. The other three contestants eagerly look out for a fumbling or failure, and buzz in to challenge, when they perceive one as having occurred. As many people in the arts did not excel in outdoor sports, their aggressive competitiveness is all funnelled into victory with wordplay. It is when the autodidacts go alpha.

From my own experience on the show, and with the aid of instinct rather than the fMRI, I believe that it requires the whole brain to light up. It is a peak experience. When waiting to pounce on another contestant, you need to be configuring your own take on the subject, while also listening intently for any 'um', 'ah' or repeated use of the word 'satsuma', 'hopscotch' or 'dowser'. When it is your turn to speak, it can seem that each word is being laid out in front of you and being checked for novelty, while also seeking jokes and ensuring that you are loosely on the subject. My problem, when playing it, is anticipating that I am about to repeat a word and pretty much buzzing in on myself, as my tongue and brain stumble and create a mash-up of all three buzzable faults. This has made it very easy for my adversaries.

It is all a bit of fun, except that it's not. It is highly competitive and one of the pinnacles of comedy show business. Unlike that TV advert for veal that you signed up for, or the all-naked panel show, it's also something that you can be proud to tell your parents about.* It's on Radio 4, after all.

Though Joseph's lab would not hold the same heart-crushing fear, I would discover that, even when alone and without an audience, comedians do not lose their competitiveness and that can jeopardize research.

The experiment required a control group. This is a group of people who should represent average ability, as opposed to the specialists – in this case the specialists being people who can just babble on and on and on, and who do it for a living. It turned out that most people are not able to keep talking about quiches or naked mole-rats for a minute, so the amount of time for the professional ramblers was reduced to thirty seconds – this being the average amount of time before someone says, 'I'm sorry, I really can't think of anything else to say about Jaffa Cakes/ Stonehenge/ naked mole-rats.'

---

* I have not advertised veal or appeared on an all-naked panel show.

The competition within the scanner was not to win, but to give the most useful performance for the research, which, as was revealed, was still enough pressure to place the brain in competitive mode. It may only have been an audience of two scientists, but to the comic, that is still an audience.

As I embarked on the process, I wondered whether my brain scan would reveal that any eloquence I thought I possessed was a sham and that I therefore had no right to perform, based on the blood flow in my brain.

'I'm afraid the structure of your brain clearly shows that you suffer from false eloquence syndrome. While you were in there, we contacted the Comedians' Licensing Body, and your right to take to the stage has been revoked. Here is a mop and a bucket; from this day on, you will be employed as our manservant. Now, go to lab room 114 – someone has been sick in the centrifuge.'

These could be my *Flowers for Algernon* days.

Lying in the cool, enclosed surroundings of the machine had lost none of its novelty since the first time. A test pattern of brain activity was taken. As a pre-scan exercise to ensure we really could gabble, Joseph asked us anodyne questions, akin to what you might be asked during a cut-and-blow-dry in a hair salon. Then the games began. A word flashed up, the clock started and the talking ensued. At the end of the hour I barely had any recall of what I had been talking about. I just knew I had been talking and talking and talking.

Once out of the machine, I wanted to know what Joseph's impressions of the other comedians were, when they first walked in. He reported that there was about a 50/50 split between those who were apprehensive and those who were overexcited, and that they all had a lot of questions. Even before the experiment began, Joseph noticed that the comedians had an aptitude for talking that was not shared by the non-comedians. Whilst the control group would soon falter on their holiday plans or how they got to the lab, Joseph told me that all the comedians would 'talk and talk and talk'; he often had to try and stop them, but even then 'they would just ramble on. All others would stall at thirty seconds – the comedians had no problem with rambling nonsense.'

Before the experiment it was explained that being funny was of no importance to the task. Over each thirty-second monologue, what was being marked was the ability to fulfil the rules of *Just a Minute*. Every deviation, hesitation or repetition would be a mark against eloquence. Once the 'eloquence' was measured, the activity of the brain would be examined. Despite these instructions, some of the comedians' results were totally unusable. They wiggled about too much, having gone into full performance-mode, desperate to prove their funniness. One of them apparently kept breaking off from the experiment to explain that he was sorry the 'gig' wasn't going very well and that he wasn't being funny enough, and that usually he was much better when doing gigs in a brain scanner. The desire to 'be best', mixed with adrenaline and fear, had usurped the ability to be functional for the experiment. Performance trumped usefulness – a common complaint from anyone who knows a stand-up.

I wanted to know, though, whether 'the comedian's quadrant' of the brain had been discovered. Was there a particular part of the brain that was peculiar to the comic? Would there be a small pecan-shaped growth below the amygdala that would be exclusive to comedic and rambling public speakers? According to Joseph's results, the comedians were not using any different parts of the brain and had no structural differences, either. Spatially, the brain activity was the same. However, whilst there were no physical differences in brain structure, the resources were being reallocated. The comedians were spending less energy on motor aspects of speech, because they were more rehearsed at it. Instead the comedians reallocated that energy to the part of the brain that involves planning – that is, what's coming next. According to Joseph, 'The pre-motor area is down-regulated and the pre-supplementary area is up-regulated.' As he summed up, 'The huge difference was the ability to talk nonsense about a mundane topic.'

So, that is my superpower.

'How did you defeat General Zod?'

'I tediumed him into submission. He willingly went to the phantom zone during the seventeenth hour of my naked mole-rat ramble, though I think it was deviation in talking about the bus routes of Poplar that really did it.'

Start the day each morning by talking for thirty minutes about a randomly chosen topic, and you too could be the Mr Universe of the stand-up comedy arena circuit.

The comedians outperformed the control group by some margin. For those wishing they could speak more nonsense, they will be glad to know that they have all the apparatus required to speak rubbish – it's just about practice and the will to use it.

Like the famous story of the London black-cab drivers developing a larger hippocampus, due to their repeated practice of knowing the routes of London – 'the knowledge' – this is a reminder that you don't have to give up on the possibilities of your brain. Even in late adulthood, you can learn to adapt your brain to new and unusual tasks; it just takes tenacity and desire.

The fMRI scans appeared to show that a comedian's brain has organized itself into a state where it is more adept at allowing its user to ramble on about nothing in particular, at length. It also shows that having become practised in such an art, that area of the brain can go into automatic mode, enabling the comedian to think ahead and insert jokes, ad-lib and suchlike. But if we are beginning to understand the mechanism of improvisation, I wondered whether a study of the brain could ever say anything about the more difficult-to-grasp concept of creating an impression with an audience, or perhaps charisma. Each time a comedian walks onstage, it is like walking into a party with a load of new people you've never met before and saying, 'Here I am! And this is how I want *you* to perceive *me*.'

Sarah-Jayne Blakemore is Professor of Cognitive Neuroscience at UCL. She is pre-eminent in her field and lives near my house, which is very useful when I have a quandary about neurons. She explained to me that neuroscience is moving fast, improving our understanding of the brain almost daily, but it is still a long way from explaining many aspects of what it means to be human, even if we dare pose that question. Smaller and smaller brain areas are being monitored and the evidence collated, but we can't be specific in picking out exactly where thinking is generated, and we are still only seeing a very broad picture.

The real advances will take place when the resolution of detail with which we can examine the brain is at brain-cell level, but

Sarah-Jayne thinks this might not happen for several decades. When even the science is so murky, this can leave ordinary people in a position of confusion, because while much is being written about the brain, it can be hard to know what is real science and what is bunkum. For instance, the oft-repeated idea that 'we only use 10 per cent of the brain' has no basis in fact, although recent research suggests that people who perpetually repeat that we only use 10 per cent of the brain may be using even less of theirs.

There is also a whole industry devoted to explaining how to tell your left brain to shut up, when you are painting a sunset or writing a poem about toad-spawning. According to such experts, if I turn off my dominant left brain, then my creative right brain will thrive unhindered by that bossy, prissy 'I'm in charge' side. The left brain is considered the foundation of logic and organization, and the right brain a place of poetry and passion, but that theory has fallen foul of late, so don't feel the need to be overly indebted to the right-hand side when you create a particularly delightful absurdist joke about vampire hummingbirds, flying kettles and singing daffodils. The left brain has the dominant language areas, so you wouldn't have been able to vocalize your creativity that well without it, unless you fancy signing up for a mime-school course. And as for where humour might originate? Well, you can't be too exact about that, either.[2] As neuroscientist Professor Sophie Scott succinctly summed it up for me, 'The left hemisphere is for most people where language is represented, but it doesn't scale up to the left equalling logic and the right equalling passion.'

Writer, thinker and connoisseur of the occult Colin Wilson talks of the Laurel and Hardy theory of consciousness, and he creates a similar division of mental capabilities, which is one to which I am drawn, if only because it involves Stan and Ollie, the most lovely of comedy-screen double acts. I would be happy for them to take control of my brain. Wilson's theory sees the right brain as prone to depression and the left brain as overly optimistic, and yet both are entirely dependent on each other for their existence. As with Laurel and Hardy, the interaction between the two has entirely predictable results – the brain eventually falling into a barrel of molasses, before staring into the camera with a look of harrumphing disappointment that says, 'I suppose I knew this was inevitable again.'

Sarah-Jayne Blakemore's particular area of specialist interest is the teenage brain, which I imagine as being very similar to the average stand-up's brain, given that both demographics can be sulky show-offs prone to mood swings, who don't like getting out of bed in the morning and worry their family by coming home way too late. Sarah-Jayne's studies into teenage brains have included research into the social self and the increased awareness of a 'looking-glass self' – the sense of how we are perceived by others. This awareness increases sharply during adolescence, and then levels out in adulthood.

Researching these ideas of a sharpened sense of how we are perceived, I wondered if Sarah-Jayne could explain what happens in the brain when we walk into a room of strangers, whether it is at a party or the moment of walking onto a stage.

I know that when I walk onstage, there is a snap transformation. The clues that something is up are there in advance, whether it is a jitteriness, an onset of yawning or a mind unable to concentrate, preoccupied with thinking about myself and imagining what might go wrong when I walk into the light. But the moment I am in view of the audience, on the vast majority of occasions, an intense concentration and wave of energy create a sharp focus and an ability to retrieve whatever I need from my mind and body.

The Australian comedian and composer Tim Minchin told me that he feels we get 'superhuman abilities onstage'. He particularly noticed this while performing in *Jesus Christ Superstar*. He had to climb up fifty metres of rigging in rehearsal – an exhausting task. He'd be gasping so hard he could barely perform the song, but in a proper performance in front of an audience he'd go up twice as fast and would have absolutely no trouble singing the song at all. Like those 'AMAZING TRUE-LIFE ADVENTURE STORIES!' of the man who found he could lift a ten-ton truck off his trapped Great Dane, or the woman who walked fifty miles carrying the arm that had been severed by her combine-harvester, being onstage can give you superpowers, most of them mental ones. Sentences and leaps of imagination that were impossible, only minutes before, trip off the tongue with no problem whatsoever.

Sarah-Jayne explained that when walking into any kind of crowded room – whether populated with strangers or not – almost all of your brain is active. 'You've got the brain area concerned with walking, your whole motor cortex, cerebellum, face-recognition areas, face-perception areas, object recognition, almost all the visual cortex, you're seeing stuff and you'll also have mentalizing areas – what we call "theory of mind" areas – trying to figure out the mental states of other people, what are they talking about, are they talking about me? About four regions of the brain are involved in mentalizing. You might have other areas – auditory cortex, language decoding areas; it is a hugely complex scenario, in which almost all areas of your brain are active.'

So if we are trying to ring-fence a specific area of the brain that might explain why comedians can feel so superhuman when stepping onto a stage, and why my feelings of wanting to be a show-off go into overdrive, then it doesn't look like we'll have much luck. She explains that in fMRI studies you want to isolate a certain system in the brain. 'You might say: I don't care about the walking-in bit, I don't care about deciphering the emotions, I just care about the facial recognition; so you show people familiar faces versus unfamiliar faces – everything else is matched – and then you would see the differences . . .'

Sarah-Jayne wants to know what is going on in the 'mentalizing areas'. These are the areas of the brain involved in understanding other people's states of mind and emotion. Such skills are useful, but also terrifyingly prone to misrepresentation and paranoia, for a performer. As the comedian begins to perform, he or she can be particularly sensitive to any suggestion that the room may not be receptive. I am consciously and subconsciously picking up on every tic or cue from the audience that may require dealing with. Are there people in the balcony who are going to be aggressive, or show derision, or just not have a clue? Is there a drunk mumbling somewhere? Is that a hen-night at the back? Does the man at the front look scared? There is an acute sensitivity to barely visible faces, half-hidden by shadow.

Such sensitivity is important for understanding what jokes might work best in what surroundings – as anyone who has mistakenly and nervously told a joke they forgot was rude, on a first visit to future parents-in-law, might recognize . . . It's only when you remember that the punchline is 'That's from the man who shat in his pants' that you know you are creating a very poor first impression. Sarah-Jayne explained to me the concept of understanding other people's hidden mental states. 'The stuff that's going on in your mind, that you're not telling people about but which I can decipher, is a critical component of comedy. That sense of "Oh my God, that character doesn't know what I know, there's going to be trouble." In comedy, it's often what's *not* being said. Theory of mind is central to most cartoons, like Gary Larson cartoons – you know something the character doesn't know, because there's something going on behind him . . .'

The human brain's ability to empathize with those around us, to predict future possibilities and pick up on varied social reactions, is part of the necessary mind-tools for sharing a joke. Whilst it seems that comedians' brains are no different in structure from those of other people, this is such an important part of the way comedians need to work that the brain's control of verbal flow has become more practised over time, allowing us (and it) to focus on really picking up these sensitive cues. What is incredible is that science can go some way to proving this, by using fMRI scans to look at the workings of the human brain in action. It is another reminder that while in most cases the apparatus is similar, it is down to us – and the advantages or shortcomings of our environment – to work out what we wish to refine, achieve and aspire to. Just as no one is born with 'the brain of a physicist' or 'the brain of a weatherman', no one starts life with the brain of a comedian, either.

*

Sophie Scott is a neuroscientist who has also dabbled in stand-up. She is the Wellcome Senior Research Fellow in Basic Biomedical Science and Professor of Cognitive Neuroscience at UCL. She is the sort of scientist you trust sufficiently to agree to having a magnetic pulse administered to the motor region of your brain, briefly making you unable to speak in front of an audience. At least I trust her enough, and it did me no harm as far as I know, and it gave the audience a blissful bout of silence.

She has also studied what happens in the brain when we laugh – the origins and meaning of laughter. She describes doing stand-up for the first time as being the most frightening moment in her life since doing exams at school when she was fifteen. Being a scientist, she didn't just move on to the next gig, but dissected her first experience in detail. 'I listened back to the recording and I sounded like a scared woman from Blackburn, which I was. My accent fully returned.'

I asked Sophie whether she knew why she found herself returning to the accent of her place of birth when she was onstage. She believes that she was speaking in her original childhood accent because we normally pay attention to how we're sounding when we speak, but fear can disrupt those mental processes, meaning that we revert back to our 'default' voice.

Sophie has a longtime professional interest in accents, and it was studying them that eventually led her to look at the origins and characteristics of laughter. She was studying Foreign Accent Syndrome, the peculiar condition where someone can wake up from a coma, or after experiencing a migraine, with an accent that bears no relation to their background or previous voice. So, from real-life examples, a woman from Plymouth who suffered from severe migraines, and had an English West Country accent, woke up one day with a strong Chinese accent. A Texan woman who had only ever travelled as far as Mexico in her life came round from dental surgery speaking with an English accent. Sophie explained that only a few such cases have been reported worldwide – around twenty, it is believed – and that the condition results from the patient having suffered a small amount of brain damage.

Some of Sophie's work at the time was also looking at 'screams and growls and sobs', and at the many and varied ways such negative emotion was expressed through facial expression. Working with Paul Ekman, one of the world's leading experts on non-verbal behaviour, she asked why there seemed to be such a limited variety of positive emotions. Paul replied that he was sure there were many still to be discovered, but that such expressions may not appear so obvious on the face. As Sophie explained, 'That got me on to laughter.'

As she is based in the Neuroscience Department, I wondered what Sophie knew about the activity in the structures of the brain whilst someone is laughing. She explained that research had not been able to elicit very much. In terms of evolution, scientists know now that spontaneous laughter has its source in older areas of the brain – areas where we share characteristics of communication with other mammals. She explained that 'There are lateral motor areas – you have voluntary control over them, and you can control speaking from there. When that goes, due to a stroke, you can still laugh.'

There is also a practical problem to overcome in conducting fMRI scans whilst someone is laughing, and which has held back scientific progress, and that is that laughing causes too much movement to create a clear picture, as neuroscience student Joe Necus found out, when trying to calm down some of the comedians he was attempting to study in the fMRI scanner. Despite his problems with jittery stand-ups, it seems it is easier to study the origins of humour than our reactions to it.

With my brain twice scanned, papers from conferences read and neuroscientists interrogated, I am still without any real understanding as to how my brain could predict or inform why I am who I am, and why I do what I do. It seems that an examination of the hardware reveals very little, save for the reallocation of some brain energy. I am no further towards understanding what goes on when I step onto a comedy stage than I was when Tim Minchin said to me, when we were talking about how it feels to be performing, 'When you are onstage, you are this uber-you. I imagine it comes from the redistribution of everything into the service of this one thing . . . performance.'

One of the main problems for scientists is, of course, that you can't yet scan the brain when it's onstage doing a comedy routine, and even when such technology for mobile brain-scanning does exist, I'm not sure comedians' brains will be top of the list. They sliced and preserved Einstein's brain, not Benny Hill's. Whatever issues with my hardware have led to a career in comedy remain buried for now, at least until our tools of scrutiny are able to dig deeper. Even my impressive occipital lobe will not mark me out for distinction, when we're all lined up on the shelves in our pickling jars.

CHAPTER 3

Talking About Myself
Behind My Back

The road to creativity passes so close to the madhouse
and often detours or ends there.

Ernest Becker

You've met Dean Burnett already, but what I previously
failed to tell you is that on the way to being a full-time neuroscientist he moonlit as a stand-up comedian. Dean was
propelled towards stand-up comedy after embalming corpses.
Previously too nervous to go onstage, he found that embalming alleviated the dread. After cutting up corpses, he thought,
'What's the worst that could happen? Even if the audience don't
laugh, they do breathe. It was a step up for me.'

I wondered what Dean thought, having been part of both
worlds, of much of the psychological research into what makes a
comedian a comedian. He is sceptical about drawing too many
conclusions. He believes the publicity around academic papers

63

which suggest that an unhinged mind is a necessity for comedy comes from a broader wish to believe it. 'Papers on comics having psychotic traits get more publicity, like papers on men having different brains to women, as it makes a good story, and we want to hear that.' The idea of comedy as a product of neuroses is something Dean sees as a stereotype rather than a phenomenon.

He also regards as a problem the idea that you can lump comedians together in one single group. 'They are, in fact, radically different individually. Rodney Dangerfield, Lenny Bruce, Lee Evans, Jim Bowen, Sarah Millican and Stewart Lee would therefore all be labelled as comedians, but the odds of them having similar psychological profiles are extremely low, given their wildly different backgrounds. A desire to stand in front of people and make them laugh is a unifying factor, but I'd argue that's not enough to expect them to be psychologically similar – any more than a golfer and a basketball player would be expected to have similar stats because they both play sports that involve balls.'

The *British Journal of Psychiatry* published a paper in 2014 which suggested that many comedians displayed psychotic traits. According to one of its authors, Professor Gordon Claridge, 'The creative elements needed to produce humour are strikingly similar to those characterising the cognitive style of people with psychosis – both schizophrenia and bipolar disorder.'[1] More than 500 comedians filled in a version of the Oxford-Liverpool Inventory of Feelings and Experience (O-Life) and the result was that they all believed they were special, which is of course what comedians always hope for, when filling out forms to ascertain their psychological state.

I took the survey, but the problem for me with such personality surveys is that I'm often not very good at yes/no answers. I just can't answer the questions on such binary lines. I don't think we are a binary species that can comfortably reply 'affirmative', 'negative' or 'don't know'. We are a grey area. Even with the addition of 'sometimes' in the question, I find myself pondering which sometimes are eligible and which ones are not; even my 'sometimes' need a subsection of certain sometimes.

The O-Life survey began easily enough. Do you prefer reading to meeting people? Yes, a very big yes. My gregariousness has sharply declined with age and my awareness of just how many books there are to read. I look along my bookshelves and shake my head with melancholy when I think of all those books I won't have time for, even if I am lucky enough to have an averagely long life. That volume two of *Remembrance of Things Past*, squeezed between Daniel Clowes's *Ice Haven* and Don McCullin's *Unreasonable Behaviour*, taunts me. When should I read *Infinite Jest*, as opposed to pretending that I've read it, though I pretend quite efficiently? When do I surrender to the fact that there are certain books on my bookshelf that I will never get round to reading? But I do know that, deep down, I'd much rather be seated in an armchair trying to read these books than meeting random people, even those people who might be as interesting as Kurt Vonnegut's *Galápagos* or perhaps even *Cross Country: Fifteen Years and Ninety Thousand Miles on the Roads and Interstates of America with Lewis and Clark, a Lot of Bad Motels, a Moving Van, Emily Post, Jack Kerouac, My Wife, My Mother-In-Law, Two Kids and Enough Coffee to Kill an Elephant* by Robert Sullivan. Perhaps I should have known that the clue was in the title and I'll almost certainly never finish that book, especially if I keep going to parties and trying to pretend to know about cars and football.

Yes, I do think making new friends is more effort than it's worth. At the time of writing I am forty-nine – I've got enough friends for the time being. As I get older, I might be up for shopping around again, or I might just be satisfied to be known by the local kids as that strange grey loner who smells of books and occasionally displays psychotic behaviour.

No, I don't find it easy to let myself go at lively parties, because I am very careful to say 'no' to all invitations that may lead to lively parties. I don't even get to the stage where I need to think about being lively or not. Life can be lively enough without walking into something specifically designed to be lively. For similar reasons, I have never found fun in a Fun Pub.

Yes, I do sometimes talk about things I know nothing about. It is a prerequisite of the job. It may even be 'always' rather than 'sometimes'.

The problem I have with these surveys – much like those surveys in my sister's old *Cosmopolitan* magazines asking, 'Are you a great lover?' or 'Do you know how to please him?', which I used to fill in on rainy days when I was twelve – is that they seem to make grey areas definite. And the answers were of course: 'Yes, I am' and 'Of course I do.'

'Do you sometimes have fits of laughing or crying that you can't control?' Isn't that the point of all laughing and crying: we can't stop and start them, on tap? Unless you are some sort of psychopath who has learnt to turn emotion on and off, in order to con others into thinking that you have empathy and soul?

'Have you ever blamed someone else for something that was your fault?' I felt this could be summarized as, 'Do you have any brothers and sisters?' I admit it now: it was me who opened all those Easter eggs, removed the sweets within and then tried to reseal them with a soldering iron, not my sister Sarah. I ask for 412 other incidents to be taken into account as well.

'Do you often overindulge in alcohol?' Of course not. I hit the recommended weekly allowance spot on and if you don't believe me, ask my doctor – it's what I tell her, too.

'Do you dread going into a room when other people are already gathered and are talking?' Isn't social dread a malleable thing? At times you may dive in, while at others you may be blushing before you are across the threshold.

The problem with being a multitude, as Walt Whitman described us, is that yeses can be nos; nos can be maybes; and changing days can change who you think you are.

And do we answer these surveys entirely honestly, or is there a brain elf that misleads you into answering in a manner that hopes you may make yourself seem more fabulous and strange – because you are, aren't you?

I took part in an abbreviated online version of the O-Life test and found that I scored very much above average on cognitive disorganization, which will come as little surprise to those who have seen the chaos of my desk or those who have chased me as the deadlines whoosh by. I was a little above average on impulsive nonconformity, which is a pity, because I probably wished I seemed odder.

I was quite above average on unusual experiences, and below average on introvertive anhedonia, which I presume is good news, as this is a reduced ability to feel social and physical pleasure, as well as an avoidance of intimacy.

It is a relief not to be average. When we do a test, we don't want to find out that we are too normal, though we also want the comfort that comes from being normal. We want to be just wonky enough to be interesting, but not so wonky that our life is unbearable or painful. We want all the perks of abnormality, with none of the pain. After my brain scans and EEGs, I was relieved that all was normal, but a little disappointed that they hadn't found a bump or shadow that was both benign and fascinating.

In the survey the researchers compared comedians to 364 actors and 831 people in non-creative professions, and the comics scored 'significantly higher' on all four psychotic personality traits. Having worked with a few actors, I was surprised at comedians having a greater number of psychotic personality traits, as I have always found actors more peculiar, superstitious and apt to talk of the ghosts they had heard rattling about a seaside theatre as they slapped on the panstick for their Falstaff.

My supposition is that some of the psychotic traits are encouraged by a life in comedy, rather than psychotic traits leading to a life in comedy. The act of trying to create nonsense can mean that you listen in to the voices in your head, encouraging them to babble more, and as long as they are whispering punchlines and not suggesting crossbow killing sprees, I think I can live with them. As the paper's co-author Gordon Claridge said:

Although schizophrenic psychosis itself can be detrimental to humour, in its lesser form it can increase people's ability to associate odd or unusual things or to think 'outside the box'. Equally, 'manic thinking', which is common in people with bipolar disorder, may help people combine ideas to form new, original and humorous connections.

As well as neuroscientists and psychologists, anthropologists have also contributed to the debate as to what personality traits make a comedian. The University of New Mexico tried to discover whether there was a dividing line between what makes a comedian and what makes up other human beings. Anthropologist Gil Greengross and psychologist Geoffrey Miller gave thirty-one comedians a standardized personality test. The result which surprised the researchers was that comedians seemed shyer than average. They also had lower-than-average scores on agreeableness and conscientiousness, which I can relate to, though surprisingly their neuroticism was average. Woody Allen, it seems, is an aberration and is not the rule.

Psychosis suggests that somehow the comedians are mentally inhabited by other beings – voices in their heads. Certainly I can be aware of my own internal voice much of the time. I remember a few years ago excitedly watching Public Enemy at Glastonbury, lost in the moment, when I was instructed to put my arms in the air like I just didn't care. I almost did; the elbows started to rise. I tried not to look, but my eyes caught sight of my arms as they were almost at ear level, and my mind snapped in. It reminded me that I always care and that such displays were really not acceptable. If I start letting go, where next? Before I knew it, I'd have been in a Bacchic frenzy, found weeks later by the farmer, daubed in mud, full of hallucinogenic fungus and still dancing in a frenzy to the music left in my head. That is where moving your arms in the air like you just don't care, can lead. While others can flail in unbridled delight, and whatever look I might be giving off, there's always a cautious internal foot in my head, just tapping along like a Baptist on a rocking chair.

When I am lost in the moment, even for a moment, there is a critical little homunculus on my shoulder, whispering in my ear and saying, 'Look at you, lost in the moment – pathetic. What do you think everyone is thinking? I bet they're thinking, "Look at that old man who's lost in the moment. We should alert someone, he looks both foolish and suspicious."' As quickly as I am lost, I am found again; no release for me, perhaps with the exception of moments onstage when I am performing. It is easier there.

So I am constantly vigilant of myself, and my inner dialogue with myself makes sure that I constantly keep myself in check. Inside my head is a very active panel of critics, the ghosts of a late-night TV arts discussion show, who might for example scrutinize all the different ways that I may have been misinterpreted while attempting small talk. Or they will explain how a casual compliment could have been interpreted as a flirtation or an advance. They are always there, nagging and critiquing. I wonder if this constant low-level hyper-vigilance could have been triggered by the car crash when I was a kid. Hyper-vigilance – a condition of heightened awareness and increased alertness – can be a sign of post-traumatic stress and can in itself become a mental-health issue. Somehow, for me, its cause no longer matters; it is there and, to my benefit, some of the panel of critics do come up with good ideas for routines.

Many comedians I know maintain a hectic observation deck in their mind, where they scrutinize their own actions, and they have a busy inner dialogue as a result. The great comic purveyor of paranoia, Richard Lewis, described having a whole jury perpetually commenting on everything he did or said. It is this sort of mix of vindictive fictional jury and negative narcissism that keeps you watchful and fearful of others' judgements. A negative narcissism that means you believe that you are worthy of sneering attention from strangers. You believe that you pop into their minds as you wander around an art gallery, and you imagine that the attendant considers you an art idiot because you didn't look at a painting for long enough; or, when you go to watch your child swimming, you think the other spectators imagine that you have no child to watch and are just an intruding paedophile.

For such comedians, it's almost as if – being constantly watchful and critical – they are unable to live in the moment, except of course when they are onstage. Then they are able to turn down the volume knob on the voices, by being watched and judged by a roomful of others, hiring out their criticism of themselves to outsiders. Doing stand-up comedy, giving a performance, provides the perpetual daily self-observation with a purpose, but whether such self-critiquing makes the performance better is open to debate. And it is behaviour far from unique to stand-ups. I've met archaeologists, architects, taxidermists* and psychologists who have similarly relentless eyes upon themselves, and yet can at times lose themselves in the moment when they are at their most focused and creative in their work.

Our inner monologue, though, is a necessary part of what being a human being is all about. In some ways not being able to live entirely in the moment, to step back and consider yourself and your own place in the world, is an intrinsic part of our relationship with ourselves and with others. This is what Thomas

---

* Yes, I sometimes hang out with taxidermists.

Nagel's famous essay on being a bat is about. Is there a state of bat-hood? If you were a bat, would you know what it is like to be a bat? Not if you were a human brain inside something with wings that excreted medicinally useful poo, but if you were the bat itself, would you have a sense of self? Do bats worry about where they are going to be hanging out tomorrow night, and how they might look when doing so?

Much of your conscious life is about thinking about things and other people, talking to yourself in your head, making decisions. Unlike a bat, most of your actions appear to involve some thought and internal debate. The human has a life of the mind, and it can be really bloody annoying as a place of self-doubt, unnecessary fear and paranoia. Are people laughing at your yellow shirt, at how you're walking, at the looseness of your wig? That is the problem with being self-conscious – it makes you very self-conscious.

Not liking to shilly-shally around with the more straightforward social niceties of conversation, I have recently got into the habit of asking people what their inner monologue looks and sounds like. Who makes up their skull panel? How many people do they have in their head? Is it one clear voice of responsibility, or hundreds of little elves of doubt?

The epidemiologist and doctor Ben Goldacre, whom I tempt out of his computer room and onto the stage every Christmas for a science-variety jamboree, told me that it often feels like there's an overwhelming amount going on in his head at any one time, and it feels like most of it is non-verbal, even if it's reasonably abstract and technical. He believes he can only fully register his inner voice when he's explicitly converting thoughts into verbal format. Once he has translated this jumble into words, Ben sees his thoughts as a dress rehearsal of possibilities. He sums it up by saying, 'A lot of the time the voice in my head sounds like a rehearsal. I'll take an idea, or an argument, and try explaining it five different ways, then remember I'm burning the toast.'

Writer and performer Neil Edmond, who used to enact an interpretative dance onstage with me whilst I read Danielle Steel poetry, told me that he couldn't describe what his inner voice sounded like, but he knew where it was. He told me it sat in his head: 'In a curved bar running over my forehead from temple to temple, about an inch out. If it ever sits "inside" my head, it's a bit shocking and usually sounds like someone else and only usually happens when I'm half-awake. I've just been experimenting with making it shout or do accents and it won't.'

And the comedian Dane Baptiste told me he has three separate inner voices: the mind, heart and ego. The first two sound like his own voice, but the ego 'is huskier and much more influenced by hip hop and Scorsese films'.

Unsurprisingly, 'bitter Buddha' Eddie Pepitone knows his inner voices well. The dominant ones are very worrisome 'pig voices'. A typical minute in his morning goes from stress over things that must be done: 'Oh boy, you really have a lot to do . . .' to 'what the hell is wrong with you that you never really focus on doing your . . .' to 'oh yeah, you've got to feed the dogs. God, I love these dogs . . .' to 'Jesus Christ look at your weight . . . I want a banana . . . God you're a failure, a major, major failure . . . No you're not, you're doing really good . . . No, you're a failure . . . I love those dogs . . . Where's that banana?' And so on.

He says that this barrage only breaks occasionally, and only on a sustained basis when he goes onstage to scream. It seems that for Eddie, as for other comedians, it's only when we are talking out loud, in front of others, that we can be loud enough to silence the voices inside our heads.

Fortunately for Eddie, he has reached a point in his life where the 'pig voices' have been turned down, though not off, and he puts much of the credit for the calming of the voices down to his ability to be discursive onstage.

'The reward of that creative work is what gets me through that shittiness. I need to be at the veterinarian with the dogs, and a dog has shat in the middle of the floor, and I'm sitting amongst it all, but there is a part of me that remembers the work I did. I am more than this human lump of flesh sitting in this vet office with dog shit around me. I try to meditate. I am constantly listening to Ram Dass or reading books like *I Am That*, constantly trying to lessen the pig voices that are in my head. Comedy consists of utilizing these pig voices. I want my mind to be like the sky and all these horrible thoughts to be like little clouds, and I have varying degrees of success with that.'

There is a delight and comedy to be had in sharing your voices with an audience, a time when 'the voices' creatively propel rather than censor or hinder.

Sometimes when I am surprised by what has come out of my mouth onstage, a series of inner thoughts becomes animated – something that may be inspired by one of my favourite early Robin Williams routines, 'Come Inside My Mind', from the *Reality . . . What a Concept* album. The piece has the illusion of a pause between frenetic routines, where Williams invites the audience to see the machinery of onstage creation as ego and superego, desperately trying to manufacture crowd-pleasing routines during fear of imminent death, while also attempting to avoid releasing the id. It is a beautiful exposition of the battle between control and mania that goes on onstage. The freedom of stand-up is that 'you' are not always in charge; when the audience are onside and you are up for playing, a cascade can come out. Afterwards audience members may approach you and comment on a routine, and you will deny it was you who said those things.

One night I did a twenty-minute piece involving a vengeful dachshund and an aggressive man in a kimono. I do not know where it came from and I was not able to retrieve most of the words I said, so I could never perform it again, but the audience members I talked to at the bar afterwards said it was the high point of the show. Some sleep specialists consider that the chaos of dreams is the mind ordering and expelling experiences of the day. There are moments when stand-up is like a waking dream. The images that occur in the excitement of improvisation can seem as if they have been dredged from an unknown place, but if I can be bothered to work backwards in the post-gig cool, I can usually find the root of such peculiarities. Sometimes, as the audience sit confused, while you excitedly tell a story about being yapped at by creatures with the bodies of shaved cats and the faces of furious Victorian children, you realize it may be best to leave the dream analysis alone and just enjoy the possibilities of 'nonsense'.

When the running internal commentary is too involved, too hypercritical, it can disable rather than inspire. My impoverished sporting abilities stem not merely from a total lack of coordination, but from a voice in my head reminding me of my inability and predicting shame and failure before I've got anywhere near a ball. In the many-worlds theory, where quantum physics suggests that every possible turn of events will happen, I can see only the negative possible events: falling over the ball, the ball going backwards, missing the ball altogether. So my sporting afternoons were spent working out ways of staying as far away from that bloody sphere as possible, because if it came anywhere near me, my body would buckle with anxiety.

In his book *How Tracy Austin Broke My Heart*, David Foster Wallace explained why he could only get so far in his abilities as a tennis player. His commentary on his actions, his imaginings of what might happen, could not be switched off, until he would find himself thinking, '. . . shut up, quit thinking about it and serve the goddamn ball . . . except how can I even be talking to myself about not thinking about it unless I'm still aware of what it is I'm talking about not thinking about?' He went on to explain that 'I'd get divided, paralyzed. As most ungreat athletes do. Freeze up, choke. Lose our focus. Become self-conscious. Cease to be wholly present in our wills and choices and movements.'

As a child, there was one film that I never missed when it was shown on television, and I was fortunate that it was shown a lot. It starred Richard Burton as a malevolent force who would intone, 'I am the man with the power to create catastrophe.' He was a man who had killed his parents, sent planes into tower blocks and caused manned space missions to fail, all with the power of his mind. *The Medusa Touch* is not in the top ten of

Burton's most celebrated films, but there is something about it that keeps me coming back to it on rainy Sundays.

I was surprised and interested to realize that I was not the only person who had an obsession with this film, and that for some it has been a lifelong inspiration. Professor Charles Fernyhough believes the film has had a positive life-changing effect on him since he first saw it when he was eleven years old. He became fascinated by the power of the mind, and has spent much of his life ever since investigating that power, though not with the end-aim of creating telekinetic chaos, as far as I can work out. From Durham University, he leads 'Hearing the Voice', which is a research project that examines the phenomenon of hearing inner voices. The project aims to show another side of hearing voices, beyond the common way of linking them to mental illnesses such as schizophrenia and psychosis. The project aims to show that hearing voices 'can also be an important aspect of many ordinary people's lives' and that they 'seek to examine this phenomenon from as many different relevant perspectives as possible'.

Though I might argue with my inner voices, I am reasonably comfortable with them. I am in a situation where rather than suppress what might be viewed by many as peculiar behaviour, I can actively reveal those voices, use them in my creative processes and get paid to do so, too. For many people in more constrained environments, the inner voices stay hidden, and it seems that the less they are outwardly expressed, the more controlling and perturbing they can become.

Am I persistently eavesdropping on my thoughts because I wonder if I can turn them into anything else – a sketch, a story, a routine, a threat?

It can be very difficult and unnerving to convey your own inner life to other people and, as such, many people would not want to. Imagine for a moment voicing all the opinions, observations and ideas that buzz around your head on any given day, or even on any particular Tube journey, and then ask yourself whether you'd feel comfortable with sharing all those thoughts with someone else? Your partner, say, or your children? The comedian Gordon Southern used to talk about being caught out at that moment when your partner looks at you, smiling, and says, 'What are you thinking?' 'Oh, I was just planning your murder.'

I can socially embarrass my wife, when I have not found a good enough alibi to avoid parties, by voicing thoughts that should frequently have been caught by the net of censorship, which is meant to guard our brain and sieve what will eventually come out of our mouths. Apparently my enthusiasm for a stuffed goat that I'd recently seen at an art event did not oil the wheels of polite conversation with near-strangers over a bottle of Campari. Similarly, an interest in cannibalism and wondering what human flesh tastes like is apparently not meant to be broached until at least a third invitation. You see, it's not just me who is not keen on going to parties; my wife is not keen on me going to parties, either – at least, not if she is with me. I burble.

As I've suggested, some of my favourite gigs, though, are often ones that just become a creative outpouring of free association, using my inner dialogue with myself to generate ideas and riff out loud. But if I'm honest, I can't say that these riffs represent every thought that passes through my mind. When I become particularly frenetic, I can imagine it is my inner mind that is being voiced, but it is an inner mind flushed out and aware that it is being watched, an inner mind that is being judged and knows it needs to be entertaining. It is my inner monologue sped up and showing off.

Charles Fernyhough believes that talking to yourself out loud would certainly be evolutionarily unwise. He says, 'The person who is hiding behind a bush saying, "I hope that sabre-toothed tiger doesn't find us" doesn't last long, plus, if you talk to yourself aloud, you are giving away your secrets.' So we keep our voices to ourselves to give us a competitive edge, and it greatly helps us, as a sophisticated social species with an impressive ability – and need – to lie.

There is something too of sophisticated evolutionary development about the reading voice we have inside our heads. Reading this page now, you can experience it as if you are not experiencing the meaning of the words directly, but more as if they are being fed to you by an internal author-voice inside your head. And yet reading quietly and internally to oneself wasn't the way one read at all until around the fourth century AD, after St Ambrose rejected the usual Roman way of reading and declaiming sentences out loud. Up until that point, libraries were incredibly noisy places.

Now, though, many outward expressions of our internal thinking are frowned upon and are seen as a little bit backward. I have sat on a bus and had a thought and then started smiling, and perhaps even gently laughing out loud, just a soft chuckle, and to judge from the looks around me, you would think I had pulled out a crossbow. The evidence of the silent thoughts of others can be disconcerting.

Charles Fernyhough thinks that if we could see other people's thoughts, it would be like Wittgenstein's lion trying to have a conversation with a human. In Wittgenstein's philosophy, 'if a lion could speak, we could not understand him'. His theory is that a lion's existence is so different from a human being's that, despite a common language, we would not be able to translate the meaning and intention of the lion's words. They would not make any sense to us, because we would not be able to find common grounds of communication. For Fernyhough, despite being the same species, the same can be said of much of our inner life. It is so unique to us as individuals – its erratic nature so attached to our personality – that any canny telepath would be quite bewildered, when listening to the minds of others.

We know so little about the nature of these internal conversations of the mind, and yet of all the people you talk to in a day, you don't converse with any of them nearly as much as you talk to yourself. Imagine attempting to keep a diary that chronicled all your thoughts; you would soon need reinforced shelves. Beyond that, you would always be trying to catch up with yourself, trying to notice the new thoughts as you jotted down the old ones.

And it does seem to be a conversation, in that there can be a toing and froing as there is between different individuals. Fernyhough describes inner speech as 'dialogic, not monologic', explaining that our inner voice is like a conversation, and not just a singular commentary or critique.

So to some degree or another, we all experience the sensation of hearing voices in our heads, having some form of interior monologue that somehow seems separate from us. For some creative professions – perhaps even comedy – drawing on those interior voices is a useful tool to have at one's disposal. Problems arise, though, if you are not sure the voice that you're hearing belongs to you. It often has that feeling of 'other', but some people begin to wonder whether someone else has entered their mind.

Most of us don't even think about how our thoughts are self-generated, but for other people, this seemingly obvious connection is not so easy. For some, the thoughts in their head become a second or third person, perhaps even a devil or god. They do not believe they are the controller and creator of the voices in their head.

Today we view such people and their beliefs as aberrant and needing of help, but is it possible that there was a time when all inner monologues were presumed to be words from beyond you? This is something that intrigued the American psychologist Julian Jaynes, who wrote just one book, *The Origin of Consciousness in the Breakdown of the Bicameral Mind* (1976), which became something of a cult bestseller. He was fascinated by introspection. He had spent some of his early years experimenting on worms and protozoa, to see how they could learn, but decided this would teach him nothing useful about consciousness, so he started to examine the history of the mind.

In his book Jaynes puts forward the argument that we did not know that our inner monologue was our inner monologue until about three thousand years ago. Until then, the two hemispheres of the brain communicated with each other, but as if separate entities, with that communication being mistaken for orders from an outside entity, maybe a god. As an example of this development Jaynes argued that Homer's *The Iliad* shows no representation of introspection, whereas the later *Odyssey* does, and so he pinpointed the awareness of the inner voice as beginning around three thousand years ago. This theory may also help to explain why throughout much of the Old Testament God speaks directly to his people, but why we haven't heard so much from him directly lately. Perhaps this is why God is angrier in the Old Testament, because we were listening to the 'I've stubbed my toe' and 'Oh shit, I've set this bush on fire' part of our internal voices and, as we know, that can consist of quite a lot of fury and not a little self-loathing.

One of the ways in which the 'Hearing the Voice' project tries to help those who have found their lives blighted by their inner voices is by showing them how artists use their inner dialogues in creativity. As a writer and novelist himself, Fernyhough explains how writers can view their inner voices as that mysterious muse that suddenly comes to them and gives them inspiration. He told me that the author Pat Barker, best known for her First World War novels, puts an imagined Siegfried Sassoon and Wilfred Owen in a room with her and waits for them to start talking. They do not talk to her, as she is not in the story, but she just has to invite them in and then listen.

Sitting in a rain-assaulted tent at the 'End of the Road' Literary Festival, David Keenan, author of *This Is Memorial Device*, told me that when he was writing his novel he would become very angry with certain characters and think, 'Why the hell are you doing that?' and then remind himself that he was in charge of controlling what his perpetrators did, or at least he thought he was in charge.

Charles Fernyhough was interested in whether stand-up comedians sit down and wait for the voices to come, as Pat Barker does. I explained that as far as I was concerned, there was no waiting involved, but that sometimes the inside of my head was like Edvard Munch's *The Scream* – one of me, the one I like to think is the main me in the me-gang, with his hands clasped over his ears, wishing the incessant babble would stop. The problem I felt was not waiting for the voice; it was waiting for the voice to say something that appeared to be useful.

I don't wait for the voices, I told Fernyhough, but I do sometimes ask them to slow down. Running away with the idea now, I told him that rather than editing the voices, for me it was a case of hacking away at the incessant stream in my head and trying to make sure that I took from it the best bits, while leaving behind the dross. Sometimes, I explained, it seemed as if five voices would pop up all at once, all with humdinger lines that I was excited by, and I would find myself getting flustered and telling them, 'Not all at once – one at a time, one at a time.' Usually, in the rapid writing-down process, I would lose one or two of the ideas, and I would have a nagging suspicion that those lost ideas were the best. Later, in bed and on the cusp of sleep, the lost ideas would come back to me and I'd leap out of bed, seeking a pencil to write them down, often injuring myself in the process. Head bandaged by morning, I'd realize the injury was for nothing, the ideas being mediocre at best. That hypnagogic state of elation at your new ideas was premature delight, at best.

Fernyhough looked at me politely, or was that sympathetically? He smiled and explained that this was perhaps the nearest I would ever get to communicating with the Wittgenstein's lion part of my brain, which he had mentioned earlier. And I realized that as well as others' brains being a mystery to us, we haven't even got round to deciphering what our own brains have to say.

I wondered again about the species of comedians, and about that survey. Perhaps we are what might be called 'self-taught psychotics': individuals who only come across as psychotic in surveys because we *want* to hear voices, we want them to energize our creative juices. Perhaps, too, because we use our eccentricities for pleasure and profit, when it comes to answering surveys we may have an acceptance of what others fear as a problem, as an unwanted form of psychosis, so we might put down what others hold back.

Charles believes that those who are distressed by hearing voices are not tuning into them clearly enough. Artists have to tune into these voices, as they often want to use them for creative effect. But for many people, hearing voices doesn't have any pragmatic use, and quite naturally they just want them to go away.

How does the 'Hearing the Voice' project help those battling with hostile voices in their head? How can you start a useful dialogue with your voices? Keith Harris would have been pleased, as Fernyhough explained how glove puppets have been used in therapy to create a physical representation of the unwanted voice, or voices, for the patient. This reminds me of ventriloquism, something that has always given me the creeps. The combination of a dead-eyed dummy that is then used as a comic prop to give voice to the internal dialogue of the ventriloquist, often instigating the most antagonistic and shocking conversation, has always disquieted me, but listening to Charles, it takes on a deep psychological relevance.

*

Nina Conti is a ventriloquist who is able to create a psycho-logical horror film onstage in just a couple of minutes. Her routine is as disconcerting as the ventriloquist episode in *Dead of Night*, the classic Ealing portmanteau horror film in which Michael Redgrave battles with his murderous ventriloquist doll. Nina's main sidekick is Monkey, a rude, lascivious id of a monkey. The interaction between Monkey and Nina is a great double act, and yet the chemistry between the two springs entirely from just one mind.

Despite the simplicity of Monkey, who is barely more than a sock puppet, he seems thoroughly alive. At the end of their act Nina continues talking as Monkey, but removes the puppet from her hand. Monkey is still alive and believable for the audience when he is just her bare hand. The puppet is not necessary. Then she drops her hand to the side of her body, mouth still closed, and Monkey becomes an invisible ghost in the room. Finally she opens her mouth, but it is not Nina's voice that comes out, but Monkey's, and her total possession by Monkey seems to be complete. I have never tired of watching the audience's reaction to Nina's show. They are amused, but even more so, they are disturbed. Who is in charge?

Nina's relationship with Monkey is a taut entanglement. It started almost twenty years ago when Nina was studying ventriloquism with the maverick theatrical shaman Ken Campbell, and from a number of basic puppets that he gave her to choose from, she selected Monkey. When she began, she believed Monkey would be just a prop, and when the act ended she'd throw the puppet into her handbag and go home. But it would not end up being that simple. She told me that now, 'I love him. I was trying to be cool about what I did and treat it like a prop, but I do care for him . . . and that's wonky.'

Her onetime tutor, Ken Campbell, wrote a part for Monkey in a play, and Nina wasn't happy. Even at this stage of Monkey's birth, Nina did not believe that Campbell could put words in Monkey's mouth. Monkey was already hers – her fabric and her mind. In this play, Monkey was in love with Nina. This disgusted her. As far as she was concerned, this was incest. 'I wouldn't allow myself to love me, because who does? – that's disgusting.

'I am very, very dirty with Monkey, and that's not normally what I say. I don't say that, because everyone will think I am a raging slut . . .' Despite this, Nina says she is rarely surprised or shocked by what Monkey says onstage because she *is* Monkey, almost as if the only prop on the stage is her, the woman holding him. She tells me that 'Nina' is on autopilot when Monkey is alive, but that doesn't stop her wondering about these 'filthy thoughts'. Charles Fernyhough told me that some voice-hearers cannot believe the voices in their head are part of them, because of either the humour or rudeness content, and they find it hard to imagine that 'they' would be capable of such things.

Nina wonders whether it speaks of some form of repression of herself that she engages in during her daily life, and then she wonders why such repression might be part of her, but she has no answer.

But comedy thrives on the repression that we all feel we must engage in, to survive in our social society. Again imagine – if you can – voicing all your day-to-day thoughts as and when you have them. If we could all express ourselves freely and without fear of condemnation, shame and embarrassment, then comedians would probably be out of a job.

When I ask Nina if she has ever had a moment when Monkey has appalled her, I am surprised that she can think of only one occasion. It was in New York. Monkey and Nina were playing to smaller audiences, and the show had a different energy. During their act* Nina spent some time in a sack, which Monkey sat on top of. Monkey was 'alone'.

At this point Nina finds that she says things that are even further removed from what she would usually permit herself to say: 'It is the freest bit of the show, and I have no idea who I am talking to.' While she is in the sack, an audience member with an obvious speech impediment calls something out. Nina can't understand him and Monkey says, 'I can't understand you

* 'Their'? It is unavoidable talking about them as two, within a few minutes of speaking to Nina.

because of your speech impediment.' In the bag, Nina is thinking, 'Are we all going to pussyfoot around the fact that he has a speech impediment, and pretend he doesn't?'

But Nina is remorseful now. 'I don't know whether that was a good thing,' she says.

What surprised me most, as we talked, was just how much control Nina has of her voices onstage. She can release this other self, but it is not wild and it is not the unruly id that I imagined. The id – the beast of desire and instincts that lives in the mind, as described by Freud and, in my view, brought to life in Robin Williams's 'Come Inside My Mind' routine, where ego, superego and slavering Tasmanian id do battle – was what I had imagined was being given free rein by the ventriloquist. But as I talked to Nina, I realized that she controlled this Lord of Misrule.

The Monkey part of her is something she is very conscious of. The taboo side is not deeply buried, but skimming on the surface.

For the ventriloquist, whilst the lines can be blurred for the audience, it is obvious in the conversations that take place that two voices are on display. For the character comedian, though, those lines can become even more indistinct and difficult to separate. Barry Humphries, creator of one of live comedy's most fully realized characters, Dame Edna Everage, has said in a way that completely highlights this split, 'She's the celebrity and I'm the puppet master. I was too nervous to appear as myself.'[2] During one of Dame Edna's New York runs, she mocked a man in the audience for wearing sunglasses indoors. Mid-mockery, the Barry Humphries behind the make-up and under the wig realized that the reason for the shades was the man's blindness – an embarrassing faux pas when Barry was himself, but now he was Dame Edna. After this brief interlude of thinking as Barry, he let Dame Edna deal with it. Acknowledging that the man was blind, Dame Edna expressed her relief that at least he hadn't brought 'his smelly dog'.* The character actor was hidden, and the ventriloquist part of the role was exposed.

The longevity of the relationship, the need to be spontaneous and creative, the total inhabiting of the role, the fact that the voice comes from inside its creator and not from a dramatist mean that the ventriloquist is not like an actor playing a part. The actor may say he has become Richard III or Mr Micawber or 'Angry Junkie at Bus Stop', but he is inhabiting someone else's creative vision and becomes someone else after the next successful audition. For Nina, Monkey's voice is not something she has created for the purpose of puppetry and entertainment; it was alive long before Monkey was sewn.

The more I think about my inner voice or voices, the more I realize that whilst occasionally onstage there seems to be more than one voice talking, most of the time it's just a single running commentary, a monologue. Occasionally, while walking down the street, a paranoid me argues with a more rational me. Sometimes they work together and come up with a routine about being paranoid while walking down the street. Nina's internal cast seems more fully formed and constantly viable. When I ask about the voices in her head, she tells me that she is plagued with contradictory thoughts. 'I find it exhausting and I want to test myself and find out what I think, and I want to find out if I think . . . that's

* It may have been 'his stinking dog'.

scary. My inner monologue is doubt and reassurance, and can you trust reassurance?'

As Nina and I are leaving, so that she can return to sitting with her acrylic writing partner, she ponders on a childhood experience of hers that may have led her down this path of having such an active internal dialogue with herself. 'As I was an only child, my mum always wanted me to play with my toys more, and I always wanted a friend round and I wasn't very good at playing on my own, which was a shame, but I think that maybe I've now become good at playing on my own. I've never said that out loud before, it's a very psychoanalytical thing.'

Perhaps comedians in the future, though, won't need such dated concepts as woolly monkeys in order to give voice to their most deep-seated fears and desires. Charles Fernyhough has been working on giving faces to other people's disembodied voices, not merely through glove puppetry, but with avatar therapy, too. This is the most recent development for people whose lives are being damaged by intrusive voices. The intrusive voice has an avatar made for it, so that the voice is given a visual identity onscreen. Animation software is then used by the researcher so that it can react to the subject. In such a way the dialogue can increasingly come under the control of the patient.[3] Doctors encourage their patients to talk back to the avatars that represent their intrusive voices. The variety of personalities for these voices range from Second World War submarine commanders who occasionally put on German accents, to voices insisting that the hearer is Jesus.[4] I wonder if, when the avatar is created, it closely resembles the typical German U-boat commander or Messiah, but Fernyhough tells me that despite the apparent stereotypes, not everyone finds it easy to create an image that goes with their voice, and some people don't find it helpful at all. The research is still at an early stage and there is much more work to be done.

We can all be disconcerted, even shocked, by some of the thoughts that enter our heads, but Charles offers some solace. He believes that most of the flotsam and jetsam of background noise that floats through his mind is not a necessary part of him. He says, 'We are all susceptible to intrusive thoughts, sometimes of a very unpleasant nature, and we can help each other to understand that it is just junk and it isn't necessarily you. Not everything that goes through your head is you; quite what "you" is, is a whole different, complex problem. There is some nice neuroscientific research out there that there is this thing called the "default mode network", which is a system in the brain which switches on when you're not really doing anything, and this is useful for creative thought. I see it as an ideas factory, as an image factory, churning stuff out all day long.'

Charles believes that the only way to be with all the stuff in your head that is churning and tumbling around is to accept that you could step forward and own it as being part of you, but that you don't have to do that. He doesn't get bothered by weird thoughts. And it is only once a thought leaves your head and you either voice or act on it that you have to start taking responsibility for it.

So I took a break from writing this chapter and went to get a glass of water and some oatcakes. I realized that I was talking to myself in my head, then singing aloud a bit of 'Sweet Caroline', and then followed that up by talking out loud in an old quavering American voice, saying apologetically, 'It's a very beautiful song,

Miriam. Please don't be like that, she means nothing to me,' and then I put the kettle on. What the hell happened there? I thought. Who was the old man? Where did that song come from? Was it just junk, as Charles would have it, or was it a useful and valid piece of thinking that needed to be voiced, creatively engaged with? Maybe I'll integrate it into my next comic performance, or maybe, if all that fails, I'll get a sock and a couple of buttons, and turn internal voices – my weirdness and malevolence – into a top-notch international cabaret act.

CHAPTER 4

Daydreaming for a Purpose

I'd hate to think that all my experiences will some
day become stories with no point.

Calvin and Hobbes by Bill Watterson

'You are the kind of man who will be found dead surrounded by carrier bags full of *stuff*,' exclaimed my wife one day, with a sense of exasperation, exhaustion and the hint of a threat.

I know she is right. The constant buzz of my internal mental machinery manifests itself in scraps of paper and postcards covered in sketches, scribbled notes and illegible scrawls. My whole office is a stacked and teetering mess.

The room reflects my conscious mental processes. Each torn corner of A4 or crumpled receipt has to be inspected before it is thrown away, just in case it has a non sequitur scribbled on it that once had the potential to be a joke or a routine or a very short story.

If I did die, then here's a brief sample from the thousands of ostensibly meaningless scribbles that would be found on the bits of paper in that plastic bag . . .

- 'toilet-door corpse horror'
- 'the dodecahedron in the cupboard'
- 'mind-envy hummingbirds'
- 'Wittgenstein suicide piano mistake'
- 'hide-and-seek dog erection'
- 'the emotional problems of living'
- 'tooth-fairy scam letter'
- 'All MIMOPHANTs now!'

Many of these brief missives to myself have been developed into whole routines, but in note-form they appear to be a sort of beat poem by someone on too much shoe-polish wine, or the frantic brainstorming of a jangly guitar band in desperate need of a name. One of the most commonly asked questions of any form of artist is 'Where do you get your ideas from?', and whilst many struggle over this question, I can answer simply: 'From out of one of my many, many carrier bags'.

Even that sort of self-knowledge is absent for some. When the artist Robert Rauschenberg was walking around an exhibition of his own work – a widely varied canon of silk screens, three-dimensional collages created from found objects and a large tank of bubbling mud – he said, apparently amazed, 'I want to talk to the guy who did all this.' Rauschenberg's imagination is an adventure we can partake in. His stuffed goat stood on a collage with a tyre around its middle, and is delightful in a way you might not expect a stuffed goat with a tyre stuck around its midriff to be delightful if told about it in passing by a friend. It is my favourite piece of taxidermy in art. One critic suggested that it is a metaphor for penetration during anal sex, but I don't always think a stuffed goat with a tyre around its middle has to be a metaphor for sexual penetration. It is instead perhaps an artwork whereby you can experience the healing balm of the imagination that others are prepared to make public, whether goat or joke.

Being creative, whether as a professional or just doodling or making cakes for the hell of it, is considered to be psychologically healthy for us. Research from the University of North Carolina found that people who were engaged in something creative at any given moment were far more likely to be happy. The more time spent on creative pursuits, the happier they were and the more open to new experiences.

So why is the imagination from which our creative impulses spring seen as so inscrutable and mysterious?

The neuroscientist David Eagleman has written of how even the greatest creative minds – perhaps especially those – were often puzzled as to where their ideas came from. In humbleness, they barely believed they had been responsible for their work at all. On his deathbed, the pioneering scientist of electromagnetism James Clerk Maxwell tried to explain that it was not him – his conscious mind – that had come up with his greatest work, but something 'within him', as if he was admitting to being guilty of thieving the idea from some other bit of his brain. And Goethe had no idea where *The Sorrows of Young Werther* came from; he just felt it flow out of him.

The other problem my wife has, with the work I do for a living, is that a good deal of my working could be confused with just staring out of the window. Coming up with ideas for shows and stories can look deceptively like doing absolutely nothing.

Surely it is possible to come up with a 2,000-word routine about seeing a giraffe in Rome zoo that had an erection while building a fence, lagging a boiler or insulating an attic? Perhaps it is possible, but it would be tricky.

For many creative people there's an awful lot of sitting around, thinking about things, before anything can really be said to have 'got done'. It's worse for a comedian, though. At the end of a working day the architect can show off the sketches for his or her new atrium, the musician ten bars of a new piece, but often all I have to show for my labours is a single one-liner beneath the two hundred that have been crossed out – and that's it. Some days not even a complete joke; some days, ten minutes of bubbling joy and nonsense. Jerry Seinfeld's *Comedian* documentary films him trying to come up with a new tour idea. He only needs to craft sixty minutes of material, so surely America's most successful comic can put that together in a couple of weeks?

It turns out that observations on chopsticks, birthday cakes and the Swiss army take time. Jokes rarely arrive bulletproof. It takes closer to a year of trying, failing, repairing, throwing away and improving, until he finds and is happy with his set and its humour, imagination and originality, which contrarily must appear as if he's just an ordinary man shooting the breeze with some people, as if a bunch of ideas had simply popped into his head.

But if it's hard to access sometimes: where does this imaginative and creative spark originate from?

Our imagination gets a lot of use in childhood, both for pragmatic and pointless reasons. Still unsure of reality (an uncertainty that it may be beneficial to maintain in adulthood), we populate our world with things from our head. Sometimes it is imaginary friends, and sometimes we decide to tell our friends that our dad plays Tarzan on the telly.

'But he's bald.'

'Obviously he wears a wig, stupid.'

One friend of mine found out that his son's imaginary friend was Adolf Hitler. In his son's defence, he would often argue with Hitler and refused to play with him if he didn't 'start to be nicer to the Jews'. Thankfully, as an adult, the son shows no signs of wishing to annex Poland or create a race of Aryan supermen.

Most of my childhood imaginative and creative ideas were, in fact, plagiarism. I used to rework tales that I had stolen from comic-book publications like *Sinister Tales* and DC's *Weird War Tales*. I also liked writing about giant rat plagues, influenced by no more than the cover art of James Herbert's *The Rats* and *Lair*. I was too scared to go beyond the cover, worried about what ghastly, gnawing, gory horror would lie within. And whilst all creative processes and ideas have in some way been subject to the influence and ideas of those who have gone before, there is a sense in which the greatest imaginations seem to come fully formed and completely unique and separate from anything that has ever previously been experienced.

*

Sometimes ideas can appear so radical and different that a majority of the population can only suppose that the creative process has been bolstered and perverted by mind-altering drugs of some sort or another.

Spike Milligan's career overlapped with the end of the music-hall comedy era and, as it grew tired and anodyne, Milligan appeared on the radio scene to create a new wild comedy rebellion. When he was interviewed by *Time Out* magazine in the late 1990s, the interviewer asked whether he had ever taken illegal drugs. It seemed an obvious question to the interviewer, who explained, 'This is a man who has written sketches in which insects prepare for an audition for a David Attenborough wildlife special; or a monologue where a man convincingly believes he is a four-poster bed.'

A wildly creative and active imagination can be viewed with suspicion and fear. It is as if society does not want people to think of the impossible or improbable and give flesh to its bones. It is not practical. What is the use of such nonsense? Those with proper control of themselves will keep their imagination focused on useful concrete (literally) things – such as building bridges, barns or gyratory systems.

The comedian and silent-movie aficionado Paul Merton was once placed in a psychiatric hospital, after a psychotic episode brought on by malaria medication. But he quickly realized that if he was ever to get out of hospital and not be eternally locked up in an asylum, then, when talking to doctors, he'd have to temper his usual descriptions of what he had been thinking about during the day. He knew that what was good for primetime – the sort of thing he'd regularly share at TV production meetings – might also lead to the straitjacket.

That line between the active imagination and the asylum, and the judgements of others in defining where it lies, can be notoriously difficult to predict. Psychologist David Rosenhan created a sanity experiment that he published as 'On being sane in insane places'. It demonstrated how, once you are placed in a mental institution, persuading people you are not insane becomes tricky. Eight volunteers became patients at psychiatric hospitals by claiming they were experiencing simple auditory hallucinations. Once admitted, they displayed no erratic behaviour and stated that they now felt fine. All eight were diagnosed as having schizophrenia in remission and had to take anti-psychotic drugs. When this problem of diagnosis was revealed, hospitals challenged Rosenhan to send more 'pseudopatients' and they would prove how easy it was to weed them out. It appeared that out of a further 193 patients, only forty-one were discovered to be pseudopatients. The only problem at this stage of the experiment was that this time Rosenhan had decided not to send any volunteers, proving that insanity can be said to be purely in the eye of the beholder.

It also shows that context is important. Someone finds a disused urinal, drags it home and puts it in the middle of the lounge. They seem to be behaving worryingly. But when Marcel Duchamp does it, a contentious art revolution begins. If anyone questions the sanity of your actions, just say it is art.

The attractive link between creativity and mental illness is bolstered by the eulogizing of Van Gogh's insanity, or the unseemly clatter that surrounds the suicide of a comedian, such as Tony Hancock or Robin Williams. Research from the University of New South Wales's School of Psychiatry into links between bipolar disorder and creativity found that 82 per cent of the patients who were questioned responded that they felt creative during their manic periods, whether it was painting pictures or generating business ideas.

Severe mood disorders have become attached to having an active imagination anecdotally and in film and TV drama, but research also seems to back up this suspicion. Nancy C. Andreasen's paper 'The relationship between creativity and mood disorders' remarks on a strong correlation between being a professional writer (in particular a playwright) and having a mood disorder such as depression or bipolar disorder. But she sums up by saying that the literature supporting this is relatively weak, and writes that 'a great deal of the work reported suffers from inadequate definitions of both creativity and mood disorders'. So you don't have to be mad to be creative, especially if we're not even sure what madness and creativity are.

One of the issues about throwing your imagination into the public arena is working out which bits of imagination are suitable for public consumption. What translates from skull to stage? Practice helps, but however weathered the imaginer, however many things they have created that have gained acclaim, ideas can still stumble head-first into the murky ditch of failure and opprobrium.

Comedian George Carlin was a revered mainstream countercultural legend, but he would spend two years on the road, honing his stand-up show until he thought it was ready for filming. Fifty years as a stand-up, but for all his instinct and learnt skills, he still couldn't simply jump onstage and know that his imagination had created all that he required for a good show. Stand-up needs an audience to shape the putty of imagination.

To have good ideas, you have to have bad ideas too, and you can't always tell which is which. Ten years ago I came up with a routine about Eratosthenes and his servant measuring the circumference of the world with sticks and shadows. Ten years on, it still remains a drawing-board idea of unsatisfying scribbles, arrows and culs-de-sac. I'm happy to share this because, even though it might be the most ridiculous idea for a routine ever, if we ridicule failure, we ridicule trying. 'If people never did silly things nothing intelligent would ever get done,' wrote Wittgenstein, which is a great comfort to those of us who feel we may be spending too much time being sillier than necessary, and slightly out of character for the way I have always imagined a man as serious as Wittgenstein. For relaxation, though, I have found out that Wittgenstein enjoyed scalding-hot baths and cowboy movies. So now I hope that the reason he only wrote two short books, with just one published in his lifetime, was because he was plagued by phantasmagorically silly ideas. Somewhere, perhaps locked behind a hidden panel of his oldest and biggest desk, we might find Wittgenstein's scrolls and scrolls of fabulous paintings and poems, which echo the sentiments and structure of the equally philosophical Dr Seuss. Sadly, reading colleagues' memories of him, it seems unlikely we'll ever find his 'The world is a totality of facts, and cats and hats and rats and baseball bats . . . not things and wings and ring-a-ding-dings.'

We all struggle to accept the creative and imaginative impulses that perhaps lie dormant within us. Seeing that even an old po-face such as Wittgenstein had a humorous and playful side could allow us all to let that playful aspect out of its box a little more often.

Sometimes, though, trying too hard can have an inverse effect. For a comedian, this can mean that finding a joke can take far longer than feels necessary. When a gag is required in the writers' room, the brain can seem to turn to chalk and an abyss of doom appears in the centre of the mind. Then, seemingly out of nowhere, but actually out of the firing of the correct cluster of neurones, the idea hurtles out. It is like the relief of hearing the first splash after a bout of constipation – you can't work out why it took so long.

On other occasions the imagination can feel even more energized than the lungs and limbs. One of the most exciting events for performers during the Edinburgh Fringe is 'Set List'. This is a place where you can watch the instantaneous imagination of a stand-up, up close. It is a game of improvisation. The stand-up goes onstage and has to perform a set based on phrases they have never seen before, and perform as if this is their best set – the big club set they do almost nightly to close the show. No humming and ha-ing or 'I'm not sure'; you must pretend this is your alpha set. You are often on the bill with comedians you fear and admire. Everyone, even the big names, is a little edgy. Is this when they will be found out? Robin Williams, Eddie Izzard, Dylan Moran and Drew Carey are among the biggest names who have risked all.

Watching from the sidelines, every comedian reacts to each set-list prompt, thinking the guy before them has definitely got an easy one and imagining how they'll stumble and falter. 'How come they got "Bestial Tap Dance Rumba" and "Jimmy Carter's Mauve Gazelle" – they are so easy.' When your turn comes, you have to fire everything up and just go, and ten minutes later, having created a story about 'John Wayne Gacy's Bicycle', 'Cat-Litter Tasting Session' and 'Mohammed Lightbulb Froth', you feel so dangerously alive and high that afterwards you will drink Kahlua or Cherry Absinthe cocktails until dawn, trying to drag down your adrenaline levels. It is the comedian's equivalent of lifting weights on Venice Beach – trying to look cool and glistening while also yelling on the inside, 'Did you see what I did? DID YOU SEE WHAT I DID THERE!'

The next day, as you sit struggling to find a punchline for a topical joke about alpaca-farming regulation changes in Northumbria, you wonder where that fired-up creative brain has gone, the one that only the night before seemed to have the wiring of a genius. Suddenly your brain feels like it's been through the equivalent of the science-fiction classic *Flowers for Algernon*, in which a bullied man with learning difficulties suddenly becomes very smart via a scientific experiment, but then loses it all again and returns to what he was. The different levels of creative function are fascinating, but it's infuriating when you are back to staring dully at a blank page.

And yet sometimes I think I'd quite enjoy not having my brain in creative overdrive all the time. As I have got older, I see every experience as having the possibility of becoming a story. As I wonder and wander around art galleries, through subways or eavesdrop on café conversations, there is a continuous process of thinking through what could be made of it: a short story, a one-liner, a routine, the arc of a whole show. It is now second nature. But as I wonder how I can use these various experiences as fodder for my comedy, I then think, 'Why not just enjoy something for the sake of it being what it is?' Perhaps the very act of letting that need and drive go would enable the imagination to work more freely, take it back to its childhood innocence, when living from one moment to the next was perhaps the time when all our imaginations were at their most vivid and creative?

One of the major inspirations of my childish imagination was the comic *2000 AD*. It was filled with peculiar worlds, terrifying dystopias and wretched outlaw alien species. One of its key writers would go on to reshape the boundaries of what was possible for comic books. Few people I know think more deeply about imagination, and use their imagination to such rich effect, as the writer and graphic novelist Alan Moore.

Moore has described his imagination as his childhood best friend. As he grew up, he used this friend to create the only comic book to be in *Time*'s Top Hundred Books of the twentieth century, *Watchmen*. Since then, often with his wife, Melinda Gebbie, he has reimagined the potential of eroticism in his work *Lost Girls*, reworked the story of Alice from Wonderland and Dorothy from Kansas and Wendy of *Peter Pan*, and, with Eddie Campbell, he created *From Hell*, retelling the story of Jack the Ripper with an unsurpassed historical and psycho-geographic intensity.

Alan has the looks and aura of an Elizabethan alchemist, with the fecund mind of a Roman snake-god sock-puppet as his assistant.* When I first met Alan, I tried to turn him from a revered

* Moore fans will be aware of Glycon, an ancient cult snake-god turned sock-puppet and an inspiration in Alan's Northampton home – a decision he made after turning forty and debating whether he should have a mid-life crisis or go totally insane. Alan's insanity is a very pragmatic insanity, for a creative individual.

and worshipped writer into a stand-up comedian, but despite a few successful gigs, he decided he was happy to remain an eloquent, funny man rather than a funnyman. I failed to destroy him with my end-of-the-pier spell.

When he was a child, Alan's imagination was drawn to myths and legends of ancient times, of fabulous beasts and vengeful gods. He was also attracted to Marvel's comic world, where awkward teens were transformed through various different radioactive events into superheroes, still fumbling in love even after they had saved the world for the fifty-third time. During this time Alan was putting on puppet shows for the other schoolchildren.

By his teenage years, the influence of the 'imaginative fiction' sci-fi magazine *New Worlds* was also having an influence on him, as teachers remarked about his school essays that they were 'quite beautiful, but utterly impenetrable'.

I asked Alan why he felt the need to express his imagination in such a way. He said that it was essentially a way of showing off. 'A lot of my creativity was showing off to my mum. My brother was a lot better-looking than me; he had the face of an angel and lovely blond curls. Showing off became a strategy.' So, for Alan, the need to be noticed incited the imagination to create the unavoidable and the noticeable.

Boredom was also the ally of his creativity. When there was nothing to distract him on long, grey days with only two TV channels, he had to fill his time with something, and that meant tapping into his own mind.

Whilst boredom was readily available and on tap in the 1960s and '70s, life now is a hectic rainbow of distractions, with computer games of zombie deaths or candy crushes. Alan worries that life is not boring enough for children to develop their imaginative capacity. It is hard to persuade a nine-year-old that being bored is better in the long term than another thirty minutes of Minecraft. 'You'll thank me for your dull, dull childhood one day; now let's walk around this DIY superstore just one more time and browse the Rawlplugs.'

Boredom creates a yawning gap that needs to be filled. Alan filled those gaps with the embryonic ideas that would grow into his award-winning comic-book behemoths.

Research from the University of Central Lancashire by Sandi Mann and Rebekah Cadman has demonstrated how boredom may boost creativity. In their experiment, one group had to copy out numbers from the phone book, while the control group was excused this tedious task. Afterwards, both groups were asked to think of as many uses as they could for a pair of cups. The phone-number copiers were more creative than the other group. In a follow-up experiment, one group copied out phone numbers, one read from the phone book and a third group did neither. Those reading the numbers – something considered to be the most boring task – appeared to approach problems most creatively. Boredom and dull tasks are a reminder that we could be doing something better with our time; they act as a contrast and incitement to fill our time more imaginatively. Boredom leads to daydreaming, and daydreaming can lead to creation. So throw away your smartphone and read a phone book instead.

The cleverest boy in his primary school, Alan was elevated to the grammar-school system aged eleven, where he rebelled against the fact that he was no longer the cleverest boy. When he was eventually expelled for selling drugs, the head teacher sent round warning letters to local employers telling them that this rebel boy was a lunatic hell-bent on destruction. Alan found himself working in the offal stink of a tanning yard and, when sacked from that, entered the Arts Lab culture of the late Sixties. The creation of spaces for poetry and experimentation (something that encouraged David Bowie too) rescued Alan and helped him put his imagination to good use.

By his twenties, Alan's imagination was his livelihood. Whatever the boundaries placed around him, he had found a way of twisting the fence posts, often straying into areas that others thought were out of bounds. He has avoided falling into a trap of 'Oh, this will do' or 'This will suit the needs of our audience'. Certainly, the hunger for success can usurp the original intention of creating things that stimulate and excite you. I have seen comedians made completely miserable when they have tried to remould themselves to become more attractive to a wider audience, searching for those illusive balms for the soul: money and fame. They have ended up loathing both their audience and themselves. Worse, changing themselves doesn't always mean they get the fame and money they hanker for. What starts as a creative exercise in expressing yourself becomes merely a tick-box job of pleasing others, and they forget why they wanted to give rein to the thoughts in their head in the first place. Leaving their imaginations behind, in search of money, can make writers crabby and bitter.

Alan makes another important point about the imagination: as in childhood, it needs to be let loose in a free and playful mind, unconstrained by boundaries, whether of your own or others' making. Even when working in a corporate environment, Alan never lost this play ethic, managing to step back from and observe his environment and then play around, subvert and undermine it. In the early days of his career, he had to work out how to keep this playful creativity, whilst also being aware of the necessity of providing a constant stream of groceries and nappies. He summarized his working philosophy during this period as 'I can't afford to turn down offers, but I can't afford not to enjoy it.'

It was at these points, these intersections of commercialism and creativity, that Alan started to wonder how his creative mind worked, how the need to make money and survive in the modern world could drive his creative juices. He did not dismiss or avoid the question 'Where do you get your ideas from?' He embraced it. As he depended on his ideas for his livelihood, it didn't seem safe to say, 'Oh well, it's just a mystery.' As he says, 'If I was a taxi driver, I'd want to know how the engine worked.'

On the shoulders of other creative and psychotherapeutic giants, he came up with the concept of Ideaspace. For Alan, the theory of Ideaspace is of a thriving mental place with connections to Jung's collective unconscious, 'The plane of reality where all our culture, ideas, identity and experience are located'.[1] In conversation with his co-creator, Eddie Campbell, who drew *From Hell*, Alan said, 'Ideaspace, where philosophies are land masses and religions are probably whole countries, might contain flora and fauna that are native to it, creatures of this conceptual world that are made from ideas in the same way that we creatures of the material world are made from matter. This could conceivably explain phantoms, angels, demons, gods, djinns, grey aliens, elves, pixies . . .' There is a geography to Alan's view of imagination, as it is almost described as a place that can be stepped into and walked over. It frees the writer from seeing themselves hunched over a desk, waiting for repetitive strain injury, and turns them into an explorer, but one who only loses their fingers to frostbite and eats their husky dogs in the recesses of their own mind.

Alan's way of imagining the imagination is a fierce reminder not to be traitorous to the potential of that imagination – not to sell out to some ill-conceived idea of what it is that an audience 'wants'. As he has said, 'If the audience knew what they wanted, they'd be the artist.'

That's not to say that a creative artist should ignore the audience, just that second-guessing what the audience wants may be a skill it can be useful to have, but overusing it can dampen your imagination. Making it worse, you may dismiss an idea, for whatever reason, because you are concerned about how far you can go with an audience. It is easy to underestimate your audience and restrict yourself – much of it out of fear that the rejection will cripple you. 'You have to assess what the problems and potential advantages of your work are, and then you've got to be right. It will all be decided by the audience,' explains Alan.

The most adored works of art are not always the most popular, but they are often the ones to which the audience shows the most commitment. They become a necessary part of the participants' life. In comedy, Josie Long's passionate and personal shows about love, politics and swimming, or Stewart Lee's slow, methodical and sometimes deliberately repetitive analyses of culture, do not follow what might be considered the usual rules of a night of stand-up, and yet people can become obsessively committed to them. US comedian Doug Stanhope can hit or miss every nail he is aiming for, depending on the night, and his audience becomes deeply involved in that element of risk. It is as if taking such risks – doing something that is so different and creative – spawns an audience/act relationship that becomes far deeper than 'Sit back and you tell jokes I like, Funnyman.' Imagination can require patience and attention on both sides of the spotlight, and the true rewards can then become greater.

The success of Alan's imagination can be measured by his audience's wish to interact with it and create from it. The corner shop at the end of Alan's street acts as a mailbox for people who wish to leave offerings for him, and they are many and varied. On my last visit to Northampton, where Alan lives, someone had delivered an intricate illustrative tree of the entangled relation-ships between the characters who exist across many time periods and places in his complex and immersive novel, *Jerusalem*. They were not satisfied with reading, finishing and moving on to the next thing; their own imagination had been fired – so potent and contagious they could not let the story go.

Have you ever dressed up as a futuristic pleasurebot, a crack fox or a yeti? If so, it is likely you are aware of The Mighty Boosh, a duo whose ideas are as original, infectious and creative as Alan Moore's. The Mighty Boosh have inspired magnificent effects with their lurid, psychedelic and preposterous menag-erie of creations. Its prime movers were Julian Barratt and Noel Fielding. Noel was from an art-school background, while Julian had engaged with experimental music, but both had become solo stand-up comedians who were more experimental than obser-vational. Their unique creation achieved arena adulation. They were adored and worshipped by a vast legion of fans. They had an outdoor festival of their own in a hop-farm field in Kent, supported by Gary Numan and The Kills.

Noel's comedy career began while he was studying at Croydon College of Art. Painting was where his imagination went first. Unlike the idea that the adult artist creates because they weren't heard as a child, Noel seems to have been supported from the outset. On the first day of primary school, the children were asked to draw birds. Immersed in his drawing, Noel eventually realized everyone was standing behind him. He wondered if he had done something wrong. The teacher asked, 'Did you do this?' and then said, 'Right, Noel's going to draw the birds, and we'll do the colouring in.' A talented artist, Noel was also warmly encouraged in his artistic output by his parents.

Whilst at art college he did a one-off stand-up routine as Jesus – clearly not fettered by lack of ambition even in his early days – and it was such a hit that he was asked to perform every fortnight. 'I built a crucifix and I'd jump off the cross and dance like Mick Jagger,' he told me, but then decided that he had to move on and drop the mask of a Messiah. Many comedians start their career hiding behind a character mask, but few start from such an elevated position as Jesus. Attempting a version of himself was challenging and nerve-racking. 'I thought, "What do I sound like? Who am I?"' When growing up, his parents had played records like Steve Martin's *Let's Get Small*, so his influences were US stand-ups, hip cats like Lord Buckley and Lenny Bruce. When Noel first heard his Jesus-less voice, he was worried that he didn't sound cool any more, because he didn't sound like Steve Martin or Richard Pryor.

I have always been impressed by Noel's tenacity. He is prepared to dig his heels in and demand justice for his imagination. I witnessed a typical example of this the first time we were on the same bill. Noel was pretty much unknown then, and he had to follow Frank Skinner, who at that point was one of the UK's most celebrated young comedians. We were gigging in this small room above a pub off Chinatown, and Frank had popped down to try out some new material for a TV show. He was in fine form and had overrun, with a series of observational routines and top-drawer cheeky smut. Noel was mentally and sartorially a very different proposition. He performed a dialogue that was taking place between some anthropomorphized biscuits in a tin. At first the audience seemed perplexed, a little lost, but Noel dug his Cuban heels into the decrepit carpet corner that was the stage, and continued to duck and weave through the atmosphere of doubt, until that doubt lifted and he eventually departed triumphant. The audience had some expectation of where Frank Skinner's imagination might go, but they had no idea where they would be taken by Noel's mind and, after some resistance, he persuaded them that they wanted to be amongst chattering wafers and ginger nuts.

The first time I saw Noel and Julian together, they were dressed as a whale and a penis for Stewart Lee's 1997 show, *King Dong Versus Moby Dick*. Not long after that, their Mighty Boosh double act came to critical and public attention, and the now-flaccid penis suit was mothballed. The Mighty Boosh became an award-winning act, attracting swathes of people to comedy who were more interested in absurdist pizzazz than in men in suit jackets and jeans telling the audience things about the lives they were already living. I was in the latter category at the time and was a reasonably lacklustre example of the genre. I spent more time drinking, complaining about other comedians and worrying about where my career was going than actually creating things that would mean my career might have a path of interest. There is a toxic satisfaction that can be found in whining about others while doing nothing yourself.

The combination of Julian and Noel was novel and inventive, as well as having something of the traditional double-act chemistry. As a joint creative process, it was an example of two imaginations becoming one. Noel explained the dynamic: 'Julian had to be more paranoid. I'd be more extrovert and he'd be more introvert, everything about us was opposite, but it became one voice, which was kind of miraculous. When we were writing, I knew it was good.'

Noel can visualize the necessary divisions of their imagination. He sees Julian's thoughts as 'a sort of panicky scream like a Russian animation, people screaming, clocks ticking, equations. His is chaos and he's always trying to create order.'

Like Alan Moore's, Noel's imagination stems from a freedom of spirit, as he explains that it's 'free like a child and very beautiful and it's surreal, but not a frightening surrealism, and I'm always trying to listen to it and get back to it, and that is why I have always animated it. I like being in that place – it's like Narnia. I'm always trying to get back to that place, and I'm always trying to take as many people as I can with me.'

Noel told me about the cab journey he had just taken on the way to our meeting. He had been talking to the driver, in the usual humdrum taxi-chat manner, about the weather and how

Arsenal's Saturday away-game was a turn-up for the books, but said that his head was elsewhere. He was thinking of people who put things that need to be thrown out into the sink, rather than into the bin. He was thinking about the elongated demise of blueberries. He was seeing the kitchen sink as a weird holding bay. He imagined the sink was a holding bay to help the foodstuffs become accustomed to the notion of change, and in that sink 'The blueberries meet a spoon with Marmite on it, and they don't know where they're going. Teabags that think they are going to heaven, but actually they're going to be boiled and squeezed; they're going to hell. So I was having a conversation with my taxi driver, but really I was thinking about that. I'm trying to write a routine about jet lag, hay fever and flu, all at a dinner party, and I'm thinking, "If I have to make a costume for jet lag, what colour will it be?"'

Noel's world may be flamboyant surrealism, but the starting point is still the mundane everyday world, the world of observational comedy. 'Hey, why do people put gone-off food in the sink, not just straight in the bin – what's that all about?' Then, the work begins. How do you give voice to a tiny smear of Marmite on a spoon, and what sort of accent do blueberries have? At times my own inclination is to stop with the initial observation, but I know that it is both fear and laziness holding me back. Part of the joy of the imagination is not letting it stop when you get to the first satisfying image or punchline. Sometimes a landscape of grandeur may arrive fully formed, but rarely. Questioning that landscape, examining it in even closer detail, worrying about it, peeling bits away, thinking and waiting for something else to make itself known – these are all still necessary. As Noel sees it,

'If you do weird stuff, people don't think you have proper jokes, [but] it's actually twice the work, because you've got to make up something completely.'

Noel believes that nowadays many people think creativity is this glamorous and cool thing, but for him personally it has always had an element of madness. It's almost as if, for him, the creative expression is a kind of release, and if he wasn't creating something, then he would start to go weird. It is not a career opportunity, but a compulsion. He worries that others may feel it's a horrible form of desperate attention-seeking, but despite this, there's something inside him that makes him want to perform and say, 'I think it is a form of madness and it is a sort of burden, because it's all you can think about all the time. But look, I've made this. I'm alive. I'm someone, or something . . .'

Back at Alan Moore's, I am still trying to find my way around the Ideaspace and, if I'm honest, I'm pretty lost. I can see that it has a connection with Jung's idea of the collective unconscious – a sort of space where ideas can congregate and develop, which is in itself . . . imaginary. But after all, what is it to talk of consciousness and unconsciousness? If you've ever watched a philosopher talking about that, you'll know what a slippery, elusive, metamorphosing mackerel it is.

Like a tourist asking for directions, I finally ask Alan, 'Where is Ideaspace?' – hoping to qualify it with the slightly more intelligent 'Where do the ideas we create with exist?'

Alan replies sympathetically, 'I started treating the world of our thoughts, the world of ideas, as a geographical shape. Then I thought: Is it possible that ideas could be alive? Flora and fauna that are not made from meat or vegetable matter, that are made from actual ideas.' He tries to view this space as physically as possible. If we take our bodily self, we have the private domestic space where we might find quiet, but we can choose to leave that and go walking in the street. He encourages us to make the same attempt to mentally leave our interior world, too. 'You've got the geosphere, the biosphere and, on top of that, you've got the noosphere.'

The noosphere is where he sees ideas existing, like a botanical garden where potential ideas can grow. Alan is up for arguing that our entire reality is a shared hallucination to start with, that it is predicated on our sensory apparatus. He says, 'We do not know that a reality is there – science can't get round this.'

The question of whether Ideaspace is a 'reality' doesn't actually matter, though, for I can see how it can be a stimulating place to imagine – a playground to run through, when you can't find the next plot or joke or tableau. Your imagination may start out as a windowbox of flowers, but it seems it is up to you to turn it into a meadow.

Once the imagination has been decanted from Alan's Ideaspace, then interaction with the audience becomes the way it is defined and given life. He knows that it's not enough just to think about your side of the equation. 'The stuff that is sitting on your bookshelf, that's not art. The art only happens at the exact interface between the reader and the creator . . . However you conceive of your audience, that ultimately imaginary figure is probably who you are doing it for.'

Alan knows that a large mass of the population have decided they are not creative people, and they think creative people

116

are a different species. He has found that many believe that in order to be creative, you have to be born to it; it's not something everyone could have and purely need a means of accessing it. Creativity is unattainable. I wonder whether such a closed-off mentality can come from childhood experiences, a lack of support or encouragement, a narrow and toxic environment. I think of myself, and of the easy path that comes from being a white, middle-class male. Even if my parents would have preferred to say they had a lawyer son, in those first stumbling days of my career, I was able to break away from that quite simply, because overarching it was someone brought up to believe that all things were possible.

I wondered what had prevented Alan from continuing on the end-of-the-pier path that I had constructed for his potential stand-up career. What was it that he had found unsatisfactory about it, as a vehicle for his imagination?

He considered that he did okay a couple of times, but that his approach to stand-up was ultimately lazy. 'A lot of the time I was just going out onstage and saying the first thing that came into my head. Sometimes that works, and sometimes it doesn't.' This instant creativity, and the chutzpah required for it, can create spectacular and surprising moments, but without some greater overarching intention, planned and thought through in advance, it can be difficult to make it interesting or coherent.

This is what I discovered towards the end of my jeans-and-suit-jacket days, my 'Hey, you know when you go to the supermarket and you can't find the coriander' days of luke-warm observational comedy. I was not committed enough to creativity.

Alan compares his stand-up to Enochian magic. This is a form of magic that involves the evocation of spirits and the summoning of angels, and is a concept based on the work of John Dee and Edward Kelley, two legendary magicians and alchemists in Tudor times. Dabbling in it, with his influence, friend and magickal co-conspirator Steve Moore, he soon realized that dabbling was not enough. 'It is a massively complex work, and to properly understand it, we would have to devote our lives to just this system, and that is similar to how I feel about alternative comedy . . .' Alan felt that he couldn't give his all to stand-up comedy and its almost-mystical processes. He realizes that to be truly creatively satisfied, in whatever realm you try to exercise your imagination, dabbling will never be enough.

Despite this, I think I learnt a lot from him about the creative use of the imagination, and much that would be relevant not just for stand-up, but for life in general. Alan told me that he sees imagination as a form of mind control: 'Art is . . . manipulating people's emotions. We use our talents . . . to actually change the audience's consciousness.' Now that is something to aspire to. The encouragement is there, the call to create, create, create, and to give ourselves the almost-childish experience of letting our minds run free. When someone complains that you haven't created what they wanted, that's really not your problem. It is up to them to find the means and ideas to create what they think the world is missing. Sometimes, if you want it, then it's up to you to make it. Build it and they may not come, but at least you have built something.

And if the link between madness and creativity is still debatable, then imagination can be a way of grabbing some of your more psychedelic or lurid thoughts and making them into an object outside your festering brain – something for others to engage with or be inspired by. It may, too, be the difference between a Booker Prize and a police caution.

CHAPTER 5

Is There a Real You?

The secret in show business is sincerity, and once
you can fake that you've got it made.

Frankie Howerd

A re you sure you don't wear a wig? Go on, have a quick
check. Sometimes you just don't know for sure.

The Young Ones changed my life. For many people, it
was their introduction to the loud, psychotic and idiotic world
of alternative comedy. One of my favourite moments takes place
in the final episode. Neil, the whining, put-upon, lentil-nibbling,
lank-haired hippy, is standing next to a refrigerator when it
explodes. The force of the blast sends his wig flying off. With
disgust and sour-faced disappointment, he looks at the camera
and says, 'Oh no, I never knew I wore a wig. Urgh.' With his
death just around the corner, Neil has discovered the horror of
his reality: he's not even a proper hippy.

It was a common preoccupation of post-modernist authors: Do the characters know they are characters existing in someone else's mind? And to take that idea further: What about us? Is there an authentic you, or are we all a slapdash amalgam of thoughts and actions that is somehow glued together to appear to be a single human?

Stand-up is about creating a persona and having these sorts of questions in the background. It is a chance to create who you want to be or wish you were, or just to exaggerate what you think you might be. And yet, isn't real life like that, too? Don't we all adapt our behaviour to fit the circumstances? Is that what we are doing when we use expressions such as 'I have my "being a dad" hat on today'?

Whose character is so consistent that they are the same with their drinking friends as they are with their grandmother? Language, accent and demeanour are all open to constant change. And isn't there a danger that, like Neil, we'll get to one of the key existential moments of our lives – our death – and suddenly be introduced to the real us, the one we never even knew existed?

Waiting at a pedestrian crossing after a late gig in Wolverhampton, I see a stretch-limo drive past me. On one side the four pink Stetsons of a hen-night protrude from the back windows, while on the side nearest to me I am mooned by three pairs of hen-night buttocks. I am unfazed, but I ruminate on the way back to my chain-hotel lodging. I'm middle-aged and dressed like a jaded sociology lecturer, so I might as well think like one. Who were those women? Why were they mooning at me?

They looked like they were having a good time, but I wondered. I thought of the day-to-day lives of the pink Stetson limo-women – behind the desk at a department-store customer complaints desk? Showing people around well-appointed bungalows, as estate agents? Curators of the Wolverhampton art gallery's fine collection of pop art? Neurosurgeons? Police officers? Stand-up comedians?

When Milly cried, 'Let's all moon the old man at the crossing!', did Kathy think she'd rather not, but joined in anyway, to avoid a to-do? Was this a gathering of contemporary friends, or had some of them moved on from their teen days but been pressured back together by Facebook invitation, for this raucous night in the Midlands?

Had some of them moved further away from the others, in taste and sensibility, but kept their increasing fondness for Dostoevsky or quantum cosmology under wraps, for fear of derision or that they might be considered to have journeyed up themselves? Or was I, yet again, projecting existential angst onto people who were just having a wondrously bacchanalian night out – the sort of night that was never accessible to me because I was always anxiously ruminating so much?

Personally, I have only mooned for professional reasons. For two weeks in Johannesburg I found myself at the end of a show naked onstage, save for a pair of socks and two balloons. I was doing the celebrated balloon-dance – perhaps the least erotic interpretation of burlesque possible – in which three ungainly men attempt to keep their genitalia covered with balloons, while slowly moving to some cha-cha music. Fortunately, my involvement occurred before camera-phones were invented. It is intriguing how sheepish genitalia can be, when placed in front of an audience.

My thoughts about who the 'real' women were behind the arses of the Stetson mooners led me to consider my own different 'hats'. I wondered how many people I had been that day.

I had been that angry, mumbling person failing to keep his swearing under his breath as he looked at the train delays at Birmingham New Street station.

I had been the anxiety-filled nervous tic leafing through his last-minute notes and wondering how many ways he could screw up his gig, questioning why he ever thought doing stand-up was a good idea, despite it having been his life for twenty-five years.

I had been the cocksure optimist talking of love and art on the stage.

Then I had been the dusty grey object being flashed while waiting for the green man.

Finally, I had been the man with a mini-bottle of wine, behaving like an anthropologist in a chain-hotel bedroom and waiting for his insomnia.

Woody Allen's film *Zelig*, about a character of the same name, tells the story of the most extreme version of a man who changes his personality – in this instance to become whatever he believes those around him want from him most. The neuroticism of fitting in leads him to tell extraordinary tales, about being anything from an orthodox Jew to a Native American to a German Nazi. He is whatever is needed to slot seamlessly into society. His wish and ability to fit in may have come from his father's uninspiring advice on his deathbed, as the narrator tells us, 'Morris Zelig tells his son that life is a meaningless nightmare of suffering, and the only advice he gives him is to save string.'

Whatever our childhoods, we are all disordered and

anxiety-filled enough to want to fit in. That said, we can also surprise people with who we might suddenly seem to be. I once went to a hockey game with the calmest astronaut I know, but leaping up and down, he was pretty energetic when it came to shouting at the ref.

Perhaps, on a sliding scale of troubled personality, a mark of your own confidence and sanity is how much you can stick to who you think you are meant to be, whatever the company. A party is a good place to watch who has the strength of personality to be only one person. At a show-business do, just like any other business social, you can stand in the background and watch the repeated transmogrifications as people kowtow, lickspittle, assert and dismiss, in the hope of snaring the juiciest career possibilities. The need to be a unified individual is frequently usurped by the ego-driven desire for promotion and popularity.

A mark of how much you can trust someone to be who they are is seeing the disparity between their behaviour towards the least important person in the room and the most important person. The greater the distance between those two personalities, the more likely they will be to cannibalize you before you're even dead, after that plane crash in the Andes.

I once spent an unexpected night out with a comedian and a group of his friends, and he played the bleeding-heart liberal with me and then the laddish, lascivious ogler with his group of pals. I've never been very good at the lads' night out, as it clashes with my cardigan and horn-rimmed specs. He became a saloon-bar Janus. One half of his face leered, while the other half took on a parson's air of disapproval.

It's the dilemma of finding yourself in one room with two very different sets of friends: 'Oh no, with Phil and Doug, I play the keen amateur white supremacist, with an interest in illegal dog fights; but with Polly and Cecil, I project human-rights campaigner and vegan flautist. How can I combine my two versions, and is it even possible to play the flute under this white hood?'

After years of practice and performance, stand-up comedians project a very specific version of themselves. It is a heightened reality or a heightened absurdity. An audience needs to know what they believe they are dealing with – the universe they occupy must be defined.

If surrealist comedy double act Reeves and Mortimer suddenly stopped hitting each other with oversized pans, and presented a heartfelt diatribe about the destruction of the North-East's manufacturing base, most of the spectators would be confused or would take it for a spoof on heartfelt diatribes. Harry Hill playing around onstage with a twenty-foot-long inflatable sausage will delight his audience, but if superstar comedian Chris Rock suddenly brought on an inflatable sausage or swollen pie, there would be mass confusion.

But with some comedians, it is expected that their onstage persona goes beyond the stage. The male comedian who espouses feminism onstage can't drop it immediately afterwards and start wolf-whistling the bus queue. The socialist comedian is under investigation if he or she underpays the support act. As Kurt Vonnegut wrote in *Mother Night*, 'We are what we pretend to be, so we must be careful about what we pretend to be.'

*

Any comedian who has to dress in a wildly flamboyant costume for their act, such as the early comedians of music hall and vaudeville, is clearly creating a separate persona for the stage. The dressing-up box of the contemporary comic is generally more day-to-day and dowdy, with some exceptions, such as the gender-uninhibited flamboyance of Eddie Izzard or the patchwork Max Miller-style of Roy Chubby Brown. And yet their offstage wear is often remarkably similar to their onstage costume, if not the same.

I have specific shirts and cardigans for my performances, but they are very close to the specific shirts and cardigans that I wear in real life. The limited change in my costume reflects the limited distance between my onstage persona and my offstage one, though I still take it preposterously seriously.

Once before a show, I had to pop onto the stage to position a book as a prop. A few of the audience had already come in, so it went through my head that, to avoid ruining the magic, I should take off my stage cardigan, which I did before going onto the stage. I take my persona very seriously, even if it is mainly the person I am. It is the great lesson of entertainment: never reveal the cardigan too early.

I played around with all manner of drab stage-garb for the first decade of my career. I started with a leather biker's jacket that I had bought from my friend Sophia. It had looked good with her Louise Brooks bob and leggings, but merely made me look like a doll whose head and limbs had been attached to the body of a bomber-jacket teddy bear. Whatever message it gave off, it was not one of Fonz-like cool. It showed someone who was clearly not comfortable in either his skin or that of a cow.

That flirtation was brief. I still had it in for cows, so the next jacket was suede. Like a uniform, it was a costume that marked you out as 'a comedian', as 32 per cent of comedians had exactly the same jacket.

Next, it was a modish suit, a lucky find in a seaside charity shop – the deceased fortunately having the same inside-leg and chest measurement as me. Now in my late twenties, I was trying to look professional: second-hand professional.

I briefly wore a Hawaiian shirt, but it made me too loud when I was loud already.

My favourite look was a drip-dry, no-iron, frilly pink shirt that I am still rather fond of. It was just like the one Carl from Cud* wore on the cover of the *New Musical Express*.

I then began to find clothes that seemed to reflect my mind – the look of a slightly shabby sociology lecturer. From biker's jacket to cardigan, I had realized that I was mild, not wild.

'What are you rebelling against?'

'The potential addition of VAT on books.'

I realized I needed to get some real experts' advice on how we put on masks and hide our deepest unconscious personas, so I decided I needed to talk to some psychoanalysts. I first read some Carl Jung many years ago, when I presented a non-broadcast TV pilot about psychology called *Right Said Freud*. I am sure that Sigmund, having written so much about the concept of the pun, would have appreciated the title. When I write that I *read*

---

* I hope you know Cud, a much underrated UK band whose output included 'Rich and Strange' and 'Only (A Prawn in Whitby)'. They also gave away the best freebies with their single releases. I still have my revolving luminous Virgin Mary that came with 'Neurotica'.

some Jung, I should say that I bought some Jung and then read a big comic book all about him. I am one of those who withers under Arthur Schopenhauer's aphorism 'Buying books would be a good thing if one could also buy the time to read them; but as a rule the purchase of books is mistaken for the appropriation of their contents.'[1] I have actually read some little books of Schopenhauer, though I still haven't got to the big books of his and the biographies that I bought, quite certain I would read them instantaneously, although I am now relying on them seeping from the shelves and into my mind as I sleep.

The first story that I read about Jung was about his dream of God doing a destructive poo that demolished Basel cathedral. That is the sort of story that sticks in a comedian's mind, while all the useful and more important findings of twentieth-century psychological research refuse to stick. Among Jung's most-repeated ideas are Synchronicity – so good that Sting decided he would use it for the title of a Police album – and Persona, so intriguing that Ingmar Bergman wrote a psychological drama with that as the title.

'Persona' is the concept of someone's public mask. It is the image that we wish to portray. Jung wrote:

Society expects, and indeed must expect, every individual to play the part assigned to him as perfectly as possible, so that a man who is a parson must not only carry out his official functions objectively, but must at all times and in all circumstances play the role of parson in a flawless manner . . . each must stand at his post, here a cobbler, there a poet. No man is expected to be both.[2]

The mask is meant to hide the true nature of the individual, so that we're all interacting as fictions. Is the real you or me, or Tommy Cooper, only retrievable when alone? Would you be a more authentic person if you were alone on a desert island, or isolated in a ruined post-apocalyptic city taking potshots with your crossbow at the thoughtless zombies that mindlessly hanker for your brain? With no one to impress, we'd never show off and seek to be impressive. But then we are not solitary animals, and we are all a bit of a show-off. Even Jesus kept upping the ante, impressing the demanding crowd with his miracles.

With my scant, cartoonish knowledge of Jung, I knew I had to seek out someone with a deeper understanding, and had a Jungian analyst recommended to me by a Kleinian with Lacanian tendencies. Our meeting of masks was not overly successful. I had come straight from interviewing a surrealist, and was dusted in fine sugar granules from the doughnut I had eaten while hurrying to the appointment. I also had mud on my shoe, which I became increasingly aware of as I looked at the pristine rug beneath my chair. At least I managed to keep quiet about the big poo in the cathedral story.

Andrew Samuels has been a therapist for forty years, describing his work as 'a unique clinical blend of post-Jungian, relational psychoanalytic and humanistic approaches to therapy'. He is also the author of a number of books about Jung and Jungian theory. The more I spoke to him, the more trivial and foolish I felt.

Andrew is not keen on comedians. I walked in, if not as an enemy, at least as a symptom of the disease. I didn't disagree with the appraisal. Comedians have become an omnipresent part of the mass media; they are a lot cheaper to film than Victorian melodramas and international drug-conspiracy thrillers. Andrew thinks this omnipresence is eroding culture. For him, I was the mildly bubonic, clown-faced horseman of the apocalypse. And one with muddy shoes, too.

He explained to me how useful comedy might be for connecting us to the multiple threads of our personality, and how it could create a discussion with ourselves. When used well, he believes comedy could put people in touch with their 'seamy side in a harmless way'. He believes that 'It is doing the confessional for you. It connects with the shadow type of experience.' Jung wrote that the shadow is 'the thing a person has no wish to be'.[3] Failure to acknowledge the shadow can be at the root of our problems when we communicate with others.

The shadow is the part of you that the conscious you tries to avoid hearing, though it doesn't only include what the conscious might deem to be negative. Creative-writing tutors may encourage people to meet 'their shadow', as Jung believed that it represents the seat of creativity. Andrew told me that if your meeting with your shadow is comfortable, then you are not doing it right, or you're meeting something in your mind that is pretending to be your shadow.

He then paused to point out that my 'quality of listening' had changed. Apparently my face had become quite solemn. He had to tell me this, as he explained, 'I'm a shrink, I can't help it.'

This did not relax me. I don't think it was meant to. He had commented on my very physical mask and, with the mud on my shoes too, I now felt hyper-vigilant. I had become aware of my every facial muscle. Was my face looking right now? What about now? Was I creating the correct look of attention? In attempting to discuss persona, I became overly aware of my persona.

My quality of listening changed when Andrew suggested that I was looking in the wrong place. It was not those who could tell jokes that were interesting, it was those who couldn't. According to Andrew, the ability to stand up and tell jokes 'is a part of individuation and maturity'. It is a demonstration of confidence of character – not just from those who tell jokes professionally, but from anyone who can tell a gag or anecdote in a social situation.

It is a mark of a certain aspect of mental health. Being able to tell a joke doesn't mean that you haven't got any psychiatric problems, but it is a very interesting organizer in evaluating somebody's personality. All those studies hoping that the joke-teller is damaged, all those docudramas about 'the private pain of a TV funnyman', may be missing the true tragedy about the private and public pain of the person who can never be funny – those who would never take the risk of getting to the punchline 'I don't know, but the Pope's his chauffeur' or 'Now *that* is how you wave a towel'. Andrew is at an early stage of thinking about this, but he summarizes it as: 'You can organize evaluation of someone around their relationships, you can organize it around their sexual life, you can organize it around work, religion, but you could also organize it around humour or the telling of a joke.'

Andrew and his PhD student wanted to work with a group of psychologically disturbed, yet unfunny non-joke-tellers. They would consider drug addicts or schizophrenics, and other 'brainy but boring' people, as possible candidates. The hope was that the psychologically damaged people would learn to tell jokes, then 'they would immediately give up drink, drugs, whatever, get a job, find a house and be terribly happy'.

I was already feeling better about myself – and I hadn't even come in for therapy. With my solemn face clearly intrigued, I waited for the next part of the story. Disappointingly, there is no next part of the story. The experiment is yet to be done.

Andrew explained that this was for three reasons:

1. They didn't have the money.
2. They didn't have the venue.
3. They didn't really have the drive to do it.

(Whether it was brain scans or therapeutic research, it was increasingly clear that finding time and focus for comedic psychological research was sparse, and it would have to be left to idiots with time on their hands, travelling from town to town, to seek the truth – and, fortunately or unfortunately, that is me.)

It is not comedy itself that riles Andrew; it is that, for him, comedy is too ubiquitous, seeping into the corners that culture used to inhabit. He believes much of it is weak and that, with the glut, the quality has gone down and, with it, possibly the honesty, too. He does not see sincerity as an advantage in any career progression. The deeply sincere person may or may not get to the top, but it is likely that 'the operator' – whether in politics or punnery – will get to the summit first.

I admire Andrew's ambition for what comedy should be. He says, 'There is a laudable idea here, which is to transmute, to chemically change, personal suffering into collective pleasure by laughter. Some people do this superbly well because they understand the game, they are faux-comedians. I don't know what happens to the truly suffering alchemical souls that try to turn the shit into gold, but authenticity doesn't necessarily mean they'll succeed.'

As I leave, I promise him tickets for a show, wondering if he'll sit in the front row, his scowling face reminding me to transmute, and not just tell phoney-baloney jokes. I hope I can manage that.

In attempting to interview a Jungian about masks, and about how we create ways to be perceived, I became so caught up in how Andrew was perceiving me that I fucked up the conversation that I had intended to attempt, and I think Andrew rather enjoyed that. He wears his mask better than me.

For the purpose of balance, I thought I had better go and see a Freudian.

Josh Coen is Professor of Modern Literary Theory at Goldsmiths, University of London, and a psychotherapist. Unlike my meeting with Andrew, I was not meeting him for the first time, so I was a little less worried about my mask. I first met Josh at a bed-and-breakfast in mid-Wales, where we shared the communal table with Sultana Bran and a man keen to tell us about his life working on the Nineties TV hit *Beverly Hills, 90210*. I stayed in contact with Josh, because you never know when you'll need to have a Freudian psychotherapist to hand. I did not stay in touch with the man who worked on *Beverly Hills, 90210*, as I don't think I'll be needing an expert on Jason Priestley and Shannen Doherty any time soon.

Josh's office has the standard flat bed, box of tissues and the *Complete Works of Freud* displayed on the shelves. I wanted to know what he felt could be revealed about a personality from the types of jokes someone told. Just as in dream analysis, isn't a banana sometimes just a banana, a joke just a joke?

He sees the process of stand-up as similar to the intentions of psychotherapy, but with an element of control that means the joke-teller only reveals what they want to reveal about them-selves. With psychotherapy, the hope is that you peel back the mask or crack the protective shell.

Josh views good stand-up as taking the model of psychother-apy's free association, where a client is asked to voice everything that comes into their head to the psychotherapist, much in the way of the hearing-voices idea. He sees a good stand-up act as being funny because it follows that odd, non-linear association, though he also believes that it is trying to control that process. What he sees is 'a tension between the wish to do what you try and do on the couch – to release the person that you really are – and the struggle to craft that into a kind of honed representation of how you would like to be seen to be'.

How honest is anybody on a psychiatrist's couch? How about a stand-up on the couch? Do they tell the truth, or do they tell the version of the truth that will increase the sense of mystery and enigma around them? Do we reveal some true self, or just some desperate self? What does it say about us when the need for a laugh, for instantaneous approbation, usurps all other ethics and niceties? Being on the couch is not, of course, about speaking the truth about some sort of reality, for all is truth and reality; instead, it is about probing the unconscious, bringing that to the fore. So the sort of jokes that you'd think of and then reject in the writing process may find their way out when you are on the couch, trapped in an ego-sucking swamp of failure.

Josh believes this may partly stem from the problem that the unconscious is not politically correct. I sometimes see this on nights of stand-up improvisation; when a comic is up against it, those more highly evolved human traits of decorum can be lost in the chaos caused by the desperation to please and find a laugh. He explains, 'If you are drawing straight from the deeper, less consciously controlled wells of your mind, you're likely to come across a person whom you might not like very much, as their thinking and feeling are not very much in conformity to what their culture says it should be.'

So in his everyday work Josh sees the boundaries of respect and decency being trampled on, and comedy is bound up with similar ideas of transgression. But much as many comedians are attacking the bounds of decency, it is only at extreme moments that they may lose their grip on the image they have control over and wish to portray. Whilst I feel that Robin Williams pushed those boundaries in his 'Come Inside My Mind' routine, he still didn't release the full, crazed, slavering id onstage, just as most people don't in their day-to-day lives, either. If comedians really did release the full slavering id, the comedy clubs would soon be closed down under laws of public decency, gross impropriety and health-and-safety regulations, but there are nights when you might catch a brief glimpse of the stocking of the id.

Josh explains that Freud saw humour and the punchlines to jokes as cutting out the usual rational processes of selection and judgement. It's almost as if our humorous mind can override all other considerations, even if just momentarily. You can hear this when performers such as Frankie Boyle or Katherine Ryan stretch the boundaries of their audience's 'decency'; when there is a laugh and then an intake of breath, where the conscious 'nice person' kicks in and thinks, 'Ooh, am I allowed to laugh at that?'

Josh explains that Freud's view about laughing was that 'when the unconscious comes to you in its raw form, that's often your reaction. It's not wry amusement. You feel a bit possessed, there is something hilarious about this person that is inside yourself – the person that doesn't give a toss about being nice.'

When watching stand-up, Josh doesn't like to feel manipulated by carefully crafted shock; he wants it to be genuine, not phoney, to come from within the person. There can be unexpected laughter in therapy, too. When Josh does free association in therapy, it can be funny when the patient's scruples are dropped. 'You find yourself in "and another thing" mode, and it can make you laugh. Patients sometimes make me laugh, as they surprise both of us with the weirdness of their mental processes. My affinities in comedy all relate to someone who is showing me the strangeness, the sheer kind of madness of their own mind and how it works. You can tell when it comes from an interior place.'

Most of us, barring the occasional psychopath or genocidally driven despot, want to be thought of as a good person and yet, as Josh explains, such a desire can become overwhelming, so much so that any perceived deviation from what a person believes to be 'good' can lead to intense feelings of shame and guilt, which are far more damaging to the individual than the 'bad' action in the first place. So, as someone who is constantly concerned about how I am being perceived – whether others think me 'good' or not – it is a relief when Josh tells me that in the early days of the therapeutic process, one of the most important moments is the realization that 'I'm not as nice a guy as I think I am, and that's okay.' This is where the exhilaration comes from, when an audience laughs at what they know they shouldn't, or wouldn't, in other environments. They are allowing themselves to be just a little bit naughty. As Josh sees it, they laugh 'Not in spite of, but because they know they are not supposed to. It is incredibly important. It's like non-pious self-education – you learn it in the most experiential way possible, without having intended to learn anything about yourself.'

And then I think back to my stand-up, and I wonder if I bumped my head on my own fears about how I might be perceived? The fear of showing too much of myself; the awareness of words being misconstrued; the constant thoughts on how many permutations of interpretation a line may have? All of these probably stopped me saying something more interesting. Do we all look back on our lives and wish we'd been freer, more open and dynamic? I also look back and still have a cold feeling of dread come over me at some of the lines I used, which even now make me feel uncomfortable; which perhaps I hope now are not a true representation of who I am, but at the time I used because I just wanted to get a laugh.

Everyone wants to know the face behind the mask, when it comes to comedians – far more so than of authors, architects or mountaineers. 'Did you ever see the real Sir Edmund Hillary?' doesn't crop up, because the real one is imagined to be the one on show at the top of Everest, even if there was indeed a dark side to the man, involving Sherpa aggression. 'The secret dark side of Edmund Hillary – new biography reveals he didn't really like going out much, and only went up things if he knew people were looking.'

Despite the fact that we are all aware we can adapt our personalities depending on the situation, people are still surprised when their mild-mannered neighbour turns out to be a serial killer. *Sure, his drains seemed to be a bit whiffy during heatwaves, but he always seemed to be so quiet and kind to his mother.*

Of course he was quiet; his head was in always in the clouds, wondering how he could get someone in the ground, or at least round the U-bend. And it turned out that 'Mother' was him in a summer frock and wig, all along.

It is much easier to think that people who commit despicable acts are just despicable through and through, that they are a stick of rock with the word 'abominable' running all the way through it. It is like the joke about the man who complains that, despite all his wonderful deeds in the local town, from bridge-building to swamp-draining, no one calls him 'Tom the bridge-builder' or 'Tom the swamp-drainer'. Exasperated, he explains to the stranger, 'And then you go and shag one sheep . . .'

And this highlights too that it is life at its lowest ebb that many people see as the most authentic version of a person, since their bubbly outward joy can only be a front for some deeper personal pain. Published diaries, letters and memoirs elevate the melancholy feelings that many performers seem to have, and yet I wonder whether, when you are happy, you are often too busy and content with life to bother writing in your diary; anyway, who wants to read about another person's happiness? This is not to dismiss sadness or depression; it is just that to sum up someone's life as 'she was a sad person' or 'he was a happy man' seems too reductive. Max Wall considered it a preposterous question to ask if you were a happy person. You might be happy and ten minutes later experiencing despair, and it might well go in the other direction, too.

And yet we seem to want our artists doomed – not laughing or indulging in normal earthy delights and passions. Author James Hawes deviated from writing novels to write *Why You Should Read Kafka Before You Waste Your Life*. He wanted to rebut the image of Kafka as miserable and dour, as he seems to be in the photo of him that is most used. You look at that photo and think: Here is a serious, gaunt and haunted man. He is not like you; he is deeper and sadder. Hawes, however, takes Kafka away from his tortured solitude, offering stories of a far more gregarious and joyous life, removing the idea that he was a neglected genius during his lifetime, and adding a stash of exotic porn to his desk. He removes some of the burden that makes Kafka a crushed man. According to Hawes, 'Kafka's porn is no real secret. The mystery is that it should seem like one.'

Some of the angrier online reactions to the work were a little antsy that an author was trying to take their misbegotten hero from them. When I was a wallowing teenager, I wish I'd known that Kafka would become incapable with laughter when he read *The Trial* to his friends.

It is easy to fall into the trap of feeling that it is only through being miserable that you can be deep and meaningful. Just as you can rush with open arms into intoxicants and, carousing, embrace the mythology of the artist, you can also trudge down-heartedly into becoming the morose, sullen-faced clown that pops up on picture postcards. It's as if life becomes a competition, and the winner is the one who seems to be enjoying life the least. In my life, after the onstage tomfoolery, you can submerge

140

yourself in weighty literature and whisky, swilling Glenfiddich as you read Fernando Pessoa's *The Book of Disquiet* – a particularly good Penguin Modern Classic to hold up high, if you want to show that you contain deep, lyrical despair on the bus to Droitwich Spa:

> I am the outskirts of some non-existent town, the long-winded prologue to an unwritten book. I'm nobody, nobody. I'm a character in a novel as yet unwritten, hovering in the air and undone before I've even existed, amongst the dreams of someone who never quite managed to breathe life into me.

It's hard to surface feeling gleeful from that. Obviously, it is a favourite of Morrissey.

I once wrote a gloomy, self-mocking blog about why I felt it was necessary to resign from stand-up. At this point a journalist contacted me and asked if I would do an interview for a glossy magazine that was more aftershave adverts than content. He had seen in the blog many doubts and fears that rang true with him, too. Unfortunately he got me on a good day, so the interview was not interesting enough to appear. Our coffee-shop conversations were timed terribly, as I had returned home and, rather than feeling exhausted in a Brisbane hotel 10,000 miles away, as I had been when I wrote the original resignation blog, I could only give the journalist a light froth of cheery thoughts, and of sometimes feeling a tad miserable when staring at dressing-room light bulbs. It was too mundane for print. The 'real me' lacked melodrama, agony and anxiety. I was the happiest I had been in a long while, and so could not believe that I had possibly been wretched.

Brendon Burns is a comedian and a wrestling fan, producing podcasts and live shows with his professional wrestler pal, Colt Cabana. I don't know if he has ever seen the Monty Python sketch in which Colin 'Bomber' Harris, played by Graham Chapman, goes into the wrestling ring to try and defeat himself. I think he would enjoy it. Brendon found himself in a similar battle with himself, though one that ended up in a clinic, rather than with an ovation at the Hollywood Bowl.

He experienced a premature mid-life crisis when, in his late thirties, he battled with what he saw as the contradictions between his loud, booze-filled and drug-fuelled rebel comic pose and his quieter, thoughtful, more caring role as a dad with responsibilities. Each night at the Edinburgh Fringe festival, the two personalities would duel. The drama of the act was balanced on who would win: the sober one or the raging id?

At the end of the first run of his show, *Brendon Versus Burnsy*, he collapsed sobbing and it was clear that an hour a night in front of a paying audience was not going to be enough therapy to sort out this particular psychological issue. Dealing with the issue would go on to become a trilogy of monologues spread over two years, but it didn't conclude even then. Near the end of the worst of the feud between himself, Brendon/Burnsy found himself taking magic mushrooms, caterwauling and climbing towards the big-top rafters of the Glastonbury Festival cabaret tent.

A documentary was made of Brendon's highest highs, including the moment at Glastonbury that was his tipping point, but the producers decided it might have been to Brendon's detriment if it saw the light of day, and it remains a locked-up curio, the secret footage of a mind at the end of its tether. Whilst Brendon fell for the mythic image of the rebel outsider and its extreme hungers, I fortunately fell only for the necessity of a pink frilly shirt and the odd whisky.

After a nervous breakdown, Brendon reached a point of questioning just how the two personalities could live side-by-side, then realized that they couldn't and so turned full-time to sobriety and life on a farm, though there is still a gleam of Burnsy behind his eyes, and his delight in the offences he committed has not been entirely extinguished.

Born in and growing up in Australia, Brendon did his first comedy gig in the UK in his late teens. Considerably younger than his two siblings, he was considered 'the funny one'. His mother said that, even as a baby, he would make everyone laugh. He was an effective show-off at school and at weddings and christenings. That first gig took place while visiting England to help his sister, who had been involved in a horrific car crash that had killed her husband and unborn child. Brendon's Australian girlfriend had also just chucked him.

They were not auspicious omens for his first live performance. He stormed onstage, screaming at the crowd, in particular the women – a crazed teenager hollering aggressively through his pain. He was reflecting the style of one of his comedy heroes at the time, Sam Kinison. The trouble was that Kinison made screaming at the crowd look easy, as he had been practising for a while. Kinison had been a preacher and had worked his way through the clubs; his aggression was honed. The audience was nonplussed by Brendon's rage, yet he continued haranguing, quite unaware of how much he had run over, until the MC had to forcefully shepherd him offstage.

That failure would have been painful enough, but it became much worse. As he walked offstage, Brendon saw that his mum and dad were standing at the back of the room, his father with a video camera in his hand. They had thought that watching their son's first gig, and surprising him afterwards, might have cheered both them and him up. Instead they watched him shouting at strangers, aggressively demanding that women use the microphone to demonstrate their oral-sex technique.

Brendon nervously asked his father if he had filmed the whole thing, and still has total recall of his father's reply: 'I stopped filming when the first tear of shame hit my cheek.' It is as close to the definition of a nightmare first gig as you are ever likely to hear.

Brendon didn't give up, though he may have been a little more thorough in ensuring that his parents remained uninformed of his whereabouts, when performing. He gigged inauspiciously in Australia and then came back to London, where his onstage persona took shape and gained interest.

At school, Brendon was known as Bogun Burnsy – 'bogun' being Australian slang for an uncouth and unsophisticated person, or trailer trash. He played this up onstage, the unruly young aggressor with a baseball cap saying 'sex' on it. Brendon told me that he reckoned he knew he was playing a game, or at least he did initially. When people who knew him asked why he was so uncouth onstage, he explained that the reveal would happen in five years. After five years, the reveal he had hoped for hadn't happened, so now he explained that it would be ten years. But at ten years, it still hadn't happened. The reveal was going to be that this bogun comedian would win a prize and show he was smarter than anyone had imagined, but after ten years the game had become real and the character had torn up his life. This was where *Brendon Versus Burnsy* was born.

Five days after volume one of *Brendon Versus Burnsy* ended, I was travelling with him to an end-of-the-pier gig in a small coastal town. The traffic was terrible and we were close to being late. The car had a breakdown at the last minute. We were both rushed and stressed. By the time he took to the stage, it was clear that Burnsy had been far from vanquished.

Now Brendon has become comfortable with himself, or himselves, and after twenty-five years of performing he offers this observation to young comedians: 'You spend ten years creating the mask, and you spend the rest of your career trying to peel it away.' Such wisdom is drawn not only from his career in comedy, but from his obsession with wrestling, too. Most wrestlers adopt an onstage persona, and many have, of course, donned an actual mask. The masked wrestler needs to keep his mask on, in order to hold on to his mystery, and Brendon suffered with the same self-inflicted struggle.

He has been sober for more than a decade now, and when Brendon analyses his onstage past, he thinks the problem was that he felt more connected and alive to the onstage persona than to the character who inhabited his everyday life. He remembers 'blaming shit' on his onstage persona, who became an excuse for his real-life irresponsibilities and errors. Now, though, he has found a more settled kind of existence and perhaps happiness, doing tours of strange small venues and ordinary people's lounges. He no longer requires such extreme diversity between 'selves', and he is closer to a single persona now, across both his everyday and his performing life. We both agree that middle age has quelled our ambitions somewhat, helping us to see our own ridiculousness and become happier for it.

Whilst many of us will not go through such extremes, we all nevertheless inhabit different personas at different stages of our lives. Leaving home and making our own way in the world is perhaps the time when we know least about ourselves and yet have the most to prove. The world is our oyster, as the saying goes; but equally, slimy, fishy, grey oysters aren't everyone's cup of tea. Which is to say that we can prance about all we like when we're twenty-two, desperate to make the right impression, to fit in, to be cool, to make it in show business or politics, or whatever. But when you reach that mid-life moment and you realize you're inhabiting the wrong persona, and it seems too late to change and, even if you could, 'change to what?' – that's when the crisis can come crashing down around you.

As Jungian analyst James Hollis says, 'The experience of the Middle Passage is not unlike awakening to find that one is alone on a pitching ship, with no port in sight. One can only go back to sleep, jump ship, or grab the wheel and sail on . . . Changing one's job or relationship does not change one's sense of oneself over the long run. When increasing pressure from within becomes less and less containable by the old strategies, a crisis of selfhood erupts. We do not know who we are, really, apart from social roles and psychic reflexes. And we do not know what to do to lessen the pressure.'[4]

Just as we all adapt our personalities to the situations we find ourselves in, I undoubtedly have a stage persona, but how I exhibit it can be dictated by the rules – some explicit, others not – of the situation. It is not a Jekyll/Hyde transformation, merely a matter of degrees. On a radio show discussing the curvature of space–time, I will present myself in a more urbane manner than when I am alone onstage being overexcited by black holes. Similarly, people who have never seen me live onstage before, and have only heard me on the radio, can be surprised by the almost insane levels of excitement I can exhibit when I am on my own, talking about Dadaism and narrowboats.

When I was performing in a pub in Chippenham for its annual comedy festival, a regular approached me to say how much he enjoyed coming to see me live, which always surprised him, as he hated me whenever he heard me on the radio. The good people of Chippenham bringing an earthy honesty to a compliment, just in case there was a danger that such effusiveness went to my head. Perhaps, confident enough in my own saggy, middle-aged skin, I can now take such criticism in my stride. But when we are younger, when we don't realize we are still only half-formed, it can be difficult to be so laid-back about such things, whether directed specifically at us or more generally.

Working out who you are takes longer than I thought. When I was a young man, I read an interview with Jo Brand explaining that stand-ups don't really know who they are until they are at least thirty. I grumpily disagreed, because I was twenty-two and I had come second in a big comedy competition, so I knew exactly who I was. Now I know exactly who I was then, and I am not best pleased: what a bloody fool! It has taken a while, but I have got used to myself. When I am in front of people, the things I say – the things I seem to be – are me, as near as damn it. They may not please you, but they are not a lie or a fabrication, or a front created in the hope that you like me. It is easier to live now than it was then. Sure, I may well still be a dick, but I am a more authentic dick than I was before. Who can spring out fully formed?

That is why we have to try on our different masks, piercings and duffel coats.

That is why there is a gentle agony when someone digs out that box of dog-eared photographs of themselves in their late teenage years from an attic shoebox. We see what we truly believed at the time to be the greatest haircuts, boots and tattoos. I once toyed with the idea of a tattoo of Oscar Wilde flying on a sunflower, before a solitary lapse into prescience saved me a lot of laser surgery. How many twist their necks and look at the reflection of their 'Brandon Lee in *The Crow*' back-tattoos and think, 'I never knew there would come a time when it was no longer my favourite film.' Now, I toy with the idea of getting Ingmar Bergman's *The Seventh Seal* on my chest, as maybe Death will see it when he comes for me and give me a free pass, because I'm a fan. With another few hundred years to play with, I could really get to know myself well, though I reckon one century of being me might be enough.

CHAPTER 6

Getting to Know Your Inner Fraud

'Hallo, Rabbit,' he said, 'is that you?'

'Let's pretend it isn't,' said Rabbit, 'and see what happens.'

Winnie the Pooh by A. A. Milne

My status as an impostor was confirmed when I was twelve. It may go back further than that, but it was in 1981 that I received the certificate making it official. It was actually a book token rather than a certificate. I had won the school book-review prize for my work on Agatha Christie. I had never read any Agatha Christie, but I made some suppositions, based on what I had heard about her work and seen on TV, and somehow created something coherent. *I'm sorry, Mr Clifton, I will return the book if you would like me to.* From this point onwards, with my trophy in charlatanism held low, my future was certain.

Now, I am a Renaissance idiot. Full-time.

I have read just about enough about a large enough number of things to be wrong about nearly everything, but as long as I am in a room with people who don't know I don't know, I can look like I know something. It just becomes a situation of waiting to have the whistle blown on you, when the Professor of Continental Philosophy or marine biologist or tree surgeon walks into the room unexpectedly.

'Hold everything, that fellow doesn't have a clue about Dutch Elm disease.'

My impostor syndrome may be because I really am an impostor when it comes to having an informed opinion on Derrida, cuttlefish or weeping-willow pollarding, but in other areas perhaps I am less deserving of feeling like an impostor.

The first thing to know about impostor syndrome is that it is an impostor itself. It is not a real syndrome, it is somewhere between a mood and a malaise. Basically, it's where the sufferer frequently believes that, despite evidence to the contrary, they are an impostor or a fraud.

The aptly 'not really a syndrome' syndrome was discovered by Pauline Rose Clance, a psychology professor who worked part-time at Oberlin College in Ohio. She noticed a number of successful women who sought counselling because they didn't feel they deserved the success they had, as if it had all been some mistake. Clance had had similar thoughts herself. In 1978 she wrote a paper with Suzanne Imes called 'The Impostor Phenomenon in High Achieving Women: Dynamics and Therapeutic Interventions'. They described the impostor phenomenon as a term that is 'used to designate an internal experience of intellectual phonies, which appears to be particularly prevalent and intense among a select sample of high achieving women'.

In Clance and Imes's paper, they noted three defining features of impostor phenomenon. First, the belief that others consider you to be better than you are.

Second, that the discovery of your true worth is just around the corner.

Third, that when you have achieved success, this has been due to outside factors such as good fortune, rather than your innate abilities.

An example of this way of thinking about yourself can be seen during Internet vanity searches. Many people will not stop looking through online comments about themselves until they find the person posting derision, spite or harsh criticism. You believe that the two hundred glowing statements that came first must have seen you when all the factors were in your favour. The one comment that considers you to have been the most excruciating experience of their entire life – 'and that includes root-canal surgery' – you believe was your most accurate analysis.

The impostor phenomenon is considered to be more prevalent among women, perhaps being partly explained in a widely circulated *New Yorker* cartoon of a man and a woman seated at dinner. The man announces cheerily, 'Let me interrupt your expertise with my confidence.' Female psychologists are particularly prone to this feeling, with 69 per cent of them feeling like impostors, according to a 1984 study by the psychologist Margaret Gibbs.

As the counterbalance to Impostor Syndrome there is Expert Syndrome, an increasingly prevalent condition, where people are quite sure they know what is best for you and the world, despite having no expertise or knowledge on the matter whatsoever. In psychology, these conditions are all part of what is known as the Dunning–Kruger Effect, where people fail to realize their level of competence, which can be loosely summed up as 'the less you know, the more certain you are that you are right'. Bertrand Russell, on whom in my impostor way I once presented a documentary, summarized it as: 'the stupid are cocksure and the intelligent full of doubt'. You will often find the cocksure at pub quizzes, usually as question-master.

I gave these up after a pub quiz in Plymouth. The question that tipped me over the edge was 'Who created the fictional detective Dashiell Hammett?' I was perplexed. Dashiell Hammett was an author who created a number of fictional detectives. Was this an existential question – a question of deep psychology? How did the real author Dashiell Hammett create himself? It seemed unlikely this was the response that was required, as it hadn't been that kind of quiz. The German new-wave director Wim Wenders had made a fictionalized account of Hammett's life, but that seemed an unlikely answer, too. We were told that the answer to the question was that Raymond Chandler created Dashiell Hammett. I remonstrated, but most of the other teams had got it 'right', and the fact that the answer was factually wrong meant nothing. When I questioned the host, I was fiercely upbraided for daring to question his wisdom. Later, I would be the only person in the room to get the answer to 'Who played Benson in the TV series *Benson*' wrong, by writing down the correct answer. In the Horse and Groom's saloon, the correct answer was Bill Cosby.*

---

* The actor who played Benson was Robert Guillaume.

I left that cocksure bar filled with doubt about Plymouth pub quizzes. Sadly, it seems the reins of political power are also currently held by those with the mindset of the pub-quiz host.

Financial success and critical acclaim are no guarantee of avoiding a sense of being an impostor. They may even exacerbate it. Tina Fey is one of the most revered comedians of the early twenty-first century. She has received four Writers Guild of America awards and nine Primetime Emmys. Despite her critical and financial success, she still believes she is an impostor. She sums it all up as 'the beauty of the impostor syndrome is you vacillate between extreme egomania and a complete feeling of: "I'm a fraud! Oh God, they're on to me! I'm a fraud!"'[1]

We are all getting away with it – some better than others – and most of us are just waiting to be found out, and yet most of us don't realize that everyone else believes they are waiting to be found out, too. Tina Fey's solution is to 'try to ride the egomania when it comes and enjoy it, and then slide through the idea of fraud. Seriously, I've just realized that almost everyone is a fraud, so I try not to feel too bad about it.'[2]

I am modestly pleased to let it be known that the Agatha Christie trophy is not the only prize I have received during my lifetime. I have bamboozled and conned others into deciding that I was worthy of receiving various pieces of extravagantly designed moulded Perspex. I am not so confident of the regularity of receiving prizes that I have invested in a dinner jacket, so I still have to hire the black tie from Moss Bros.

So whilst I am embarrassed to be offered a prize, I am keen to receive a prize. And then if I do receive one, I feel I can only have pulled the wool over the eyes of others, to be considered worthy of the gong or Perspex block. We demand prizes and then blush, 'Oh, really, you shouldn't have.'

Such feelings have been studied by Mark Leary at Wake Forest University, North Carolina. While many people have inflated views of their abilities, Leary wondered why people with impostor phenomenon don't. The conclusion was that these people may be pretending to feel like impostors, making this impostor-impostor syndrome. These frauds may be frauds. I think it is more convoluted than that. You don't suffer from 'impostor syndrome'; it's not there every waking moment and so it is not a set-in-stone condition, but rather a state that can emerge and vanish and re-emerge, depending on numerous factors, including how cocky those around you seem.

I was at the British Science Association conference, receiving a fellowship. Awkwardly, I sat amongst those who had changed the potential of humanity, offering futures to those who would previously have died prematurely perhaps, or had at least invented a more effective type of pump. I was getting my scroll for being silly about strange quarks, sea squirts and quantum indeterminacy. My impostor syndrome glowed with a bright and eerie light. I was definitely entitled to feel like an impostor, but was perhaps so wrapped up in my own feelings of inferiority that I was surprised when the respected physicist next to me told me she was quite flummoxed by why she was getting her award. This was not mock humility; she seemed befuddled, yet she totally understood why I was getting mine. I took umbrage. I was just doing jokes, while she was changing how we understood our universe. She refused to give any ground. So did I.

'You are deserving of the scroll, and I am not.'

'NO! You are deserving of the scroll, and I'm not.'

'Shut your face. You are the scroll-deserver.'

'NO! You are the scroll-deserver.'

It made no difference. We both got a scroll anyway and then we drank too much red wine, in the hope that we could drink away our fakery.

Later, we were joined by a Nobel Prizewinner. Now he wanted to declare his impostor status. This was getting ridiculous. We had to find another bar to keep the argument going. Then, on the way out, the Nobel Prizewinner displayed his total inability to work out how the taxi door opened. And we all felt reassured that: sure, he had transformed the advances of cellular medicine, but we knew how to lever a door handle open, so he was not superior to us on every level, just on most of them.

The length of time you have supposedly been getting away with the fakery doesn't necessarily reduce the suspicion that you have of yourself as an impostor. We judge ourselves on the terms of our own inner monologue, and others by their outer appearance, which will never be an equal match. Everyone else looks so confident at the party, so are you the only one terrified of picking up a vol-au-vent, for fear the prawn filling will splurt down your top or you'll have pastry-plastered teeth, just as a stranger decides to make conversation with you? Will your conversation be too polite? Or insufferably dull? Why is everyone else in the world vivacious, except you? Are you the only one who has Stevie Smith's 'Not Waving but Drowning' on repeat in your head?

Could it be that the man over there, gesticulating with a cocktail stick, is screaming on the inside, 'Why did I start this story?

There's no punchline. How can I bail out? These people must hate me. Make your excuses and leave NOW!'

See that woman over there, passionately describing why she loved the latest *Star Wars* film? Is she really paddling wildly and thinking, 'They know I haven't seen it, I've only read the synopsis, but I thought it would help me fit in. I am not even sure Chewbacca is in it.'

See that guy over there, throwing his head back in laughter as he eats a devilled egg? He doesn't know what he's laughing about, and he just imagined throwing himself out of that open window. I wonder if the secret of the social human is to tactfully conceal the fact that you're screaming on the inside. Or am I just projecting my scream onto others?

I had thought that most comedians I asked would break down and confess to being shackled to their own impostor syndrome, but it seemed I had been living in a bubble of self-confessing pseudo-charlatans, and when I popped the surface tension, there were fewer doubters than I had imagined. Of all the comedians I asked about impostor syndrome, the only one who immediately recognized it and kept on replying 'constantly', as I described its symptoms, was the comedian and writer Jason Cook, which was a relief to me. Nevertheless, I began to feel quite concerned at just how much of a minority I was in.

Did the composer and comedian Tim Minchin, for instance, find himself thinking, 'This shouldn't be me' when, in under a decade, he had gone from being unable to get a record company interested in his album or an agent interested in his acting, to drinking pink gin with Stephen Sondheim and having a musical opening on Broadway? 'When you are as talented as me, you just don't feel that' was his deadpan reply.

Tim has mastered the ability to spot other people's faults as well as his own. He is comfortable knowing that if he is incompetent at times, then so are all those around him. 'I look around and I can see the incompetence of everyone else as well. I can have self-doubt, I know that people in the room can sing better than me, or write songs better than me, but some of them can't make people laugh as well as me, or hone in on a common human experience and make people feel emotional about things. When I am with scientists and people who I know know more than me, I compensate by being able to construct sentences well. I often feel self-doubt, but I don't deify others. I know others have limitations, too, just maybe different ones.' Tim Minchin could savour his pink gin with Sondheim.

Sofie Hagen, whose stand-up work frequently tackles personal anxiety, told me that she didn't feel like an impostor; she only worried that she might one day lose her abilities.

Neuroscientist Sophie Scott didn't feel like an impostor, either, but she did feel that once she had achieved something, it must have meant it was far easier to achieve than she had imagined.

As these conversations with comedians and scientists went on, I increasingly suspected that I must think I am an impostor because I am one.

I have tried to contain my impostor moments by saying No to some of the offers that I think will trigger my feelings of being a charlatan, even if I reckon I could get away with it. I have been asked to be on the BBC's political debate show *Question Time*, but have always shied away from it. Partly because I think there are too many idiots like me already on these shows, and I really would like to see people on television more often who properly know things. I also worry that I would be seated next to an acerbic newspaper columnist who, whilst I might try to be controlled, I'm sure would eventually bring me up in hives of rage.

The one time I attempted such a show, I soon became goggle-eyed with frustration, as I found myself trapped in a constant impotent harrumph whilst others wittered on around me. It doesn't help matters that I have usually been offered a place on such a panel show when I have been tweeting about the despots and fibbers on it, from the drunken comfort of a bed in a chain hotel on the Leicester ringroad. By the time I am sober, my confidence in my own vigorously held opinions has gone, to be replaced by a deadening thud of empty ennui. When I asked Alexei Sayle about his experience on *Question Time*, and for his advice if I was ever still drunk enough in the morning to say Yes to one of these requests, he reminded me that it was possible to do it once, but try it twice and, like H. Rider Haggard's *She*, you may be destroyed and turn to dust.

How do those who make a living of holding strong, coherent beliefs and opinions keep it all going? How do dim and venal politicians keep stepping forward spouting codswallop time and time again, even being proved wrong time and time again? It's as if, through a remarkably muscular cognitive dissonance each time they open their mouths, with no sense of impostor syndrome whatsoever, they may really think they are right. The game has become transparent. Our political leaders do not even bother to attempt to create the illusion of knowledge or depth; they just make up bilge and aggressively dismiss all other, better evidence with nothing more than 'That is a lie.' The charade has become far less nuanced, it is a swill-bucket hurled. And perhaps that is why comedians have found themselves on political panel shows – not because they are any smarter, but because the political class has fallen so low, and it's just not funny.

I wondered what thoughts someone would have about themselves if they had made a living making people laugh by doing stupid and funny things for most of their career, and then turned to something seemingly completely different and far more serious and esteemed. Would they feel out of place, like an impostor?

Lenny Henry has been a British comedy star for forty years, though in the last decade he has reduced his attempts to make people laugh and has increasingly concentrated on both performing and studying dramatic art. It is the oft-told tale of the comedian who wants to play Hamlet, though in this case it was a critically acclaimed Othello.

Lenny won the TV talent show *New Faces* when he was seventeen years old, and then spent more than twenty years starring in sitcoms and sketch shows. He was quickly celebrated as a loveable, family-entertainment comedian but, arriving on the scene before the ground-breaking alternative comedy had begun, he was moulded by the variety scene and by producers who wanted another 'beloved entertainer'. One of the first jobs that his management got him after *New Faces* was as the comedian on a tour with *The Black and White Minstrel Show*. Onstage, Lenny was the only one who wasn't an impostor – everyone else was blacked up. He was also one of the stars of *Tiswas*, ITV's rowdy Saturday-morning children's television show.

Lenny now has a BA in English Literature, a Masters in screenwriting and a PhD about the representation of black people in the media. He had only just finished his PhD when I met him, on his lunch break from rehearsals of Bertolt Brecht's *The Resistible Rise of Arturo Ui*. This culture is very different from the clubs he first played, and I'm sure most of his fellow actors never had to go onstage after a juggler and some men in blackface singing 'Camptown Races'. Lenny remembers the period in general as a time of 'othering', when the 'others' were the subjects of the jokes – people who weren't like the audience. They were the ones to be laughed at: blacks, Irish, blondes with big breasts, landladies. Lenny felt the acts were often talking down to the audience. It was not easy to be a young black comedian. 'Offstage I was this young black kid that listened to funk and went to discos; when I was onstage I became this sort of middle-aged, white semi-Northern club act, who knew how to get laughs based on a certain agreed set of complicities, and it took me a really long time to say, "I don't want to do jokes like that, I want to do other jokes."'

With his life now taking a turn into academia and dramatic acting, he thinks he has experienced 'the slow blossoming of my own thing, my own point of view and my own sense of humour'. He no longer has to feel, or be, the impostor.

Lenny realized that what he had become wasn't him; that he was meant to be an actor, not having to come up with ideas from scratch, but waiting for the boom of a solid text to drop through the letterbox. He may have been nervous and full of anxiety, but he doesn't seem to have felt like an impostor when he took on Othello. He had found what he wanted to do. He thinks it is easy to see how unhealthy being a stand-up can be, both mentally and physically. Lenny thinks comedians imagine they must be pirates for the first ten years of their lives: 'I will sleep around, I will eat stupid food, I will stay up late, I will drink too much. A deal has been made that they have to nearly kill themselves, before they come out the other side. You don't have to do that to get where you want to be; you can just be kind and be a good person. You can be a mensch. You don't have to go through that horrible phase.'

Lenny's thoughts are similar to Brendon Burns's feelings, now that he has come out of his pirate years. Lenny doesn't believe that the onstage-you should be the place you are happiest, the place you feel nearest to being complete. 'It is the rest of the day that's important – it's the other twenty-two hours that's the most important thing – and I think we don't understand that, so we self-medicate and we end up doing terrible things, because we don't know how to deal with the other twenty-two hours. Onstage guy, if that's your best self, and the audience are laughing and laughing and roaring and roaring, then you're living a lie; that guy's not you. You have to work on the other person . . .'

At a time when there have never been so many ways of having criticism delivered to your door, at every hour of the day or night, it is increasingly difficult to believe that you really are your own worst critic, when so many others are auditioning for the part. Perhaps it is more likely that you are just your own most methodical critic. It is also piteous to observe that the most intense and violent criticism has an ugly gender bias. Australian feminist Clementine Ford summed up the problem of relentless social-media abuse in her book *Fight like a Girl*: 'Who would willingly sign up to being called a pig-faced slut every day?'

In 1949 the anthropologist Margaret Mead wrote that the successful or independent woman 'is viewed as a hostile and destructive force within society'. When social media gave us access to so many human thoughts, it led to an unpleasant realization that things had not changed as much as we might have hoped. Josie Long has been a comedian since she was seventeen. Now thirty-six, she has won multiple awards and has been critically revered. She has also received vicious and relentless personal attacks on social media – something that would undoubtedly make me doubt my own ability. These attacks have affected her, although not by making her feel like an impostor, but just by inserting that little bit of doubt in her abilities and, more importantly, in her desire. She wondered, 'Is it worth all this violent language and threat?'

It knocked her confidence, just when she was at the point of getting a lot of offers to do television. She thinks the Internet trolls succeeded in their goal of holding her back, which she considers to be 'as bleak as fuck'. She now reckons she is totally impervious to it, but there have been times when she was very scared.

Josie's advice is 'call it out in public straight away – get people to look after you; acknowledge that if it is upsetting you, your feelings are legitimate; try to separate it from you and your life, and you and your goals. The creative life is long and wonderful, no matter your age or gender; you always have your own power – that is to make and to showcase – and you mustn't let these people take that from you, as they are always sad, pathetic and bitter people. I'm a comedian and I got death-threats, it's fucking nonsense . . .'

Not long after I spoke to her about this, Josie received another barrage of abuse, filled with violent language and threats. Her ability to overcome this has helped to make her more certain of herself, but if there weren't so many pointless aggressors in the first place, this would not have been necessary.

Even if you don't think you are an impostor, sometimes there are those who are determined to persuade you that you are. It is a pity that so many people spend so much of their time brutally dismissing other people's achievements and existence, while doing nothing whatsoever with their own lives. Malice is an odd hobby, time-consuming, and you don't even end up with a model of Chichester cathedral made out of matchsticks to show for it.

At the other end of the spectrum, I am perhaps someone who puts too much emphasis on searching for malice that is aimed at me – an even odder hobby.

I know it is not merely me who waits for the tweet after a big show that says 'You suck' and takes that as gospel. Play to 4,000 or be broadcast to two million, and it can still only take one comment to crumble, to ask what's the point, to presume that everyone else was suckered, but one far-seeing oracle has torn back the curtain and shown the ugly, charlatan truth. But if you are a proper impostor, you know you are the only true charlatan. I have been a comedian for twenty-five years, but place me in a room with ten other professional comedians and I wonder why I am allowed to be there. Everyone else is a real comedian. They do comedy properly, not my ragbag nonsense.

As someone who has spent some years looking at how proper science works, too, I am keen on evidence as a method of appraising a situation, and yet despite the evidence that I have made a living as a comedian for all this time, it doesn't take much to make me feel like an impostor. It is the suspicion that you are Truman in *The Truman Show*. For all these years people have been paid to find you funny; some have even been paid to heckle occasionally so that it seems real, and then everyone else took another cheque to laugh even more heartily at your heckle put-downs.

I have generally hung around with comedians who will talk of their defeats far more than of their triumphs. Defeat normally has more anecdotal permutations, while victory is dull. 'I went on. The crowd seemed restless. Someone heckled. I said an amazing thing. They gave me the keys to the city and slaughtered a calf for me.' Victory stories usually follow roughly this pattern: it was a tough night, some people who are good did not do well, but I faced a tough crowd and was worshipped.

Defeat stories can go many ways, from fist-fights to projectile vomiting; to being attacked by a man dressed as a Klingon, who then runs away in tears when his prosthetic spiny forehead falls off; to having your car pushed into a quarry by an aggressively inebriated rugby team. Some people – the ones I don't trust – will always keep their failures hidden under a bushel. They are protecting an image of impregnability, for fear they might lose work otherwise. They are probably right. It was either Sun Tzu in *The Art of War* or Eddie Izzard on a TV chat show who said, 'It isn't what you've done that matters, it's what you can make believe you have done.'

Now, you just have to convince yourself.

CHAPTER 7

Anxiety and the 'Imp of the Mind'

I'm the Descartes of anxiety. I panic, therefore I am.

Richard Lewis

It probably won't surprise you to know that I think I am an anxious person. Even the act of reading back over this chapter will lead to me feeling anxious about whether I looked stupidly anxious, or whether I really wasn't anxious enough to write anything about anxiety.

Søren Kierkegaard defined anxiety as 'the dizziness of freedom'. At least this means I am free. Anxiety is evidence of existence. Anxiety is one of those special treats that goes with having evolved a brain so big that we almost break our mothers during birth. It gives us the delight of imagining our possibilities, and the worry of predicting all the ways they may go wrong.

For many years when I was onstage I kept any anxiety under wraps, hidden beneath a glaze of chutzpah and bonhomie, keeping most of it for the dressing room/broken-cistern toilet cubicle that doubled as a dressing room, and a little bit for the train ride home. At times, my anxiety and the things that I was anxious about felt so ridiculous that I was sure such feelings were unique to me, which in itself fuelled my anxiety further. One night, though, I was onstage and, in a moment of bravado, I wondered aloud about a particular paranoia that I had; and as the audience fed back to me, I was surprised to discover that, in terms of anxious thoughts, I was just one of the crowd. That's stand-up comedy as my own personal crowd therapy, thank you very much.

One of Christopher Walken's early film appearances was in *Annie Hall*, playing Annie's depressive, possibly suicidal brother. He confesses to Woody Allen that he sometimes has an urge to drive into the oncoming traffic – and then proceeds to give Allen a lift to the airport. Allen sits in the car, petrified, all the way to the terminal.

Have you ever been the passenger in a car speeding down the motorway and imagined grabbing the wheel and swerving into the barrier at high speed, towards conflagration and death? Have you ever been holding a baby and imagined dropping it down the stairs or hurling it off that nearby cliff? Maybe you imagined hurling *yourself* off the cliff, even though, as far as you can tell, you have no desire to die. If so, stop worrying so much. It's highly unlikely you'll go through with it. The fact that you've been thinking about it so much might even make it *less* likely.

The first time I looked at an audience and said, 'Who, here, when holding a baby near an open window or sheer drop, has suddenly imagined throwing the baby?' I had no idea how they would react.

Slowly, is what I discovered. One hand rose, and that encouraged a few others. Eventually it was almost 10 per cent of the audience. The 90 per cent looked nervously at the 10 per cent. The 10 per cent looked nervously at me.

A pause. Who had trapped who?

Then I looked at the first person to put up their hand and pointed him out. 'Now I need to explain something. This man was keenest. So what I need all of you to know is that this man . . . *this man* . . .'

No one knew where this was going. Was it going to end in relief or shame? Was I a front for some hostile lunatic asylum, on a recruitment drive to repopulate the cells?

'*This man* . . . is the best man to hold your baby. If you're looking for a baby-holder, he is the safest pair of hands in the room.'

There was palpable relief.

But how can this be? He readily admitted to having an infanticide fantasy! Such thoughts are a trick of the mind – a useful one, but one that you can misinterpret. In situations of jeopardy, such as holding a baby, your mind will play you a little public-information film, like those ones that used to be on the BBC, warning against eating lit fireworks or going swimming with 1970s TV celebrities.

You're holding a baby, so remember: when holding a baby, don't throw it down the stairs, says the portentous voiceover artist in your head.

Unfortunately, the warning film is delivered in such a way that you could easily mistake it for a desire. In severe cases, this can lead to obsessive behaviour and chronic fear – and all because of this misinterpretation of an internal broadcast.

The problem with thoughts is that they can take you by surprise, and it's not always easy to shrug them off and detach them from the you-ness of you. Some people have an easy-going relationship with their mind-burbles, while others can get hung up on the more extreme thoughts that seem to come from the 'I am/I do/I will' section of the brain.

I had been plagued by these thoughts – living nightmares when holding babies – but now that I had found out it was all a cognitive error, I wanted to share it with others, so that they could be as relieved as I was that they were not as homicidal as they might have imagined.

It makes sense, then, that sharing anxieties is often suggested as a good thing for the sharer. They're able to get things off their chest and somehow, if and when you discover that everyone understands your anxiety and is on your side, then that anxiety will ebb away, even if just a little. However, what happens if you decide to share your innermost thoughts, concerns and fears about things that are perhaps shaming to you, and which have worried you for many years, in the hope that others will warmly smile and offer you a similar story – only to find that you're holding a candle for that particular worry and source of shame on your own? Is it possible that your personal paranoia is unique?

My stand-up experiment with confronting anxiety had begun over a decade before. I decided to play with the comedian's rejoinder for a failed gag ('Just me, then') and write a series of 'Do you remember when?' jokes that really could only be 'Just me'. They were extremely specific moments of toxic nostalgia from my own memories.

'Do you remember when you used to get the school bus home and it was driven by Mr Duffy, and all the other boys used to say

"Thanks, Duffy" when they got off the bus, and you were a bit shy. But you wanted to be cool like the boys that said, "Thanks, Duffy", so one day, as you got off, you went to say it – but it accidentally came out as "Thanks, Mr Doughboy". And he was quite a fat man, and he grabbed you by the arm and started shouting and shouting at you, and you got so scared that a small amount of urine came out and splashed on the inside of your shorts. Do you remember that?'

And thus, 'Just me, then?'

This is one of the many embarrassing incidents in my life that cannot be deleted; my recall of shame is annoyingly robust. Even typing this school-bus grotesquerie now, forty years on, I feel a little sick. It seems that some people have an ability to coast and delete, while others prickle for decades.

My sometime double-act partner, Josie Long, told me how she is still haunted by guilt and shame about the terrible things she did to her sister. Fearing her actions may have caused long-lasting damage, she decided one day to apologize to her sister, at which point her sister told Josie that she had no memory of them what-soever. What had played so negatively on Josie's mind for so long had meant nothing to her sister.

My 'Just me, then' experiment expanded to include broader observations, to see how much of my own behaviour, which I considered peculiar, was actually quite mundane – or at least not exclusive to me. I became an onstage market-research pollster, polling idiosyncrasy.

I would start with: 'Who, here, when they find themselves alone in the house, sometimes dances to a song they have made up in their head?' A few hands would go up. Then I'd move on to what I considered to be the next level: 'Who, here, sometimes talks to themselves in a language of their own making?' This would normally see a decrease in the number of hands going up, as it was perhaps a little odder than the dancing, and a little less safe to admit to. Sometimes people would be nudged by their partners, who knew they were concealing the truth. I would then mess it up by asking who sometimes danced to a song in their head that was in a language of their own making – and watch to see whether the level of public honesty was increasing now.

After a ramble through other peculiarities, I would get to: 'Who, here, when they were a child, would sometimes sit up in their bed in an awkward manner until their back really started to hurt, just so they could feel the benefit of lying back down again and thinking, *Mmm, even more comfy now?*'

The number of raised hands was surprisingly high, and a surprising number of people would come up to me afterwards and fondly recall their previously forgotten memory of making their back ache, so they could then feel the benefit of a comfy bed – though they would explain that they had never before wanted to acknowledge that memory publicly.

By admitting my own absurdity early on in the set, most knew it was fair game to join in, but what became apparent with these further conversations was that there was undoubtedly a trust element to revealing previously hidden anxieties and memories, with some audience members never quite feeling confident enough to join in and admit theirs, for fear they were being set up for a trap. They had further anxieties – that they'd admit to body-popping to their own form of Esperanto and then a spotlight would burn into their face and I'd let out a noise like Donald Sutherland at the end of *Invasion of the Body Snatchers*, half pig-scream, half human bellow, and they, the outsider in the room, would be torn apart and devoured.

Surprisingly, the question that people were most bold – even joyous – in answering affirmatively was: 'Who here stands on a train platform in the morning and looks at the person in front of them and thinks, *Fuck it, I'm going to shove him in front of the train?*' For some reason, homicidal musings were less embarrassing to admit to than solitary dancing.

The only time I can remember an utterly lone hand going up happened on a night when the discussion was about human breast-milk. Having visited a friend who had recently given birth and gone on to attempt to make a pudding out of her breast-milk, I wondered why it was that if most of us were offered a dessert made from a friend's breast-milk, we would not be very keen to partake. Some people, I would imagine, may even go so far as to react with barely concealed revulsion, before making up some alibi about 'lactose intolerance', hoping it had been forgotten that they had just poured milk into their tea. But why not drink human milk, when we drink milk from cows, and they plod around muddy fields with their hooves in dung all day? That night, in another moment of psychological pollster work, I asked the audience who would eat a pudding made from the breast-milk of a woman they knew. A hand shot up eagerly from a man in the front row, who then turned round to see that he was the only person in the whole audience with his hand up.

'You seemed eager. Are you thinking of one woman in particular?' I asked.

He explained that he was, and then sheepishly continued that he was a bit disappointed, as he was meant to meet her this evening and she hadn't turned up.

Five minutes later, she turned up. As she walked all the way to the front to join her date, the audience sat attentively, all aware that they were now the keepers of a secret. This was a rare case of a 'Just me, then' being not the man onstage, but the man in Row A, Seat 6.

The nagging *Just me, then* in our heads is often what stymies our social conversation. When we are at events with strangers – at a school do, for example – where pleasantries and niceties are necessities, outrageous or impulsive thoughts sometimes creep towards our mouths, with the words even forming on our lips before at the last minute being hastily turned into a cough. We think, *Don't say that – it's probably only you. Stay on safe ground.*

I had become intrigued by these impulsive thoughts, like the fear that you might deliberately drop a baby down the stairs or suddenly shout out, 'God is dead. Satan is king' during a minute's silence in a cathedral. Impulsive thoughts are sometimes called the 'imp of the mind', or even the 'imp of the perverse', after a short story by Edgar Allan Poe. They can be ignored by some, are bothersome to others – and even get to the point of causing distress that can hinder the thinker's life. The imp is the deliverer of images of the extreme, the outrageous, the worst-case scenario.

The most shocking imp I recall (and I warn you that this is horrific) was imagining accidentally putting my thumb *through* the soft spot of my sister's baby's head. It had come to me in a dream, before I met my new nephew. I woke up with a start, wide-eyed and clammy. When my sister arrived from Australia with her new offspring, I nodded at him from a distance.

'Don't you want to hold him?' said my sister.

'*I certainly do not!* I mean, I have tennis elbow or something similar that makes baby-holding problematic. I would like

172

to make it clear that I'm not avoiding him because I imagined putting my thumb in his brain.'

He has left school now and is training to be a carpenter, and his skull is devoid of extraneous holes, as far as I know – and if there are any, they were not made by me.

I have built up a list of the impulsive thoughts from audiences across the UK. *Grabbing the steering wheel and propelling you and the driver into oncoming traffic* is high on the list. Also, concerning car shenanigans, there were admissions to having had a sudden urge to lean over to a grumpy minicab driver and give him a kiss. On the inappropriate-kissing list, there were thoughts about French-kissing a very elderly relative and, more specifically, doing this in the midst of the relative's telling a melancholy story of his experiences during the Second World War. Shoving other people in front of a freight train ranked highly, though slightly higher was the sudden fear of throwing *yourself* in front of a train – an urge that could seem so worryingly real that some people said they would grip hold of the bench they were sitting on, as a train passed through the station. Inappropriate thoughts about pets also cropped up. Later, I was told by someone who had researched this academically (rather than merely in the bars of arts centres) that a common impish thought occurred when seeing a dog walking in front of you with its bottom on display, which was to imagine yourself briefly and unpleasantly in congress with it. I had never had this impish thought before, but it became harder to avoid, after knowing such notions existed and were 'common'.

This is the problem with researching the imps – doing so can feed your imp imagination with new unpleasantness. Dog congress became hard to shift from my mind for a good month after being told this – getting off the train in Nottingham to find myself stuck behind an Alsatian proved particularly disconcerting, and I even gave up going greyhound-racing on Tuesdays. I remain suspicious of the academic. I don't know what the dogs are like in the area where he walks, but I presume those mutts must roam in a considerably more flirtatious manner than anywhere else in the world. Perhaps certain psychological studies are merely the hunt for an alibi for the researcher's strange peccadilloes – and I include my own onstage research in this.

So, like Freudian psychotherapy, going to a stand-up gig can be a talking treatment for both the talker and the listener. It may not cure you, but at least you'll know you're not the only one who is ill. That's the potency of cheap gags.

Not everyone wants to be cured. At one gig I was collared by an audience member who complained that he had always thought he was weird – until that night. His internal peculiarities helped define him as not being 'like the others'. Having sat in a room where he noticed so many other hands going up, when it came to baby-slinging and railway-track-leaping thoughts, he had realized he was not as uncomfortably unique as he had hoped.

The good news for us psychologically, and also for the conceit behind the *Just me* strand that I've been mining for my shows, is that scientific studies in the 1970s and '80s showed that around 90 per cent of us have experienced these 'intrusive, unwanted thoughts, images and impulses'. What started as a niche piece of stand-up is now accessible and comprehensible for even more people than I imagined.

But it's not just *having* these thoughts; crucially, it's what we *do* with these thoughts that counts. For most of us, whilst there might be a momentary feeling of cold dread and disgust at ourselves, we see them then for what they are – momentary brain-glitches. They may be primal and a bit weird, but this baby's pretty safe with me and I don't want to spend the rest of my life in prison, so I'd better just pass it carefully back to its mother and get on with my life. For some people, though, the anxiety and fear that such thoughts create can become completely overwhelming, obsessive and 'stuck'.

Those with some form of obsessive–compulsive disorder, or OCD, can be particularly prone to taking impulsive notions and running with them, literally, as if their life depended on it. For them, their one-off and unusual impulsive thought about throwing the baby across the room becomes something that defines them. They might avoid any contact with babies, or people with babies – and have a belief about themselves that they are twisted, horrible and weird. In order to avoid babies, they might decide not to go outside the house; and if a baby does loom into view, then they might experience massive fear and anxiety.

Cognitive behavioural therapy (CBT) works by changing the way we think about the world, in order to affect our behaviour, which in turn can then affect the way we feel. As you can imagine, if you believe you are a potential evil baby-thrower, a danger to yourself and to others, then you might also feel pretty anxious and sad. Looking at the real evidence behind such thoughts can help a person overcome their negative thinking, so the anxious potential baby-thrower will be asked for all and any evidence as to why they believe they are a danger to babies. Once the patient can see that there's no evidence of this whatsoever, then the cure can slowly begin to take place; the anxiety and shame that have come about, purely because of intrusive thoughts common to us all, can begin to subside.

The English are known for their fatal addiction to public shame, and yet using CBT as a cure for this can only take place if the person is willing to seek help and share their problems and anxieties. We stand-up comedians can draw much comedy from playing with the British desire to maintain a stiff upper lip, to keep our worries and shameful behaviour secret. I'm sure that in certain parts of the world, people regularly get together over a beer and have a good laugh about their thoughts that morning of taking a chihuahua from behind, but the British national mentality is a little more circumspect. By gently – and not so gently – creating an atmosphere of mutual trust, a stand-up can pierce the mask of propriety and control that we often present to the world. We hope, of course, that the anxieties within *us* are the anxieties within our audience – or it can lead to a very cold time onstage, and to the anxiety of unshared anxieties.

On the whole, the anxieties of comedians used to be kept offstage, which made producing revelatory documentaries about their pain and depression so much easier. Dramatists and documentarians delight in showing us that our favourite post-war clowns were paranoid depressives hooked on painkillers with a predilection for booze and violence. However, when the newest generation of comedians dies, it will be tough times for the revelatory-documentary industry.

Imagine: *What many people didn't know was that, despite her onstage mettle, Polly suffered from . . . Hang on, what's that? She turned her dark secret into an award-winning solo show? How sad it is that the funny people no longer spend their lives tormented and racked with hidden inner pain. Ah, those were the good old days of agony.*

Australian comedian Felicity Ward has been both public and funny about her internal struggles. She explains, 'You can see how skinny or overweight you are, you can get on scales and there's a measurement, but there's no measurement of how happy you are.' So perhaps this is why she and others have a need to seek external recognition and acknowledgement of their problems with anxiety.

Felicity came to prominence in Australia portraying a nihilist, a child and a lawn-bowls instructor (not all the same character) in the TV sketch show *Ronnie Johns Half Hour.* She has performed shows about leaving a bag on the bus and worrying about where a toilet is, both of which imaginatively and usefully took advantage of her anxiety to create psychotherapeutic entertainment. Her comedy reveals, rather than conceals, her mental-health issues.

At her first stand-up gig Felicity hadn't a clue what she would do, so in advance she ordered two toy tanks that could electrocute members of the audience, hoping to use them as some sort of prop. Stuck on the phone when the delivery man left the dangerous replicas outside her apartment – a mistake General Pinochet would never have made – she had them stolen by a would-be torturer who got lucky before Felicity reached her front door. The only option left that night was to talk to her audience instead.

Fortunately, Felicity already knew that her anxieties were funny to other people. 'The nature of my mental-health issues is that I am very up and down, so every night my fiancé gets to play "Guess Who's Coming to Dinner?" . . . I've got IBS, I've got anxiety, I've got depression. I'm what the doctors refer to as a triple threat.'

A central part of the anxiety that Felicity suffers from takes the form of insomnia, something that she talks about in her routine, and something that I too have suffered from a lot over the years. Insomnia is now commonplace – we may not have to worry so much about smallpox, the bubonic plague and other carriers of premature mortality, so we worry about our worry and how it will interfere with our sleep patterns. It means we are unable to fulfil all our daytime tasks, generating further anxiety and bringing about further disappointment with ourselves. It is another battle between the rational mind and the Tasmanian devil that lives in there too, impishly scuppering our lives – often with a free internal-music sample.

The internal soundtrack to Felicity's insomnia is Eiffel 65's 'Blue (Da Ba Dee)' – don't look it up if you don't know it, or you'll be infected too. My insomnia came with a seven-second loop from Serge Gainsbourg's ballad 'Bonnie and Clyde', a peculiar piece of production that sounds as if Serge has placed a howler monkey in the studio with Brigitte Bardot – a scenario that further stimulates my sleeplessness anxiety.

In a way that echoes the sharing of anxieties with audiences, Felicity and I discuss the long, dreamless nights of sleeplessness. There's the pacing of thin-fibred hotel-bedroom carpets, with their sharp-edged patterns of orange and turquoise that levitate towards the eye. There's the psychotic emails sent at 4 a.m., the start of the insanity hour that marks the sixty minutes of total darkness before the dawn chorus. There's the feeling of utter helplessness and anger when the last creative impulse remaining is inventing new swear words, usually around the time you hear the first songthrush of the day. 'You warbling cock canker, shut your bubonic beak gash.'

After a few months you can have an individual swear word for each species of bird, from wren to starling. Twenty-seven minutes before you leave the hotel, you will fall into a deep and worthless sleep. Your day will be spent apologizing and retracting pre-dawn tweets, emails and blog posts.

Sometimes, returning to a hotel you once spent a night at, you have no recollection of it whatsoever, until you see the ceiling of the bedroom that you spent seven sleepless hours staring at on your last visit: I recognize that fleck of spider blood smeared directly to the left of the light fitting. I must be at the Coach Inn, Daventry, again.

Try taking G. K. Chesterton's advice: 'Lying in bed would be an altogether perfect and supreme experience if only one had a coloured pencil long enough to draw on the ceiling.'[1] You start drawing on the ceiling with the imagined extended pencil. You aim to sketch a pastoral scene, but somehow it always ends up like a pastel Pollock or a Hieronymus Bosch.

Felicity reminded me that you will always have unwanted but kindly meant advice from people who have forever slept like spindle-pricked princesses, but reckon they know just what you need.

'You've got insomnia? Have you tried chamomile tea?'

'You've got insomnia? Have you tried listening to recordings of dolphins being fetishized?'

'You've got insomnia? Have you tried screaming into the night and weeping? It might just tire you out.'

As someone who has suffered from insomnia, I feel I can share my best practices. I have found out that giving up alcohol helps; rather than helping you sleep, drink can mean you have to argue with a pissed demon that is trying to keep you awake, so you end up having a bone-encased street fight in the gutters of your amygdala. Sobriety aids sanity when sleepless. So I have tried giving up alcohol, buying plenty of melatonin tablets when abroad, and then concentrating first on what my toes feel like and then slowly moving the point of focus up to my knees, which is a sort of mindful distraction technique that is so pointless and dull that sleep has sometimes come unexpectedly.

Earthier acquaintances have suggested masturbating whilst drinking large quantities of whisky, but I've always been fearful of the dangers of inebriated onanism. I can only see it bringing on further anxiety.

I attribute my insomnia directly to anxiety and stress. It reduced when I didn't have so many deadlines and worries, and it came back again the moment I was on tour. It becomes a self-fulfilling prophecy: my anxiety fed by the fear that tiredness is going to lead to over-slack-wittedness onstage.

Felicity's insomnia is also brought on by stress and anxiety. She gets stressed and anxious, so she gets insomnia. This means she's tired, so she makes poor choices. Then she goes to bed and starts to worry about the poor choices she's made, and that brings on insomnia again.

She now finds that meditation apps calm her and allow her to reason with herself more rationally, enabling her anxieties to reduce and sleep to come. She's learnt not to freak out too much: 'I lie there and remember that relaxing my body has almost the same impact as sleep, and also that I can – and have – completed very important things the next day after having insomnia, so ultimately it's an inconvenience more than anything else. Then occasionally I just go full tantrum; cry, curse a god. You know – proper toddler shit.'

The anxiety that fuels the insomnia, though, is also the anxiety that led to her *What If There's No Toilet?* show, the title referring to the IBS, or irritable bowel syndrome, that can accompany anxiety. 'This show is sponsored by Imodium,' she would announce at the start of the gig and, as the laughter came, she would explain that it really, really was. The show dealt with both the anxiety that causes IBS and the genuine and very real anxiety brought on by the fear that can arise about being caught out in toilet-less situations.

IBS is described as a 'syndrome' because much of the seeming physical discomfort may well live in the mind, though this is not to say there isn't a physical manifestation, too – it is just that quite often it may well have its worst flare-ups when restrooms are at their most elusive, or the seat-belt sign is on in the plane, or Sir Ian McKellen has just started a very long soliloquy and you are in Row C, Seat 9.

Felicity's show dealt with how anxiety and IBS are inextricably linked. Get on a train where the toilets are all out of order and your brain drops into your bowels, but approaching the final destination – a gleaming station inundated with public conveniences – and the mind travels back out of the guts and explains that it was all a false alarm. Walking onto the concourse, there is a sign explaining that the toilets are closed, and the mind calamitously falls back into the bladder.

Felicity's show was close to my own colon – too close for comfort. I once found myself sitting next to Germaine Greer at the Royal Court Theatre and enjoyed the play, even though I spent most of it wondering which direction would be the best exit route if my bowels began to explode. I decided I was going to either climb back the two rows needed to get to an aisle or crawl under the seats, which had the added jeopardy of getting trapped, rather than disturb Germaine Greer. As usual, the discomfort disappeared three minutes from the curtain call. The power of the mind to create false jeopardy is the shabby gift that comes with self-consciousness and imagination.

My anxiety, merely an English cliché, is nothing to Felicity's. Though the 'talking cure' of stand-up seems to have helped her somewhat, during her worst attacks of anxiety and IBS she would go out wearing numerous pairs of pants stuffed with sanitary towels, just in case something happened.

Performing the show hasn't eradicated the issue for her, but it has got it out into the open and has increased the sense that there are more people to talk to about it. She does not insist on the aisle seat in the theatre any more. She reasons with herself that if you are in the middle of a row and an IBS attack strikes, you can get up and leave and no one will die. I am not sure I would be so brave – you should see the look Germaine Greer gives you, if you make so much as a rustle.

The power of the mind to take what is in the world around you and play on your worst fears of it – even when those fears are completely irrational, and to the extent where you are physically changed – is remarkable. Yet again, it is intriguing that some anxious people like Felicity find respite from their anxiety by doing something that many consider terrifying, which is speaking publicly on a stage in front of an audience. For Felicity, the problem is not getting *on*stage, though; it is the *off*stage existence that is where the trouble lies. The balm is what perhaps should be the horror.

During her most recent Edinburgh Fringe run, Felicity was experiencing depression. Every time she feels well, she thinks she'll never be sick again as it just doesn't seem logical, but when her mental health falters, logic – so frequently tenuous – crumbles. In 2016, Felicity counted how many shows she had performed while experiencing depression; she did nine, which she considers 'very unfair, when you are doing shows and the audience are experiencing joy, and it just seems very unfair. It literally inhibits my career.'

It seems hard to imagine how someone can go onstage beaming and beamish while feeling lost, confused or melancholy. Before one show, Felicity had a huge panic attack and she thought: *You've got to put this out of your mind*. But then she realized she shouldn't try and conceal it; her performer's instinct kicked in and she said to herself: *No, you've got to take this onstage with you. If there is one place you are allowed to be anxious, it's onstage doing a show about anxiety.*

For me, it seems there is a mysterious figure known as 'Doctor Theatre', who will apparently cure all your ills from the moment Dick Dale's 'Misirlou' comes over the sound system and you know the show is about to begin. It's not always Dick Dale's 'Misirlou', but it will be 43 per cent of the time; 18 per cent of the time it is 'Let Me Entertain You' by Robbie Williams; 0.1 per cent of the time it's the theme from *RoboCop*.

Doctor Theatre does not always work. Sometimes you know he has sworn the Hippocratic oath and you've got the real deal; at other times, he sells a potion he says is made of mermaid tears and unicorn rind.

Chutzpah and adrenaline and five hundred people staring at you are not always enough. I have seen the norovirus kick in onstage: a visual, aural and olfactory spectacular of anxious vomiting, which then made the club unplayable for everyone else for the rest of the night. I saw people just stop and stare, and then someone come on from the wings, hug the performer and walk them offstage. However, I've also seen decrepit elderly performers, who can barely walk, leap onstage, do a little tap-dancing, sing a song, bow, smile and then collapse in a chair the moment they are out of the spotlight.

I asked Felicity if Doctor Theatre had had an effect on her mental health. She told me, 'Sometimes I've done a gig when I have been depressed, and it's been transcendent and my depression has gone, but there have been times when I have been depressed or anxious and I shouldn't have been gigging, because it's too hard to be funny.'

The nearest *I* came to having a complete mental collapse onstage, unable to continue, was during my addiction to painkillers. To say I was addicted is a bit of an exaggeration, but apparently these sorts of claims can help with book sales and publicity. I had broken my arm three days into the Edinburgh Fringe festival after a clumsy cartoonist, unaware that the rules of animation do not exist in real life, pushed me over in the road and I failed to bounce back up. Rather than spread my painkiller usage throughout the day, as instructed, I would down them all before going onstage and then feel the warmth and confusion that can come with such hasty pill ingestion. One night I was onstage and I paused and then found myself unable to depart from the pause, so I just stood there, looking at the audience, feeling myself starting to well up in the confusion and stillness. I learnt my lesson – I never crossed the road with an animator again.

Before she became a stand-up herself, Felicity considered it just too frightening a prospect. Now she thrives on the thrill of the peril, the knife-edge that is made sharper by performing shows of such honesty. There is no hiding behind a character. For her, it is indeed a trust game: 'You've got to get them to trust you until the punchline . . . before I start I think, *How is this gonna go?*, because sometimes it doesn't go well.' In a life of anxiety, she has found a way to turn at least some of that anxiety into a thrill.

Sofie Hagen is another comedian who gives voice to her own anxiety onstage, even going so far as to set it up as being first on her agenda the moment you walk into the venue, taking her feelings of social unease and using them as a theme for her show, and for the way the entire auditorium and venue amenities are organized. Aware that the style and content of her comedy may attract other people with social anxiety, she has organized her tour to remove as many potential stressors as possible – from ensuring that you have the seat you require, to making the toilets non-gender-specific, just a choice of urinals or cubicles.

She encourages her audiences to write to her to explain their gig-going anxieties and then she tries her best to ensure they don't occur. For one individual, it was about whether a certain word would be used and, if so, when it would occur, as it would make her less anxious if she knew roughly when to expect it. Some people may harrumph at this point and grumble, 'Generation snowflake!', but I find it quite appealing. After all, what is the harm in trying to make an individual's life less stressful through a single simple action? Human experience is the frequent chaos caused by the unexpected and unpredictable, from birth to death, and comedy is meant to be about making people happy, so what's the problem with occasionally making things less unbearable? What's so funny about love, peace and understanding? If we can develop a little empathy, why let those things shrivel and be ignored?

When I meet up with Sofie she tells me her social anxiety is not particularly active just then. But when she *is* feeling on edge, she has to sit in the corner of a room, needing walls on either side of her. She becomes especially seat-aware on public transport. She says, 'I need to sit in the window seat on planes and trains. I [once] sat in the aisle and had a four-hour panic attack. My mum always jokes that if I could build my own bed, it would be a coffin. When I was young, I wanted to sleep in a cupboard.'

Sofie first became truly aware of her anxiety during her childhood, in what many of the nervous amongst us considered to be the most anxiety-inducing building in the school, especially if you were one of those who had a dimpled chest: the gymnasium. It was for her, as it was for me, a place of shame and ridicule, coupled with an overt consciousness of your own body and its apparent peculiarities. The nausea would rise as you saw the wooden horse that you'd career into after a mistimed spring-vault, and the rope you'd be hanging six inches off the ground from, as all the others monkeyed to the roof.

Sofie hated gym class, she says, 'Because it was a big gymnasium and there were no corners anywhere, and the shouting and balls flying everywhere, and I ended up not attending gym class, which is illegal in Denmark [her country of origin]. I fought the school system for three years, because I would get panic attacks every time I did gym.'

Even as Sofie explains her anxiety, she voices a strange scepticism about it, because when she's not feeling anxious – like today – it seems like a lost fairy-tale piece of her life.

I'm aware that the mind seems to have a handy habit of rewriting itself when it is distant from the anxious or more neurotic self. The anxious human is a stranger, when the calm rational one is in charge. Yet the rational voice that says: *Hey, don't you remember last time? It was all fine in the end, so why shouldn't it be this time, eh?* is drowned out by a voice that says: *But this time it's different. Your anxiety wasn't real before, now it sure is.*

Watching Sofie Hagen onstage, and the warmth and ease she seems to exude, you can't imagine her ever being gripped with anxiety, but for her (as for other stand-ups) it's all about doing the performance. There have been times in the past when as soon as a gig has ended she has fled the building, even forgetting to pick up her pay. She says that the moment she doesn't have the microphone in her hand, she can't talk.

Even in the midst of the show, Sofie can find herself at a loose end for just long enough for her anxiety to make ripples. If she should get an applause break, she is uneasy. I can recognize this, too. It's as if once you stop talking, it gives you time to think, and anxious, unneeded thoughts can intrude. A little like Cinderella without a watch, working out when your control of the anxiety is going to run out is difficult and anxiety-inducing itself. Until a few years ago, my gigs used to stop dead, when the confident persona I'd inhabited onstage would suddenly disappear. I'd get to the last line that I had planned for the evening performance, hoping against hope that it felt like it had drawn to a satisfying conclusion – and drawn at least a reasonable round of laughter – and then I'd say, 'Thanks' and walk off. Before I'd even got to the edge of the stage it was as if the anxious offstage me would return, tap me on the shoulder and say: *I'm back now. What the hell have you been doing while I was gone?*

For Sofie, part of her show begins with her greeting the audience as they enter, and ends with her saying goodbye to them from the door, almost as if they are personal house-guests; but once the door is closed, the relationship between audience and act ends and the real-life social anxiety returns. She explains that if she is offered a drink by two people, she can't say yes, because 'I am way more scared of an individual person than an entire 650-seater theatre.' Her shows are very personal, but despite the intimacy of the material, it is an intimacy that can only exist with an audience, and within the parameters that are created when a confession becomes a performance.

Onstage, Sofie appears utterly free to express herself in any way she wants. What would be terrifying in humdrum, close-contact, eye-to-eye reality is possible with the heightened reality of talking from the stage. She likes to create 'moments' onstage. One night, she went onstage and explained that she was in love with the compère. She was unable to express that love to him personally, but she could tell him, and eighty other people, when she was performing: 'I will do something onstage that is terrifying, and it was so thrilling and I didn't even care what he said. This rush, yeah, holy shit, something just happened, something just happened.'

The need for an audience at times of revelation is starkly revealed by the poet Lemn Sissay. First fostered, and then brought up in a care home, Sissay believed that the care system had been negligent, and he launched a case against the local council. As part of his case he had a five-hour psychological assessment. When the report was completed, rather than face the document alone, he waited, hearing its contents for the first time at the Royal Court Theatre with an audience in attendance. Seated onstage, he heard the report being read to him by the actress Julie Hesmondhalgh. The story of the institutional failures in Lemn's care and upbringing is not pleasant, and their impact has been so severe that he can suffer from crippling depression and disappear from public life for months. Lemn explained in the *Guardian* his reasons for making this report into a live event:

I feel good onstage. I feel, in a bizarre way, like I'm with family. This is the best way for me to look at those files. I couldn't be in a safer place. I feel more comfortable having this out in the open, because they fucked me up when I was on my own.[2]

Perhaps that is what many anxious performers really need: the space in which to share their pain, their anxieties, with others – many, but anonymous – because often being with those anxieties on their own is too painful.

While performing one night in Denmark, Sofie saw a man she recognized in the front row, someone who had previously broken her heart. As she worried backstage in the interval about what to do, another comedian said, 'Talk about it' – so she did. She told the whole love-torn story about the boy who had broken her heart, and then she looked at the front row, pointed and said to the audience, 'It's him, by the way.' What a twist!

With a confidence that deserts her in day-to-day life, Sofie looked at him and asked, 'Why couldn't you love me?' and then handed him the microphone. 'It made me so happy. I felt strong and brave.'

It needs to be said, of course, that this is perhaps the worst nightmare for anyone unlucky enough to find themselves in the front row of a comedy club. It is one thing to be picked on with 'Hey, what do you do?' or 'Why are you wearing that lousy jumper?', but 'Why couldn't you love me, and why did you break my heart?' is in quite a different league. That said, Sofie had found the courage to express something deeply painful for her, which she hadn't previously been able to do. She explains that part of her drive to create shows is because they are a way of telling people that she is okay. 'I think I've been pitied a lot in my life, for various reasons. I don't look like someone who has got their shit together, I'm not an alpha. When I talk about something a bit dark, people go, "Ah" and I want to punch the audience. Why would you think I would stand here to get your pity?'

We all attempt to control the environment around us, and part of that is trying to influence the way people think about us. I think that, for anxious people, it's losing control of this situation – and having the horrible reality of our apparent fakery exposed to us – that is the greatest fear. When a comedian has an audience laughing at their act, even when that act is seemingly self-mocking and highlights their flaws and anxieties, then in that moment they have mastered some form of control over what people think. And so for comics, as for a person at a party, the greatest frustration comes from being misinterpreted – when you think you have presented yourself in an indisputable manner, but the subjectivity of the observer gets in the way.

Sofie had just started another relationship, which floundered when the boyfriend saw her show and said how great it was that Sofie showed her 'weakness' onstage. 'I thought "he knows who I am", but he had seen something else. He didn't understand. What he thought was my weakness was my strength. It's scary when people get it wrong. The only reason I want to be a good comedian is so I can control exactly what you think of me. After five minutes, I don't let latecomers in, because they won't get the full context . . . Now that you mention it, I might need help . . .'

I returned to Josh Coen's Freudian couch with my pitiful tales of social anxiety, public incontinence and compulsive, intrusive thoughts, such as French-kissing elderly uncles.

According to Josh, Freud believed that to really enjoy a free and happy life you have to have contemplated incest with your mother or your sister. Don't worry, he explained, it doesn't have to be that literal – it's more the sentiment that counts. It boils down to the need to have contemplated the worst in yourself, and realizing that there is a difference between contemplation and desire. So you can stop thinking about incest now.

Josh said, 'It's not the desire that generates the prohibition, it's the prohibition that generates the desire. I don't see it as an inbuilt desire to sleep with your mother and kill your father – that

191

makes absolutely no sense to me. Our early life is built around rules and prohibitions.' We need to confront what is prohibited in our society, to imagine ourselves in that situation, in order to understand ourselves.

He imagines that every stand-up comedian, however outrageous and uninhibited they appear, has an intimacy with inhibition and repression. It is the proximity to repression that might make some of us eager to expose ourselves, as long as the environment is right – and that environment is being on a theatre stage in front of an audience of people. That said, Josh doesn't think all use of outrage by comedians is of the same worth or delivered with the same intention.

There is a difference between the calculated, naughty-child *This will outrage the audience* outrage – a sort of extreme cheekiness for surface effect – and the type of outrageous comment where the comedian reaches the point of *My God, this will outrage me; I can't believe I'm thinking this, and I really can't believe I am saying this aloud.*

But then the question *I* want answered is why things that are left unsaid with your closest friends can become sayable in front of a large group of strangers. It seems such a peculiar part of our psychological make-up, even when we take into account ideas of control and power over others.

In a society that worries so much about status and perception, Josh sees social embarrassment as absolutely non-trivial. When we are trying to maintain an appearance of cool sanity, where keeping the lid from blowing off is exhausting, it might take just one impolite jab, one paper cut, to lose control. The fear of being found out can leave us in a precarious state, with the veneer always on the cusp of cracking. It is that which we cannot control that dominates us.

As Josh says, 'No grown-up wants to be seen shitting himself on a plane. It evokes a primal humiliation.' It is our battle with our physical selves, our instincts and our reflex actions; we want to show that we are in charge, and every time our bodies look as if they are about to fail us, we fear that we aren't really in control. We run from our own fragility.

There was a point when I became so certain that I would need to urinate just before I went onstage, despite thirty visits to the urinals in the fifty minutes before start time, that I took to wearing a duffel coat for performances. Fortunately, it was during one of my shoutier phases of stand-up, so it added to the 'street' crazy-chic look, as if it was deliberate set-dressing rather than protecting a peculiar anxiety. Also it meant I didn't have to hunt around looking for a hook, or worry about where I'd left my coat when I was leaving the venue. It seemed to me that if your anxious bent peaked before going onstage, then when old anxieties have run their course, new ones will replace them. In the early days you panic that you'll suddenly dry up and have nothing to say. Once you are aware that you have a body of words and a set of improvising skills that can get you out of that situation, the mind brings a reserve paranoia off the bench and finds new things for you to be anxious about.

Josh tells me that this anxiety is a form of vulnerability, and that an unconscious fear of being exposed could be what makes a performance work, what gives it its edge. 'In a situation where we aim to control perception, the neurotic mind will always remind you that some functions are beyond your conscious control.'

So, what to do?

Josh explains that he doesn't see the psychoanalytic cure as being about a behavioural transformation or a transformation of personality. He tells me that when people ask him how analysis will deal with their problems, his response is, 'What do you mean by *deal with*?' For Josh, it is instead about making contact with the hidden things within yourself and trying to use them creatively, rather than allowing them to be a prohibitive force that looms, unidentified but toxic, in the shadows.

He explains that you need to know and love your anxieties. They need to become your friends. He sees this as meaning many possible things: 'If you have a set of anxieties around anything, does working those through mean you no longer have them any more, that you just breeze through life? I don't tend to think so; it's just that you are able to get closer to the anxiety, you are able to talk to it and about it. If you think about it in that way, then you are no longer in conflict with the creative person. People who come to me with a creative block, it is because they have put a boundary between them[selves] and some region of their head. It is introducing themselves to this region of themselves they've blocked off, but not to get rid of it.'

Can comedy be psychotherapeutic? If so, is it more for the act or for the audience? In moments of ego-fuelled pomposity, is there a secret desire to stride onstage and announce, 'I come here to cure you', before the laying-on of hands and puns?

Perhaps don't throw away your pills when your booking confirmation arrives, though – not just yet.

A Sunday night in Nottingham sticks in my mind. While I was on tour with a couple of friends, someone saw something onstage that evening that changed her life. Suffice it to say, it was nothing to do with me. A woman was sitting in the audience looking unhappy. It wasn't as if she was unhappy with the show; it looked as if something heavier hung over her. Not being ones to pick on the audience, we all let it be. Grace Petrie, a friend, folk singer and frequent stage ally, came on and did one of her sets that manage to rouse and move. She is funny – but that is her secondary show-business characteristic; her primary talent is singing songs of fury and beauty about love and politics. Her love songs are about her relationships with women, with emotions and paranoias that are universal. We finished the gig and drank beer on the train home. It had been a good audience, but for us no more or less remarkable than usual.

Six months later, after doing her own show in London, Grace received a note. It was from the sullen woman in the audience in Nottingham. She explained that she had not wanted to go to that gig as she had been feeling bleak. During Grace's set, in a Damascene moment, the reason for the woman's bleakness suddenly came into sharp focus: she wasn't who she was trying to be. She was in a heterosexual relationship, but hearing Grace's beautiful songs was the tipping point for her to know for sure that she was a lesbian. Six months on, she wrote that her life was far better.

Ever anxious, I wondered whether that was the difference between Grace and me: that she illuminates people's true sexuality, and I make people less worried about their fear of wanting to throw babies out of a window or have sex with a terrier. If people aren't cured, or at least ready to make friends with their anxieties after our shows, you can't say we didn't try.

After my years of onstage research, I can confidently say that whatever your anxiety, however seemingly irrational and unfounded, however strange and unique it feels to you, someone else somewhere will share it.

Breast-milkshake, anyone . . . ?

CHAPTER 8

Morals and Temptations

I'm not offended by all the dumb blonde jokes because I
know I'm not dumb . . . and I also know that I'm not blonde.

Dolly Parton

'You're not allowed to make jokes any more,' I was told by a sulky man.

'You are,' I replied.

'Yes, but not funny ones – they've banned the funny ones,' he continued.

I tried to explain that comedy is subjective, but he insisted that political correctness had stolen all the jokes that brought him joy.

'What jokes in particular are you missing?' I asked.

There was a moment's pause while he considered how delight had been stolen from his life by a cabal of mirthless despots who despised happiness.

'Well, you're not allowed to make jokes about the disabled . . . or the truth.'

197

That is some Venn diagram of where mirth is to be found. I either want a joke that clearly accepts energy is mass multiplied by the speed of light squared or one about people in wheelchairs falling off the end of piers. Preferably both in the same scene.

People like aggressively picking apart what they believe is allowed speech and banned speech. People take jokes very personally. Make a joke about an archdeacon but don't follow it up straight away with a jibe at an imam, and the complaints logs will fill up.

A joke is a shortcut to understanding someone's ethics, morals and beliefs. What outrages us tells us what we care about. The jokes that come out of our mouths may also say something about who and what we value, and who we consider worthy of our derision, though this is susceptible to gross misunderstanding.

We've already seen how comedy and humour can work best by pushing at the boundaries and yet, inhabiting a very public space, comedians run the gauntlet between humour and offence – even to the extent that people will be offended not only by what you have said, but by what you haven't. Every performance, you run the risk of overstepping one person's boundary of what is acceptable, while falling far too short of someone else's.

You can play it too safe, and you can go too far. Some people make a career out of 'going too far', though this often lies just within the limits of what will keep an audience coming back, and TV commissioners interested, so those same boundaries still apply. If those comics promoted as 'saying the unsayable' really were saying the unsayable, they'd be driven out of every town they performed in, and would be playing to seven people before being found dead, weighted down in a canal.

I have never been a comedian who deliberately courted controversy. When I was younger, I liked sick humour, as best exemplified by the bad-taste movies of John Waters. These are movies full of faecal matter and vomit, and things that really should not be done to chickens. You don't need to be a prude to be repulsed by Divine, star of a number of Waters's movies, eating dog excrement and then smiling at the camera with his famous, truly shit-eating grin.

I drew a lot of inspiration from Waters's onscreen atrocity, but this made much of my early comedy repulsive, rather than morally offensive. When I left my twenties, I left those jokes behind, too. There is a time to leave behind the poo, wee and peculiar sex jokes and at least pretend you are an adult. Part of growing up is finding those things that your parents don't under-stand and revelling in them, to show that you are not the same. This was the joy of *The Young Ones*; it was snotty and loud and stupid, but it turns out that my mum quite liked it too.

A psychological study has shown, though, that whilst there are age-related differences to how we view the offensiveness of certain types of humour, even this statistic can vary greatly from country to country. In *Good Humour, Bad Taste: A Sociology of the Joke*, Dutch Professor of Cultural Sociology Giselinda Kuipers carried out a large survey looking at how different cul-tures react to different types of humour, particularly in the US and Holland. Whilst many of the jokes were considered to be the best matched across the two countries, the way we take offence at particular types of comedy differed greatly, and the professor even had to remove some 'ethnic and sexual jokes' from the US part of the survey, because the Pennsylvania University board where the survey was taking place deemed them to be breaching regulations.

So where you come from can also impact on how you react to a joke and whether you find it offensive or not, or funny or not. Irrespective of whether you were offended by the *Charlie Hebdo* cartoons, many British people objected to them because they didn't find them funny. Some comedy travels and some fails to make it across the border. I was surprised when I started to get missives of fury over my use of the term 'Chinese whispers' in a tweeted joke, now long forgotten. I'd not really thought of it as a racist jibe, as it seemed pretty distant from my view of the people of China. 'What is it with these Chinese people failing to pass on messages effectively – it's almost as bad as when they all jump up and down at once and create earthquakes.' Then I discovered that it had been re-tweeted by someone with a large American following and the anger was universally stemming from there. I have referred to it as 'the telephone game' ever since, though I would like to stress that I do not consider the Chinese ability to whisper to be lacklustre or ineffective. This is the problem of the speed at which a joke can travel now; you have no idea who will be in your virtual audience, and the presumptions they may make.

The first public upbraiding for a joke I made concerned a gag about animal experiments. It had initially stemmed from seeing the newspaper headline 'Scientists have discovered how to make mice live one-third longer'. This headline became the set-up to my punchline, 'They've stopped injecting them with cancer.'

In my mind, this was a joke more against vivisection than for it, but the man in the second row of the gig in Kings Heath didn't think so. He heckled angrily and then cornered me at the bar, to air his concern that my one-liner was a vigorous promotion of pointless mouse-death.

Explanation of intention is no use – he was certain he knew what I really meant. I was probably from the propaganda wing of the biomedicine animal-destruction institute. I left a man standing in a fetid puddle of dissatisfaction, being unable to relieve him of his offence.

I realized after the incident that, in telling a joke and being questioned about it, I began to gain some knowledge of how comfortable I was in defending the joke, something that had never really crossed my mind previously. In the end I dropped the joke, not because I was concerned about its offensive impact, but because I realized it just wasn't funny enough. But since then there have been jokes that I have questioned myself about and have dropped, for reasons other than their humour content.

I was particularly keen on the phrase 'He had the kind of face that in the old days you'd have to pay a shilling and go into a tent to see'. As a youthful fan of Tod Browning's *Freaks*, I liked the circus sideshow imagery, but decided I wouldn't be happy justifying it to audience members at the bar afterwards. Similarly, I used to describe a particular journalist during a performance as 'a septic tank housed in a human-skin sack'. I liked the rhythm of it. It wasn't intended to be about appearance, but about the toxicity and stench of her opinions. I kept it in for many shows. It was not meant to reflect her physical structure, which does not in any way resemble a septic tank housed in a human-skin sack, but later I felt uncomfortable about it and decided I should focus on her writing and opinions, and not just create a rancid image. I am fond of the rancid image, but now I only mumble it to myself in times of solitude.

Almost every day my tediously hyper-vigilant brain debates what is offensive and why; it picks up the slack time when one of the multitude of online voices isn't explaining why I am a monster. I once tweeted the philosopher Eric Hoffer's aphorism, 'What monstrosities would walk the streets were some people's faces as unfinished as their minds.'[1] I hadn't realized it was offensive. I was informed that this quote was quite unacceptable and was offensive to people with physical deformities.

Once, when tweeting that I was debating whether to watch a panel show which featured a particularly toxic panel of contrarians or to wrap myself tightly in barbed wire and roll in broken bottles, I was informed that this was very insulting to people who self-harm.

I once tweeted Einstein's comment about the nature of time: 'Put your hand on a hot stove for a minute, and it seems like an hour. Sit with a pretty girl for an hour, and it seems like a minute. That's relativity.' I wondered if Einstein would have faced a space–time quandary if he burnt his hand on a robot kettle that had been welded into the shape of Marilyn Monroe. However, again people took offence and told me my tweet was misogynistic.

It is easy to be an -istic nowadays, either intentionally or unintentionally.

I realize that, being a stand-up, I do have a platform for such humour, and perhaps some people would argue that because of that, I even have some sort of social responsibility. But these were not even jokes, just very idle, foolish thoughts shared broadly enough to find the offended. Just as it seems, if you look hard enough, you can find someone with a sexual predilection for any species or object or idea, so you can find someone who will be offended by almost any loose collection of words. I used to be infuriated, but I'm not any more. I have been educated almost as much as I have been exasperated.

Are we more sensitive now to taking offence at things around us, or is it just that there have never been so many ways of publicly expressing your outrage? What is the research into why we take offence at what we do, especially when it may have little to do with our life or experience?

Belonging to a social group is an extremely powerful marker of who we are. US social psychologists Diane Mackie and Eliot Smith have written extensively on how strong emotions can be triggered as part of a social reaction within a social group, rather than on an individual level. In their studies they have found that when an individual is reminded of belonging to a particular group, and then asked a series of questions about emotional reactions, their emotions are different than when they are asked the same questions, but from the standpoint of a different group. In the same scenario, an individual might feel a high level of happiness when thinking about themselves as an individual, but when asked how they feel as a woman, they might feel angry and upset.

Just as laughter can bind us, so can outrage. I probably get too hung up on working out what may offend people. Joan Rivers, whose life included struggle and tragedy and who was one of the finest purveyors of acid-tongued barbs, said, 'Part of my act is meant to shake you up. It looks like I'm being funny, but I'm reminding you of other things. Life is tough, darling. Life is hard.

And we better laugh at everything; otherwise, we're going down the tube.'[2] She got into particularly hot water when she joked, a few months after the 9/11 attacks, that some of the widows might be happier with the compensation they received than they were with their dead husbands. Rivers revelled in her outrage onstage, but a documentary made a few years before she died showed that, behind the outrage, she was frequently worried about losing popularity and success; her drive to prod and goad also came from a sweet, almost melancholy neediness to feel worthy of the audience's attention.

Further studies show that when a group feels angry and threatened by something, it lashes out beyond the group – a study in the US showed that those most in favour of military action after 9/11 were, unsurprisingly, those most angered by the attacks. What seems to be key in this lashing out is a breakdown of any form of empathy towards those in the 'out-group', or outside the 'in-group'. Social media, in a frequently positive way, has allowed many individuals to see themselves as belonging to a number of social groups; it has given them a voice and a strength that perhaps previously as individuals they didn't have. And we only have to see the recent #METOO campaign to see how important that can be. But empowering people, and giving them a sense of belonging to a group, has also enabled any and all people at any one time to find something somewhere to be offended by. If you can take offence at something, drum up a bit of righteous indignation – safe in the knowledge that, when you put it out there, you won't be having your own personal 'Or is it just me' moment – then you become more confident in taking offence at something.

This virtual unity can lead to dogmatic positions, as well as lashing out without allowing the slower-thinking parts of the brain to say, 'Hold on; before we voice our opinion, shall we just think about this for a moment?' We used at least to have to put pen to paper, and the act of taking the top off the biro and finding a sheet of A4 may have given us time to reason; now the phone in our hand is ready to be red-hot with fury and, once you have publicly declared your rage, it is harder to take it back. Once we have stated our position, it may seem embarrassing to back down, so we cling to it even more vehemently and find others to confirm our bias.

When you look back nostalgically at what you were furious about the year before, sometimes you may find that you appear to have got rather carried away with it all.

This perpetually leads to the question: 'But where do you draw the line?' And for many people, the line just happens to coincide with jokes about them and their most dearly held beliefs. Any moment in the debate where it gets to 'I'm all for free speech but . . .' is one that will lead to shifting ground and quicksand.

A joke about Jesus will lead to an outcry that it is unfair there aren't more jokes about Mohammed, as if the upset Christian would be quite happy to be mocked, as long as there was some form of parity in mockery. At the end of the year the Council of Comedy would collate information on all jokes told per annum and ensure that, when placed on the scales of ribaldry, the number of jokes about Jews was exactly the same as the number of jokes about Muslims and the same as the number of jokes about Anglicans; any disparity would lead to an airborne task force with state-of-the-art megaphones swooping over cities and reciting one-liners about whatever denomination had been unjustly treated with too much kindness. There would also need to be some measurement of the strength of the jokes, because one harsh joke about Ganesh might be worth three gentle jokes about the Archbishop of Canterbury.

If the solution that I propose is not viable, then what can we do? Must humour have victimless punchlines? Is the fault with the teller or the listener? Have comedians become more offensive, or audiences more sensitive? Is it because the news media has become more opinion-based than event-based, so that the lack of foreign correspondents has meant that Twitter has become the foxhole from which to observe the flying shrapnel?

It is difficult to make sweeping generalizations when considering such questions, especially when such questions are often spurred on by sweeping generalizations. For instance, it could be argued that context and how well the audience knows you, and you know them, is a vital part of the play. A hilarious joke amongst friends does not always translate to the stage. Sadly, you often only realize that after it has come out of your mouth. This is the danger of sharing jokes on social media. Those jokes stand alone, with no context – often nothing more than an avatar to give any representation of who lies behind the joke.

Unlike television, radio or newspapers, or even being online, the useful thing about being offended at a stand-up club is that you can immediately respond and be heard. Sadly for all those involved, it is usually only the drunk who have the courage to voice their feelings, and rarely does it lead to a Platonic dialogue. Sometimes the response to being offended swerves past the straightforward heckle and goes straight for the physical. YouTube has an impressive archive of comedy stages being invaded and comedians being attacked by inebriates. Sadly, we frequently don't know why the punching begins, as the filming only starts when an audience member gets that exciting buzz that says, 'I think there is about to be some violence – what should I use my lightning-quick reactions for? Should I stop it or film it? It's the twenty-first century, so let's make sure I've got the frame-ratio correct.'

Fortunately for Australian comedian Jim Jefferies, The Comedy Store in Manchester has a camera that can film acts at all times. Jim has gone on to become a TV star in North America, and has angered audiences to the point of death-threats with routines on religion and gun control, but for quite a while his most-watched clip was a drunk's fumbling but passionate attempt to punch him in the face. The footage of this is still the fourth most-watched clip of Jefferies, behind 'USA and North Korea are in a nuclear diss battle', 'Jim Jefferies explains a coke wank' and 'Jim Jefferies's awkward Justin Bieber run-in'.

Ricky Gervais spent a couple of decades testing the borderlines of taste and decency in the privacy of his own home. Then, when he was in his late thirties, he decided it might be fun to test the boundaries of decency in public.

I have known Ricky since he was an entertainments officer who had a sideline managing a Queen tribute band. Somewhere in the early part of this century he made the transition from booking discos to becoming the UK's biggest international comedy star. In 2005 he asked if I would support him on his UK tour. Being a support act was a negligible part of my duties on tour, with the main job seemingly to be manhandled, buried and hanged by Ricky, whose need for distraction can lead to a jovial torturing of whoever is within reach.

Ricky wakes up each morning and thinks, 'How much fun

can I have today?' He doesn't care what the collateral damage to other people's egos is, or indeed the damage to other people's skin, as they try to peel off the masking tape he has wrapped around their arms, legs and head whilst they were sleeping. 'Collateral' makes it sound accidental, but part of the joy for Ricky is deliberately making people do ridiculous things and placing them in uncomfortable situations.

The further away we got from home on the tour, the more Ricky seemed to require such distracting activities. These included burying me on a grey beach (for my birthday), hanging me upside-down on coat rails, covering my face in make-up and having people hide in my shower, so they could leap out when I least expected them. Some days it would just be Ricky insisting on singing 'Halfway down the stairs is a stair where I sit' for an hour or so.

Onstage, Ricky plays with the ethics of the audience. He plays with the perceived principles of a liberal audience. It is a position of knowing mockery and mild outrage. It requires the Alf Garnett/ Archie Bunker paradigm of laughing both with and at. It is a difficult balance, and it is almost impossible for the entire audience to receive the joke as intended, and that can create problems.

When I meet up with Ricky, he is about to embark on a tour whose theme is offence. The critics wrote of the tour, 'Those sensitive to transgender issues, say (or jokes involving rape or cot death), should take a deep breath before booking for *Humanity*. And yet, it's Gervais's best and most considered standup show so far';[3] and '*Humanity* finds him lampooning the snowflake sensibilities of those who take offence at the slightest thing'.[4]

Ricky likes to mock and goad, but he has added a layer of commentary, expressing the purpose behind his offence, and perhaps putting his philosophy degree to good use with his well-argued rhetoric. His onstage persona has had to change a little, as it is harder to punch upwards as a comic when so many people are below you. It is harder to play the lowly scamp from Reading, when you are a multimillionaire with a first-class-cabin lifestyle. If you are punching up, you've only got a few dukes and presidents above you – and, obviously, the illuminati, whoever they may be. I suppose it could be him.

The other problem is that some of the bigotry that he knowingly toyed with and mocked a decade ago has gone politically mainstream in the last two years. Rather than kicking against a society that is too polite for its own good, mainstream media and politics are flooded with galumphing lummoxes, brattishly spraying spite and aggression for the purposes of social-media trends, advertising revenue and political promotion.

Ricky is fully aware of the oddness of his stand-up situation. 'This isn't a societal norm, it is already beyond the realms of how we feel people should treat us in society. You've paid me to potentially offend or annoy you. You've paid me to make you laugh initially, and with that comes the chance you won't like everything.'

The audience has to accept that it is a game. It is dangerous. Is everyone laughing because they know they shouldn't or because they are in full agreement with this persona? Sometimes he crosses a line where a section of the audience feels Ricky's professional offensiveness has now become too offensive. They've come to revel in the 'naughtiness' of laughing at what they shouldn't, but is that an alibi to pretend they have some intellectual distance from the ideas he is sharing, which only become raw and angry when he butchers their own personal sacred cow?

While playing in New York, he received a complaint letter from a Jewish group who had enjoyed all the jokes about fat people, AIDS and famine, 'but we did not appreciate the jokes about Anne Frank'. I wonder how that audience has been interpreting the rest of the show. Has their laughter come from the frisson of naughtiness – 'Oh dear, this cheeky man really shouldn't be saying these things' – or have they enjoyed being in a 'safe space' for laughing at others, people outside their own social grouping: fat people, cancer sufferers and those enduring famines? Why are the victims in the jokes by 'edgy' comics so frequently people who are more likely to be victims of abuse in real life, too?

As in real life, comedians have to ask themselves whether they should edit their opinions, depending on who they are with. If you have a joke about wheelchair users, do you drop it if you see a wheelchair user in the front row? How robust is your game of offence? Are our apparent ethics flexible, depending on who is looking?

Veteran comedian Jim Davidson delights in offending those with 'liberal media elite sensibilities', but when he was playing a theatre in Plymouth he pulled a gig at the last minute, because he found out the front row would have quite a few wheelchair users in it. He likes to converse with, and mock, the front row and decided that would be quite impossible if some of his front row were in wheelchairs.

Whether onstage or at a dinner table, we are creating our context and are surrounded by the context projected onto us by others. When writing his material, Ricky doesn't feel the need to change a joke due to an onset of gag-guilt – the sense that a joke is not tellable because of a particular audience. He believes he can stand firm with his offence, whoever may be watching. He sees himself as able to do jokes about people's -isms: 'You can't justify the joke if the -ism victim is there and you drop it. It's no good to say, "Oh no, I didn't see you at the back, I'd never have said it if I'd known you were there."'

One of the more contentious areas in recent years has been jokes about rape. It became a focus at the Edinburgh Fringe, where some felt that too many comedians were relying on quick and easy laughs from jokes about rape. Around this time I was asked to sign a declaration that I would never make a joke about rape onstage. I believed the petitioner's intentions were good, but I couldn't sign, despite the fact that it would be a promise I could easily uphold – unless I was doing a routine on the necrophiliac behaviour of mallard ducks.

I've never thought of a rape joke so funny that it created a conflict between what I think I should say and my need for laughter. However, I still wouldn't want to sign something, as I think a vow like that is an alternative to actually being thoughtful about what you write and what you express: 'I can't make a joke about that – I've signed a pledge', rather than 'I'm not going to make that joke because it may well ruin someone's night and, frankly, it's not worth it, for one punchline or two-minute routine. I'll think of something better.'

The taste and decency line used to be drawn at 'I'd never make jokes about disabled kiddies.' You could see the sense of nobility as this gesture was announced, but it felt like an alibi. It's like saying, 'You can't criticize me for making jokes about violence towards women, cheap cracks based on race or my grotesque homophobia, because I don't make jokes about disabled kiddies. I am a good human being.' It is not as if they are sacrificing a deep well of zinger material by not doing those jokes about disabled children. On reflection, I think it might be true that you can joke about anything, but why you *want* to joke about them in the first place is the bigger question. 'It's just a joke' seems a weak response. Humour and comedy, as I think I have expressed in this book, can be incredibly important and powerful: individually, socially and politically. If jokes are so unimportant, why do people get so exercised by them, and why do certain dictatorships ban them and imprison the tellers?

Ricky's most well-known rape joke was in *The Office*, which he wrote with Steve Merchant. It takes place during a role-play exercise. Ricky's character, David Brent, a needy man desperate for love and attention and deluded about his personal popularity, is pretending to be a dissatisfied customer in a hotel, while the corporate trainer plays the surly, inattentive hotel receptionist:

> **Brent:** I'd like to make a complaint please.
> **Corporate trainer:** Don't care.
> **Brent:** Well, I am staying in the hotel . . .
> **Corporate trainer:** Don't care, it's not my shift.
> **Brent:** Well, you're an ambassador for the hotel . . .
> **Corporate trainer:** I don't care what you think.
> **Brent:** I think you'll care when I tell you what the complaint is . . .
> **Corporate trainer:** I don't care!
> **Brent:** I think there's been a rape up there!

Brent's employees and the corporate trainer look on aghast. In Brent's mind, he has shown that he is best.

Brent: See, I got his attention. Get. Their. Attention.

The joke is clearly on Brent. This is not a joke about rape, but about a desperate little man who wants to 'win' at any cost.

Recently Ricky got into an argument on social media with someone who asked, 'Can you ever make a joke about rape?' Social media is not the best place to argue such thorny issues – even the canny use of emoticons may lead to a misunderstanding of tone. Socrates would have drunk his hemlock with greater haste, had he been debating on social media rather than in the market square, but it is interesting for our purposes to see how the argument played out.

Ricky's first reply was, 'It depends what the joke is.'

Others soon joined in, replying, 'No, it doesn't', and someone added, 'I will laugh at a joke about rape when I know no one in the audience has been raped.'

Unfortunately Ricky was unable to resist a joke and replied, 'What a weird door policy.'

Discussing this exchange, he later told me, 'This is a nice person worried about this. Offence is the collateral damage of free speech. I should add: these arguments fall down when someone goes around shouting "rape is funny" or "black people are inferior". I am not defending someone's right to be racist or support rapists, I am supporting my right to make a joke about that subject, which is very, very different.'

Ricky believes that offence usually comes when people confuse the target of the joke with the subject of the joke. He made a joke about paedophilia on Twitter after a story about Operation Yewtree, the police investigation into high-profile child abuse, which then became a headline story itself. Ricky tells me that what most annoys him is 'where idiots treat jokes about a bad thing with the same fury as the bad things themselves'.

The question for the offensive comedian is not merely how far can they go with their audience, but also how far can they go with themselves? Do they have a line that they'd rather not cross? Do they watch other comedians who mine offensiveness and think, 'I wouldn't go there'? Have they lost all right to be offended by anything in their life and experience?

I've met very few people who are offended by nothing. They may despise the fact that they have been offended, with their brain arguing against their gut instinct of outrage, but they can't totally suppress it. I know Ricky never really gets offended, but I wonder which comedians he watches and thinks, 'Wow, that is further than I would go.'

Nothing springs to mind, although I know that he is a keen campaigner on animal rights, so I wonder whether perhaps his line is drawn at animal cruelty: 'Skinning dogs alive, I just can't find that funny.' Perhaps it is easy for people like Ricky and me to spend less time being offended, as our existence is pretty comfortable, and the antagonisms of our daily existence are fewer than they are for many others. One of Ricky's most-troubled outrage incidents was for using the word 'mong'. He argued that it was now so distant from being a derogatory term for people with Down's syndrome and that it was simply a playground form of abuse. After the story started to gain some traction, he spoke with a disability campaigner and was informed that, sadly, this was still a common catcall aimed at adults and children with disabilities. He refrains from using the word now. Sometimes our bubbles lead us to believe that civilization has moved on at a greater pace than it has.

Our biggest difference of opinion, though, is on how the way a joke is received can affect us. I think that if you believe a large enough number of people are not getting the joke in the way you hoped, then the joke has failed. If you write an anti-misogyny joke or an anti-skinning-dogs-alive joke and you start to get very positive feedback from women-hating dog-skinners, then you might want to rework the wording. Ricky disagrees: 'If anyone gets your joke in the way it was intended it was gettable, you can't open the doors to thousands of other people and expect everyone to get the right message.'

Being a bleeding-heart liberal, I get very tangled up in working out what and why things that I have said have been found offensive. If I find I am going to antagonize people – whether they take my joke the wrong way or the right way – I think hard about whether that antagonism is worth it, for the sake of a joke. Ricky seems far more pugnacious than I am. He knows what the joke is meant to be about and, if you have misunderstood it, that is your fault. He tells me that he feels he should come down on the 'right side', and he does get into discussions: 'I'd rather more people got jokes than less, [but] nothing makes me more uncomfortable than someone without a sense of humour.'

So what really seems to offend Ricky is people being offended. It is the nearest he gets to having the same tone of outrage that others may have with him, when they take issue with his jokes. Being offended by the offended is a catch-22. Much of Ricky's act is about overstepping the mark to provoke the correct amount of shock to make people laugh, but making them feel like they have been risqué or improper in doing that, so of course some people will go from laughter to feeling offended. If the line between the acceptable and the offensive was straight and solid, there would be no fun in toying with it.

It is said that offence is taken, not given, but sometimes it is just shoved in your lap. A popular stance, amongst those offended by the offended, is summed up by a statement from Stephen Fry: 'It's now very common to hear people say, "I'm rather offended by that." As if that gives them certain rights. It's actually nothing more . . . than a whine. "I find that offensive." It has no meaning; it has no purpose; it has no reason to be respected as a phrase. "I am offended by that." Well, so fucking what.'[5]

It's an easy dismissal. Sure, there is a lot of being offended out there and, through the publicity that people know they can generate by being offensive, it has been monetized, but it can be useful beyond the realms of increasing ad-revenue and public profile. Some days it is not worth getting embroiled, especially with the perpetually offended, but other days it is worth asking why.

Once people have decided they are offended, it is difficult to shift their position. Mark Twain wrote, 'It is easier to fool people than convince them that they have been fooled.' Equally, once someone has found their viewpoint from a position of high moral outrage, it is hard to talk them down. Perpetual dismissal of the offended gets us nowhere. Though both sides often go into a discussion howling and screeching, if you can go into a discussion calmly, sometimes – after you have weathered the first couple of blows – you can find yourself talking rationally.

You can find out if they really know why they were offended, and you can work out if you are content to have offended them and think it was worth while. Well-thought-out offence is so much more fun than scattergun offence. It seems a pity to squander the coinage of offence just to be an arsehole. As another bleeding-heart liberal comedian, Marcus Brigstocke, has said, 'Offence is important; that's how you know you care about things. Imagine a life where you're not offended. So dull.'

Tim Minchin's comic songs are clever, witty, catchy, mocking and celebratory. They have also been criticized as being offensive. In 2012, for instance, Minchin was booked for the Henley Festival, with the organizers professing to be unaware of his standing as 'comedy's most renowned atheist'. When locals criticized the show as being 'crude, blasphemous and unbelievably bad', the organizers' only defence was to plead ignorance.

Minchin uses his songs to shoot arrows at organizations and ideologies that he wishes to question and criticize. Outside of the good burghers of Henley, his is an act that seems to be deeply loved, not just in an 'I loved that show' way, but someone whose work permeates his admirers' lives.

When we performed together at a benefit for libel reform in a London theatre, Tim only played one song. His worshippers were not disappointed, as he watched the rest of the show behind the curtain from the side of stage. The next day's Minchin comedy forums contained comments such as 'Tim only did one song, which was brilliant, but we could see his feet for the whole of the second half.' Other comments were more effusive about his toes, while some ogled and described his ankles. They are good feet, better than mine. I have stubby toes.

It is an indication of Tim's charm and musicianship that even some of his most vitriolic numbers rarely lead to angry placards and off-key chanting mobs, but he has still had his songs pulled from TV shows that might think of themselves as rebellious. 'Woody Allen Jesus' went unaired on *The Jonathan Ross Show*, despite Tim's ability to find a rhyme for 'parthenogenesis'. Lyrics like:

Praise be to Jesus
Praise be to Woody Allen Jesus
(Woody Allen Jesus!)
Praise be to magic Woody Allen zombie superhero komodo
    dragon telepathic vampire quantum hovercraft *me* Jesus!

were too much for late-night British TV's arbiters of taste and decency.

Tim's most pugilistic songs are often on the theme of religion, and what he considers to be scientific woo-waa and charlatanism. His song about the Pope is less likely to be aired on television. It is not as wordy as 'Woody Allen Jesus':

Fuck the motherfucker
Fuck the motherfucker
Fuck the motherfucker
He's a fucking motherfucker

Fuck the motherfucker
Fuck the fucking fucker
Fuck the motherfucker
He's a total fucking fucker.

It continues in a similarly jaunty fashion.

I first heard 'The Pope Song' when we were performing together at a comedy karaoke night. I was about to go on and murder REM's 'It's the End of the World as We Know It' – a song too fast for karaoke, I would discover – when Tim beckoned me into a corner like a shifty rhyme-dealer selling couplets for coins. He wanted to play me something he had just recorded, which he wasn't sure he could ever play live. He wondered if it was too much. It was 'The Pope Song'.

I was putting on a benefit the following week and suggested that he tried it out there. It wasn't for a Catholic orphans' charity or to replace the rubies on the Vatican roof, so it would be fine. A week later Tim played the song at another benefit show and within a few months, far from being un-airable in a public space, it was a momentous sing-along in an arena.

Since then, Tim has written a song called 'Come Home' about Cardinal George Pell, a leading member of the Catholic Church in Australia, who was suspected of being involved in covering up child abuse there. It is a song that comes from a deep rage, and yet it succeeds in getting across a very important message with real humour. A Catholic journalist wrote that it 'provokes hilarity and horror in just 4 minutes of melody', and that she cackled when she first heard it, and wept by the third listen.[6] Tim worries about shaming, believing that shaming bad people – even those who, a burden of evidence would suggest, deserve it – doesn't always help. This is a moral dilemma that he had to think about with his Cardinal Pell song.

It is a powerful mix of pop melody and furious intent. Tim viewed it as more personal than 'The Pope Song', 'because by calling it "The Pope Song" you are focusing on the institution, but in Cardinal Pell, I called him George over and over again. I called him scum and a buffoon. It slightly broke my personal rules, and I don't know how I can defend that. Either you condone shaming or you don't.'

The song has had a profound effect on people, although it broke with Tim's own current ethics. I don't write 'current ethics' because he is an ethical flibbertigibbet, but because whenever someone takes a stand, there is usually a fearsome queue of snide and wearisome trolls eager to claw at the soil to unearth some historical inconsistency. It is for this reason that Tim has created the word 'apathete'. He wonders, 'Can I be consistent? Being ethically consistent in this world is impossible. It can be more consistent to do fuck-all all the time . . . I'd rather be a well-meaning hypocrite than a consistent apathete.'

Much thought has gone into Tim's approach to taboo. He is also aware of the malleability of our ethics. They are not cast in stone, at age eighteen, unless your upbringing has been defined and moulded by an overbearing dogma. Lacking a cult leader or deity to pay homage to, Tim celebrates the lack of 'stagnant boundaries'. He worries that creating such boundaries lies somewhere between virtue signalling and 'a salve for your own uncertainty'.

I ask if the moral purity of what you create should be governed by its popularity? 'The answer is no, it mustn't be. Is what you're writing a positive thing for the world, where weak people are not the victims, and can people swallow it?'

Although Tim remains uneasy about the song, he also believes that he did the right thing: 'There was a positive effect, and the money raised was tangible.' ('The money raised was used to send the survivors of abuse to Rome, to publicize and argue their cases against the Church.)

'I had to be very mean to an individual who I fucking loathe, but seeing as I don't really believe in free will, he isn't to blame for being a fuckhead.' Sometimes your small hypocrisy can be trumped by the enormity of another one.

Tim told me, though, of two songs whose good intentions did not surmount the problems of giving offence. The first song that he dropped was about obesity. The subtext was about parents not looking after their kids properly, but he realized that it came across as humiliating towards the big people in the room. In a comedy show, explaining your intentions can really dampen the effect of the entertainment. If they don't get it at first, sometimes it is best to drop it. Had Tim been physically bigger, it might have changed the way the joke was received, but a skinny man with a fat song may be presumed to being punching down, before the chorus of explanation is reached.

Similarly, material about racial identity is made thornier, depending on how the audience identifies you. Tim wrote another song about misuse of the N-word. He noticed that it made black people in the room uncomfortable. He realized that he had chosen a topic that wasn't his to satirize. 'I realized I wasn't really allowed to speak on that . . . You absolutely should adjust and, if you don't adjust, you're an idiot and belligerent.'

This comes back again of course to context, and many comedians, myself included, have argued that the context in which a joke is told is crucial. Perhaps for many of us, where we draw the line is about how we view the question of context. I only feel comfortable if I think a good percentage of the audience understands the irony of a potentially offensive joke – they understand its sometimes quite deeply hidden messages. Ricky Gervais perhaps stretches that line much further and is far less concerned – and, he would argue, not concerned at all – about who gets a joke or doesn't. Thomas E. Ford, a Professor of Social Psychology at Western Carolina University, has looked at the psychological consequences behind jokes that denigrate a social grouping, and as a result of his research he strongly believes that such humour, even when intended ironically, can negatively influence someone's behaviour, if they already have a leaning in that direction. His worry is that a man, say, who consciously or unconsciously has elements of his thinking that are sexist in nature, on hearing a sexist joke (whether told ironically or not) is then more disposed to sexist behaviour or sexist thinking in the future – he's had his biases confirmed.

The late Barry Crimmins was a veteran comedian and campaigner, who died of cancer in 2018 at the age of 64. His work was politically challenging and forthright, but he was a comic with a code of ethics. One night particularly stuck in his mind, when he thought about why he too believed that it's more than 'just jokes, folks'.

He was headlining a club and noticed that a couple in the front row really seemed to light up when he was on. Their reaction to him seemed to go beyond just being delighted by an act. They came up to Barry after the show and told him that they had a severely disabled son. Once a year they could get a special babysitter whom they could feel safe leaving their son with. For this year's night out, they had decided to go to a comedy night.

The first two acts that night repeatedly used the term 'retard', and they had felt deeply upset and uncomfortable. Barry didn't use it once. The couple said they soon realized that they would be safe with him. Barry commented, 'I became aware of the shrapnel you can spray out, that there's a lot of collateral damage you can do out there. That's why I don't do cancer jokes . . . randomly picking on people in the audience; people are often absolutely terrified of being picked out – "Oh, good, the bully isn't picking on me."'

Is your joke worth the collateral damage it may cause?

Barry believed that you've got to have a conscience onstage. 'I'm filtering out stuff – stuff I know would get laughs, but it might get taken the wrong way . . .' He had little time for those 'edgy' comedians who are often heralded for their unpleasantness. 'I don't know when a lack of conscience became synonymous with bravery; it seems cowardly to me.'

Different people are always going to draw the offensiveness line in different places. As we've seen, those 'different people' don't have to be individuals in a bubble; it can depend on their age, gender, social background, what country they come from, their religion or lack of religion. We all have social rules that we live by, and which enable us largely to go through life without causing great offence everywhere we go. And whilst social media has given power to certain groups to take offence at a far greater range of perceived slights, by and large there have also been some very positive effects of such sharing of experiences and feelings.

I think if this look at causing offence shows anything, it is that comedy by its very nature thrives on walking that narrow line. From the moment you tell your first rude joke to a group of the opposite sex in the playground at school, and you either want the ground to swallow you up or you become the most popular person in the class, you know that comedy is a tightrope-walk. If no one anywhere is offended by your comedy, and you don't get the occasional lurch of nausea about whether you've crossed a particular line, then it's probably not working.

Equally, I believe we all need to think about the power and impact of our words on others. Words are not 'just words', and whilst laughter can often be an important and powerful release, we have to consider how our humour is impacting on all those who are listening, and then decide just how much we give a fuck about whether we offend them or not. After all, some listeners might still be idiots.

Outrageous humour can be an outlet for the festering, spitty sores of being human, but so can bullying, and sometimes it's a precarious balance between relief and repellence. It's not dissimilar to eczema, in that there is the right balance to be had between scratching it and feeling blessed relief, to the point of then needing bandaging . . .

Sorry, is that image repellent?

CHAPTER 9

Death, Where Is Thy Punchline?

In India if a man dies, the widow flings herself onto the
funeral pyre . . . in this country the woman just says '72
baps, Connie, you slice, I'll spread.'

Victoria Wood

It was nearly four weeks after my mother's death before I made my
first joke about it onstage. I had planned to say something about
it, but didn't know what, until the actual joke came to me as I
walked to the stage. On the back of that came the thought 'Is it too
soon to make jokes about this?' and then 'And is it funny enough?'

'My mum's just died, which is predominantly a bad thing, but
on the plus side, I can have my hair cut any way I want now.'

Fortunately, it got a laugh. I'd hate to have wasted all that
trauma on a gag that sucked, but it touched the correct nerve.
One woman came up to me afterwards to say she had recently
lost her mother and that a few days later she'd thought, 'Now
Mum's dead, I can dye my hair green again' and then felt guilty. I

told her it didn't seem that she was actually glad her mother was dead because it meant her hair could be green again; it was just one of those little moments of contemplating life's changes when you lose a parent. She agreed and reckoned she was unlikely to dye her hair green now, as she had long since realized that the band that had inspired her hairstyle was rubbish, and some of them had since been investigated for sexual offences. I couldn't even ponder growing back the psychobilly quiff that my mum had taken exception to, as by the time she died the genes on my father's side had robbed me of the number of follicles required for such lacquered exuberance.

I had taken a break from doing stand-up, so when my mother died, I didn't think, 'Great, I've been going through a bit of a dry patch – this is just what I needed for a few new routines' in the way that I did when my son was born, or my basement flat flooded with sewage, destroying most of my LPs and the collection of B-movie publicity posters that I kept under my bed.

Nevertheless, a few hours after she died, I couldn't help but wonder what material might come from the situation. Comedy and death. Death and comedy. There's a link, you see; those moments when, no matter how upset or traumatized we are, something comic slips into our mind to make it absurd enough to cope. It's finding the humour in the noise of the squeak of the shoe of the undertaker carrying the coffin; it's the bum note of the organ as the organist starts playing 'Guide Me, O Thou Great Redeemer'. It's almost as if the sadness becomes so great that it has to burst out, even if just for a moment, and be replaced by some humour, even if it's the most inappropriate or juvenile humour – in fact, especially if it's inappropriate and juvenile.

The process of working out how something becomes a joke or a humorous story is part of the way we turn something strange or traumatic into something of manageable proportions. It ring-fences distress into a shape that makes it easier to perceive. Is it good for you? I think it can be, for some people.

I rang up my friend Tiff to get a slot at her new-material night, where comics try out material they are shaping up for tours and telly. I wasn't preparing for a tour or TV appearance. I had no plans to go back full-time to stand-up in the immediate future. I was just going to make use of it, as stand-up had been my method of expression for so long. 'My mum died, and here's a funny story about it.'

Even before this one-off stand-up show, I had had another brief public performance, on a day when I was pretty sure you are meant to be kept away from the spotlight and microphone.

I went to an awards ceremony on the day of my mother's funeral. I had been instructed to, by my dad. We had the funeral, I delivered the eulogy, we ate the egg-mayonnaise sandwiches, and then I went to the British Museum to see if the radio show I present had won either of the two awards for which it was nominated. Going to a media awards do with lots of free booze and miniaturized Yorkshire puddings with Borrowers' gravy in them seemed like the most preposterous thing to do after burying a parent, so it somehow felt like the right thing to do. It was another moment of bookending sadness to shape it into the story. As the evening went on, I became desperate to win the award, because I wanted to say something about someone who had shaped me, in a way that meant I ended up being able to go to the British Museum for small food and gongs, however unhealthy such a public admission on such a day might seem. We won and, filled with boozy adrenaline heightened by the peculiarity of the day, I went to the podium.

'Thank you very much, everyone. It's been a funny old day. This is my second speaking engagement; the first was the eulogy at my mother's funeral . . .'

There was some confusion in the room at that point. Was it the right thing to do? Did it belittle all that had gone before it? Fortunately it is not something I can make a habit of, as this was my one shot at dealing with the day.

Despite the fact that I think we all have experienced that link between death and humour, death is still one of the more sensitive topics, where the boundaries of taste and what people might find offensive are hidden and murky. In keeping with his onstage persona, Ricky Gervais didn't treat his mother's funeral as hallowed. Knowing there would be tears, he had taken a box of tissues to the funeral, for himself and to share with others. He had written a personal message on each one: some with 'snotty pig' written on them, others 'snivelling bitch'. When the vicar was preparing the funeral speech he asked one of Ricky's older brothers what his mother was like and was told that 'she was a keen racist'. When the shocked vicar said, 'Oh, I can't say that', the brother replied that he should just say that she liked gardening then. The family also ensured that the list of their mother's children's names was not entirely accurate. Rather than saying Ricky, Robert, Marsha and Larry, the vicar said, 'She leaves behind four devoted children: Ricky, Robert, Marsha and, of course, Barry.'

When comedians talk about death onstage, their stories often reflect the life of the comedian as much as that of the deceased. Doug Stanhope is widely admired as the rebel comedian with a libertarian approach to existence. He celebrates hedonism and futility. He is one of those wild figures you go to watch so you can imagine that you don't give a shit too, before rushing back to your parking spot because the ticket is almost out of time and you told the babysitter you'd be back by eleven. He tells the audience, 'When I go onstage, it's like leading you into battle. You're not all going to be here at the end.' He mauls topics, with no regard for your sense of impropriety. He did not shy away from talking about his mother's death onstage. In an exuberantly dark routine, he discussed assisting the suicide of his terminally ill mother by making the alcoholic cocktails she wanted to ease her into the afterlife. She chose White Russians, as she thought the milk would help line the stomach for the drugs she would be taking.

'My mother killed herself in 2008. Don't worry, this is a fun story,' he begins, before taking us through the story of the night of his mother's death. He rang around and found the morphine dosage required, told her not to kill herself on Sunday and Monday, as those were football nights, and advised her to break her Alcoholics Anonymous pledge, because 'You're not going to kill yourself sober.'

'I didn't so much assist the suicide as barback,'* he explains. Despite discovering that thirty of the morphine pills would definitely kill her, his mother took all the ninety she had, not wanting any risk that it wouldn't work, much to the chagrin of Stanhope,

---

* To 'barback' is to carry out the duties of a bartender's assistant.

who hoped that a few of them might form his only inheritance. It is a routine about suicide that is scurrilous, profane and fond. As she guzzled cocktails and pills, she said, 'There's times to be dainty and there's times to be a pig.' Stanhope then struggled to ensure she said nothing else, as those are pretty darned good final words.

I've no such story to tell of the day of my mother's death. It was instead a quiet fading, with carefully and correctly administered morphine by a qualified nurse while Classic FM played light and popular symphonies in the background. There was plenty of morphine left over, which, despite my protestations, was all returned – as legally required – to the pharmacy. We are not a family of rebel libertarians; we abide by the pharmaceutical code of honour and obedience.

Her last weekend had been a busy weekend for me. In between visits to the family home I was speaking at a one-day event on counter-culture, a talk about science communication for a festival in Folkestone, and was on a panel-discussion evening, talking about what it is to be a man, with Mark Steel and Jeremy Hardy. Each event seemed somehow entirely detached from the separate reality of my mother approaching her death. It was only in the pauses between the events – the train journeys and green-room silences – that aneurysms of emotion would briefly burst.

The final thirty-six hours of my mother's life, which we were not expecting to be the final thirty-six hours, but diarizing death can be tricky, had just enough absurdity to become a story to tell. Unlike Stanhope's, this story was more about Imodium than morphine. Annoyingly they had already sponsored Felicity Ward's show that year, so there was no commercial opportunity there.

The weekend had passed and I was preparing to record an *Infinite Monkey Cage* Christmas special when the texts started arriving, suggesting that things were speeding up. True to my English roots, this put me in an awkward situation, as I didn't want to cause any bother; after all, the physicist Fay Dowker, the comedian Ross Noble and the former Dean of Guildford Cathedral, Victor Stock, had all been booked, and the *Radio Times* listing had already gone to press. Meekly and apologetically I explained to the producer that fortune might be against us, but I really would do my utmost to postpone any impending death.

'I'm so sorry this whole death-thing is rather up in the air. I mean, it might not be until next Tuesday – sorry for bringing it up really, but, you know, if the death-thing does look like it's around the corner, I'll have to pop off. I'll try to be as quick as I can. I'll see if someone can have a word with her about hanging on, at least until we've got the retakes in the bag. Trust the bloody finite existence of us all to get in the way of the *Christmas Special*. What are the chances of that, eh? Oops. I shouldn't have said that, on a show with physicists, I'll have distracted them into working out the probability.'

On that last day, there was also a documentary on general relativity to record and a guest spot on a music show. Everything was fine – I just had to keep busy; best not to ponder, that was where trouble would be waiting.

Busy. Busy. Busy.

About an hour before the Christmas show, something in my abdomen didn't seem quite right. There was a gurgling urgency. Though I have no scientific research to back this up, it seemed that my body was saying, 'You can have the use of your brain or you can have the control of your bowels, but with all this stress-control going on, you can't have both. Now pick a card.'

I made a hasty search for some pills. Brimful of Imodium, I became more granite than flesh, and prepared to go on. The combination of diarrhoea, science communication and an audience is a good distraction from the rest of existence. It can take your mind off imminent death by making it concentrate on particle behaviour and strict muscle control.

I decided it would be best to set up with the audience the possibility of me having to scarper. I explained that the *Christmas Special* we were recording included a special bonus experiment, in that we would be asking: 'Is Imodium effective for the entirety of a ninety-minute recording?' Professor Brian Cox, being as empathetic as any particle physicist can be, repeatedly uncorked and re-corked a bottle of sherry, in the hope of creating some psychosomatic effect. Then we began the Christmas carnival, with the funereal undertones hidden behind tinsel and Santa hats.

Though my memory of the recording is scant, I know my mind was operational. I think it was working quite fast. It was creating jokes with Ross Noble about velociraptors, working out questions about relativity, general and special, keeping a close watch on my sphincter, and then interrupting itself with brief bursts of 'Bloody hell, my mum's really dying, but enough of that, let's get on with comprehending the nature of space–time.'

About fifty minutes in – somewhere between explanations of how matter tells space to curve and how space tells matter to move, and an Anglican take on Doctor Who's TARDIS – my colon declared it was close to defeat. I generated a question: 'Fay, looking at the new understanding of the cosmos over the last hundred years, and the changes in what we believed to be the laws of physics – in particular the change from a Newtonian to an Einsteinian universe – I wondered: how do you feel theories such as the unifying of space and time have affected late twentieth- and early twenty-first-century science fiction? And you have as long as you want to answer that question.'

And with that, I upped and ran to the restroom. It was fifty minutes from set-up to punchline, but it got the laugh required to cover my personal shame. I was not gone long, but having left the stage to physics, I returned to find it was now in the hands of the former Dean, talking beautifully about knowledge. Despite what the listening public might think, it turns out that I was the one who had kept the show on the track of physics all these years. Brian was desperate to ask questions about the functioning of the General Synod and the laws of physics that could allow for transubstantiation.

Adrenaline plays havoc with sudden outbursts of uninvited emotion (goddammit, isn't all emotion uninvited?). None of the panel knew what was going on; well, they knew about the bowels, but not the parental illness. Once out of my chair, I ran off the stage. A cab was waiting to take me to my mum and dad's house. Ross caught up with me. Out of the spotlight, everything was real again and the only way to maintain control was to get away unobserved. Ross said it was a good show, and in my attempt to reply, I burst into tears. I gabbled, 'Sorry, I should explain – my mum's about to die,' and then I was gone.

How rude!

The cab driver was edgy, having been placed in the unenviable position of being told that I was being driven to a dying parent, but that I was also ill and he might have to suddenly lurch into a lay-by. Anytime I leant forward to mention something about the route, he panicked towards the roadside, presuming he was about to see the ruin of his upholstery. I arrived home and sat in my mother's bedroom, right next to the room I had been born in forty-six years earlier, and I stayed up with my youngest niece, listening to Classic FM and breathing and wondering what to do, and that's all you need to know.

When I first interviewed the psychotherapist Philippa Perry for a BBC Radio 4 documentary examining the cliché of the sad clown, she told me that if you are still joking about a sadness in your life, then you haven't come to terms with it. This means that, after forty-eight years, I still haven't come to terms with the whole of life one bit, because I still think jokes are often the best way to confront and comprehend reality.

Fortunately, when I visited her two years later, I found out that I hadn't been listening properly. I told Philippa about the haircut joke that I related after the death of my mother, and was relieved to find out it didn't signify that I was completely emotionally disturbed. It does not fall into being an example of 'grief avoidance', as the set-up to the joke acknowledges the loss, so I am not trying to deflect from the reality of the situation. Phew! The joke acknowledges the pain, and it is when you don't acknowledge the pain that the therapists begin to scribble more enthusiastically in their notebooks.

Philippa shared with me the story of a night out, when she had been wanting to forget the day-job. She went to a comedy night, to see a one-man show about the comedian's relationship with his late father. Booking a seat at the last minute, she found herself in the front row, which she knew was always a bit of a risk. Philippa could not relax, but she realized this was not because of her seating position, but because she began to watch the act like a therapist and started to see what the effusive newspaper reviews of the show had not seen. To her, this was someone deep in the midst of grief avoidance. While the critics saw the show as a brave exposure and an honest revelation, Philippa thought something was still hidden. She could see the pain.

The jokes the comedian was telling didn't seem to her to lay his anxiety to rest, but instead skipped gaily around it, and it became so obvious to her that she couldn't laugh. The gallows humour was clearly defensive. He was fending off his loss. She explained the problem of being a psychotherapist watching confessional comedy: 'You are blotting paper for someone's awful feelings. I was listening to him, and I picked up all the grief and anger.'

The comedian, though, doing his job properly, spotted her in the front row and picked up on her mirthlessly resistant face. He pointed at her, 'She's the only one that's not laughing. I'm gonna get her laughing by the end of this.'

Philippa knew that was unlikely to happen. 'It was almost like he wanted everyone to collude with his defence, and one thing we therapists don't do is collude when it's damaging to the person.'

She does not think laughter is the most healthy coping mechanism when dealing with trauma, but you can't just take it away, without replacing it with something else. When her first therapist asked her to tell her about her life, Philippa told stories of her life and family in a jaunty, carefree style. She put on an entertainment.

The therapist coldly admonished her, insisting, 'Why are you laughing? It's not funny.'

The problem for Philippa was that the therapist didn't replace it with anything. 'She took away my defence, and I spent a week crying around Sainsbury's . . . So these jokes are very important; they stop you crying around supermarkets.'

Perhaps. And this returns to the question of when it feels right to start making jokes about someone's death and the grief that goes with it. The comedian in question hadn't moved through the various stages of grieving for his dead father. He was still stuck somewhere, unable to accept what had happened.

In the late 1960s, Swiss-American psychiatrist Elisabeth Kübler-Ross wrote a groundbreaking book about how we respond to death and grief with the forthright title *On Death and Dying*. It was a title that pulled no punches. You couldn't take it back to the bookshop and say it was mis-sold to you, under the Trades Descriptions Act.

She wrote the book in a mere two months (this book has taken more than two years, but I am easily distracted!) and it went on to sell millions of copies worldwide, helping to change the way we feel and speak about death. Working in a hospital with dying patients in the 1950s, talking to them about their impending death – something that in itself was groundbreaking at the time and seems quite shocking – Kübler-Ross suggested that there are a number of stages in a cycle when we are confronting death. There is denial, which often comes first, a sort of 'They must have got it wrong, this can't be happening' stage, or indeed a complete avoidance of the situation. Then there often comes anger and frustration, the 'Why me?' stage. Then there's a bargaining stage, where the patient might argue with themselves about what they can do to lengthen their life, or search for some sort of meaning from others, telling stories about their situation. There might then be a period of sadness or depression, where they feel overwhelmed or have a desire to run away. And finally there's a stage of acceptance: 'This is going to happen to me, I might as well just accept it.' Kübler-Ross thought that not only were these stages of grief relevant to those facing death, but they were also highly applicable to those left behind by the death of a loved one. The stages aren't chronological, either, and instead a person might swing in and out of each 'stage' quite randomly, with different things triggering different feelings, until finally reaching that point of acceptance.

My desire to talk about the death of my mother onstage, I now realize, was a type of bargaining – a moment when I perhaps wanted to share the story of my grief, however briefly, in order to acknowledge her death, and perhaps imbue it with some meaning, with a punchline tagged on as my alibi.

Since Kübler-Ross's book was written, the ideas behind it have been expanded by some and criticized by others. However, it's hard to deny that she started a more honest discussion about trauma that continues today.

'Trauma – what is trauma?' asks Philippa. 'There's a little girl crying because the leaves are falling. You're going to cry as hard as that, because you have the grief in you. Everyone is individual about "stress points". We all have the capacity for grief. You might lose your glove and be as angry about it as when your mother died ... [The] best way of being soothed is someone really getting your trauma. Grief knows no reason.'

Sometimes the only way of approaching the great traumas and losses is by concentrating on the trivial and day-to-day, something that is almost certainly part of the avoidance process; something almost institutionalized in the British psyche by the need to offer to 'a nice cup of tea – and I think we've got some Garibaldis somewhere'.

Philippa tells me of how old women would ring up the counselling centre seeking help or someone to listen to their discomfort or pain, but would then be unable to go straight in with their story of loss. They would ask apologetically, 'I know this is probably not what you are really here to deal with, but I couldn't think of who to ask. I just wondered if you know of a charity shop that takes men's clothing? I have quite a lot to get rid of, and I don't want it to go to waste.' Most counsellors worth their salt will know immediately that this is not really a call about recycling woollens and using tweed to finance a clean-water well.

So the counsellors' strategy, whilst no doubt flicking through the telephone directory looking for the number of a local charity shop, will be to say, 'By the way, why do you have a lot of men's clothes to donate?', usually soliciting the reply, 'Oh, my husband died last week'; although 'He's finally gone ahead with the operation' might also be a response.

The comedian doesn't need to ring a counsellor for permission to speak about their grief, although to be effective it still has to be entertaining grief – not necessarily funny, but interesting.

David Baddiel reacted very differently after his mother's funeral. He didn't stop at a joke or two, but instead was inspired to write a whole stage show, *My Family: Not the Sitcom*. Listening to other people's memories of his mother at her funeral, he was annoyed at how they were immediately reducing her to the straightforwardly saintly or wonderful, something he knew was difficult to reconcile with how he knew her.

He was interviewed in the *Guardian* about the show, which highlighted the problematic reality of a family, rather than an image cleansed of turpitude:

> What comes out of me when I feel an untruth happening close to me, like I felt when people were talking about my mother at her funeral, when I just saw this idea of who she actually was slipping away, I just want to tell people the truth. And that's where it comes from. For me that doesn't feel necessarily brave; it's kind of an urgent thing that comes upon me when I see the world slipping out of what I perceive as the reality.[1]

You can almost see here the different stages of the grief cycle rubbing up against each other, causing friction and tension. There are the people who don't wish to confront the reality of his mother's life before she died, the reality of who she was, so in a way they are avoiding the whole truth of her death; and then there's David himself, who doesn't want to avoid that, but who at the same time wants to bargain with the world, wants to give some meaning to her life and – through it – her death, in order to move further towards the peace that might come with acceptance.

Despite her enthusiasm over the years to tell me about even the most mundane incident at a village produce show, so that I could turn it into a routine, I couldn't ever have imagined writing a show with my mother about her ill health or anything that was too close or personal, because it is not just my story to tell; there are too many other living people to consider. If I am the last one standing, then I may well return to the theme and write it myself, but that's unlikely, as I have a shoddy diet and my sister runs marathons, while I don't even run for a bus.

Jason Cook's honest depiction of loss – an active collaboration with his father – was very different. His 2007 show, *My Confessions*, detailed the trials of his sixty-year-old father's stroke. Jason became aware of his ability to turn personal difficulty into entertainment at an earlier gig, when he told just one joke about it. He told me that it was 'a victimless joke about my dad having a stroke, and me and him getting drunk. My mum was carrying him upstairs and he was getting a bit frisky, and my mum said, "We'll check the blood pressure on the machine and then I'll think about it." Finding that one bit opened the door to thinking you can talk about things that are a bit heavy and real. I like to take something that, on the face of it, is very sad, but to find something funny. It is difficult, but it's also very honest.'

From that short routine grew a whole show. *My Confessions* was very warmly received and was deeply affecting for many. Jason described the first three outings of the show as 'sweating out the club comic', ridding himself of his normal need to be bulletproof in trying situations. By the fourth night, he had found his ending. After taking the audience through the love and difficulties of family life and his father's stroke, he would tell the members of his audience to ring their dads, make contact with them, and many did, and some wept. Jason became another comedian facing the embarrassment of doing something that was not merely funny at the time, but useful afterwards. He felt that it was more like a mission than a gig and that he 'really had something to say'.

Creating the show also gave Jason and his father, Tony, common purpose and a reason to talk, not that there had previously been any frostiness between them. Jason had joined his father in the Merchant Navy when he was nineteen, and they were drinking buddies.

But Jason found that they connected to each other on a deeper level after he did the show about the stroke: 'My dad was at sea when I was a kid, so I only saw him for a quarter of my childhood, so we never had a very deep relationship. He was a kind bloke, a very honourable bloke – the kindest bloke I ever met, all these very positive qualities. After he saw the show, he saw the effect it had, and I'd forward the emails I got and he'd see what *we* were doing together, what *our* story was doing . . .'

Tony cried when he first saw the show, and also showed great understanding over the moments in it when Jason told how he had felt great anger towards his father, when he first saw him motionless in a hospital bed. This should have been the beginning of an intriguing partnership between father and son – talking and creating from their own lives and relationship – but, sadly, it wasn't to last.

Shortly after the run of *My Confessions*, which took Jason across the world, Tony was diagnosed with pancreatic cancer. One of his first comments to Jason's mum after the diagnosis was, 'Well, that's Jason's next Edinburgh show sorted then.'[2] Sure enough, Jason's next show was about his dad's diagnosis, short illness and then death.

Working with his dad on the show gave him another excuse to talk about real things, because it was for a show. Jason felt that it was 'a conduit for an emotional discourse . . . He was a sixty-two-year-old Geordie raised in the 1950s. I'm not sure he would have had much time for "Come on, everyone, let's get into the talking circle; now who's going to hold the story stick and start talking about their emotions . . . ?"'

Talking about it – through talking about the shows to come – seemed to help provide a purpose in the most pessimistic of times. Whether or not you believe there is an afterlife, there were small crumbs of comfort in knowing that you have an afterlife of being centre-stage in a story for a while. There was a catharsis for the family in knowing this would be a story told to thousands. Looking to Kübler-Ross again, Tony had found some way to give the last stages of his life some meaning and, through that, he had moved perhaps towards some sort of acceptance of what was to come. When his father was in hospital, Jason expressed his worry about what he would do without him. They held hands and Tony said, 'Son, just have a wonderful life. I did.' And they both started crying. And as that poignancy reached its crescendo, the man in the next-door bed let out a boisterous fart. Jason's dad smiled – he knew his son now had a punchline for this scene in the show.

Jason asked his father if he had a message for the audience of the show about his illness and death. He replied that his message would be 'Buy more tickets for Jason's shows.' Jason says that Tony then 'pissed himself laughing', saying 'It's not even a joke . . . it's not even a funny joke.' It got a round of applause and a laugh every night. 'He howled at the mere notion of that being in the show . . .'

But what is it like to stand up every night and recount a parent's illness and death when it is so recent? Can it all be cathartic? Jason suffered bad anxiety after the shows and experienced panic attacks. He described the most difficult moments onstage: 'There was a point in the show where I would say something like about when Dad would hold my hand, and it would be very much there in my head – the smell and everything. That became problematic in that way, but I was never afraid of doing it, because it made a better show . . . I was as honest as I could be then.'

The comedian's desire to turn all into comedy leads to creative quandaries. At times you imagine that nothing cannot somehow be turned into an anecdote, but it's not just up to you; it requires the audience to feel they can find it funny, too. Jason was worried that he was prostituting his father's death. He told me of the bits that never made the final cut, in particular something that occurred at the point of death, which on the one hand is both funny and dark, but perhaps was just too personal and difficult to relate in front of an audience. 'We were watching the numbers going down on the heartbeat, at one point down to twelve, and the nurse came in and said, "He's dead now." I leant forward to kiss him and there was a sudden exhalation like a gasp and I sort of jumped . . . I tried it a couple of times in warm-up shows, but it seemed a bit jarring.'

Now each member of Jason's family waits for the moment where sickness or bad luck will mean they can provide him with his next tour show or prospective sitcom. He tells me that his mother has recently had breast cancer. 'It's the best stuff, she's had a mastectomy and she's living with my sister, and she wandered into the room and just said, "Ignore me, I'm just trying to bring the nipple count up to an odd number" . . . Thank you, Mother . . .'

Rebecca Peyton used to be my agent, then she ran away to become an actor. She wanted the 85 per cent, not the 15 per cent, and she wanted to be the show-off rather than wrangling with the show-off.

She enjoys being playfully rude to people from the moment she meets them. She has the knack of them understanding that it is a game. She is whip-smart and her life has been shaped by two harsh deaths: her father's, when she was six years old, and her sister's, when she was in her mid-thirties.

The first thing Rebecca says, before we start talking about her sister's murder, is: 'It's not dull, like your mother's death . . .' It's true. My mother's death was a fade over a week, a last withdrawal until the lungs finally failed for ever. The deaths in Rebecca's life have been significantly more traumatic. 'Grief is a big plate of gristly food, and you can eat it or not eat it, but it's not going to go away. It's just going to sit there and congeal' is how she explains it to me.

On 9 February 2005, Kate Peyton was killed in Mogadishu. She was working as a news producer for the BBC at the time, and was shot in the back and died. She was due to be married a few months later, and Rebecca was helping plan the wedding.

Four years later Rebecca performed *Sometimes I Laugh Like My Sister*, a monologue conceived with Martin M. Bartelt. When the show came to London, the *Guardian* wrote of Rebecca:

What she does best is to show how a death can change a life. She reminds one that grief can be an out-of-body experience;

news of a sudden death reaches the head but takes a while to catch up with the heart. She reminds us, too, that death can be a jump-start to the living . . . At one point, she says: 'I never want to turn away from how my sister died.' And she generously makes us feel part of her continuing observance.[3]

Sometimes I Laugh Like My Sister is about loss and it is about Rebecca. It is about the partying and drinking, in the hope that she can find an escape and that Kate will come walking through the haze of oblivion and admonish her for her behaviour. Rebecca tells me the play 'is things that I would tell anyone . . . if they wanted to know'. It is her chance to stand, unquestioned and uninterrupted, and say what she wants to say. She doesn't know if it was hours or days later, but very soon after Kate died she knew she needed to make something: 'You are full of everything when something like this happens – fear, misery and creativity.'

What must it feel like, moments before you take the stage for the first time, to perform something so personal and so tragic? Rebecca's main fears were actorish ones: would she forget her lines? Beneath that fear was her 'uber-worry' that people would think she shouldn't speak, that she didn't have the right to speak: 'Who the hell am I? People go through horrendous things – why should I talk about my thing? The sense of "do I have a right to speak?" was very, very powerful.'

This is a reflection of what Philippa Perry had told me about the question we often ask ourselves concerning our grief: 'Is my trauma traumatic enough, or do I just shut up and get on with it?'

As Rebecca developed her story, she knew that it was not just about the death of her sister, but about the death of her father, too. When she was six, her father was killed in a traffic accident. She has spent forty years considering the ramifications of her father's death. 'My experience of that, and the sense I've made of it to myself, was that my trauma was utterly unacceptable and that I should be okay. This idea that children are resilient, it sends me wild. They are as resilient as anyone else, except they aren't fully formed, so that things will go down in the hardwiring. They will be established in their instability.'

Her father was the show-off. He was adopted, but the birth certificate put down his mother's profession as 'actress'. With his death, Rebecca believes she lost the permission to show off, and she lost the person to show off with. But she gained the position of being the weird one in the family – the eccentric offspring with the desire to perform.

From this early age, she felt that the expression of her troubles wasn't acceptable. 'I learnt as a kid that I shouldn't talk. Adults can't look you in the eye if you are a traumatized child. They can't bear the fact that you have experienced something they haven't experienced. They are kind of terrified of you . . .'

Having experienced the loss she had from such an early age, Rebecca believes that she has learnt the importance of showing emotion at those times. 'If you don't show any emotion when your mum died, it will be difficult for your son.'

I worry about this. I didn't, of course, share any emotion with my son. The shame and embarrassment of non-stage emotional sharing – the lack of any sense of knowing what would be the right and proper thing to do – meant that I was just blocked, and that overrode any need to share feelings, to be an emotional dad, to be fully human.

Before my mother's funeral, my son had apparently expressed a worry that he had never seen me cry, and he wasn't sure how to react if I did. I explained that I might and I might not, and there was a possibility of tears at the funeral, but they were nothing to worry about and could even be welcomed. As it was, I didn't cry and I hope I haven't traumatized him too much, in blocking my feelings and trying to reduce the trauma.

Rebecca sees nothing useful about feeling shame around expressing emotion. 'It should be exposed to air and sunlight,' she says with some passion. 'I feel besieged by my inability to function in the light of what has happened in my life ... I feel mostly pointless without my sister, but I had the show to work on – a show that is really by the six-year-old whose father died. I didn't realize until after the first show. Martin and I had been working on it for two years, and then I realized – it is that six-year-old who wanted to speak.' It took thirty-two years, but eventually that voice was heard.

In twenty-five years I think my wife has seen me cry only once, quite fulsomely, at the conclusion of an episode of *Inside No. 9*, a TV series of weekly terror tales. This story, 'The Twelve Days of Christine', ended with a car crash where a child lost his mother, and it made me blub like Sally Field, on three consecutive viewings. Rather than offering my wife a window of understanding on the immensity of my own childhood crash experience, she simply presumed I was having a nervous breakdown. That's the problem: if you keep it in for too long, when you do have the opportunity to let it out, it comes as a little too much of a rude shock to those around you, and they go hunting around the house for a noose or a pill stash. I'll try to make sure I don't let out the demons again for another twenty-five years.

Despite comedians' usual easy flippancy with the tragic and the troubling, one night I saw a surprisingly subdued collective reaction to death amongst a gaggle of comedians. Just as any music fan remembers where they were when they heard the news of Elvis's death and John Lennon's death (I was placing an image of a Wellington bomber into a sticker book on news of the former, and I was making a clay zombie in art class on the latter), most comics recall where they were when they heard the news of Robin Williams taking his own life.

Robin had been one of the biggest influences on my life and career. Even if I talk too fast, I cite his influence. His death was announced halfway through the Edinburgh Fringe festival. It was my last night of performing there that year. My final show of the fringe was *Cheaper than Therapy*, a nightly mental-health charity event where comedians perform routines about their own therapy, their own insanity or experiences of mental health in general. Some acts are not keen to partake, while others may be too keen. As with most nights in Edinburgh, I was late for this last gig of the day and had to rush. It was a hot night by the time I arrived, near midnight – considered early evening in Edinburgh.

The audience was framed in dream-like condensation. Ranting on, I cleaned my spectacles on the corner of my cardigan. (This is the nearest I ever get to that Elvis moment when he would dry his sweat-sodden brow with a silk handkerchief, before handing the salty treat to a screaming fan. No one screams for my condensation-tainted cardigan, and they can't have it anyway; I can't just keep giving away my cardigans willy-nilly.) I finished with a story whose invective was propelled by images of William Blake sitting in a tree with Billy Bragg while some angels played 'Jerusalem' on lutes and Stanley Kubrick's films were being injected directly into someone's eyes mixed with some heroin.

Not wishing to punch the clock too early on my last night, I had suggested to the promoter that he added a second half, where we would discuss the myths and realities of comedians as morose, melancholic or just plain mentally ill. This was at the forefront of my mind, as I had found a black dog increasingly hanging over me as I toured. I had not lost my sanity, but the cracks in it had widened. I had thought a discussion on comedy and mental health with Eddie Pepitone, the other stand-up on that night, would be a good idea. Eddie was an explosive cauldron of precise fury and neuroses. It would make an interesting panel, and it would slow down the first hour of post-gig drinking.

During the interval I walked into the bar, where the air was a little less toxic. Once outside, everyone had switched on their phones, fearful that social media might have moved on without them during their sixty-minute incarceration with me. My phone was antiquated and so, embarrassingly, it only functioned as a phone – something akin to a Quentin Crisp level of eccentricity, in the twenty-first century. Ordering a beer, I became aware of a ripple of gasps behind me. The giggling, smirking and sense of jollity were suffocated by a miserable silence. A line of people stooped over their phones, looking uncomprehendingly at the screens. One comedian walked straight out of the bar, looking distressed. Usually a gregarious fellow, especially amongst media folk who might hasten his career, he said nothing as he went, not even to the TV producer by the door. It still had a hint of showmanship: 'I think you'll find my look of fleeing distress will get five stars in *The Times* tomorrow.'

Then I heard the news that knocked the flippancy out of me. Robin Williams had killed himself. Rarely have so many comedians been dumbfounded. We were about to go onstage and talk about comedy and mental health, and one of the world's most famous comedians had just taken his own life.

Eddie Pepitone had been friendly with Robin Williams on the West Coast comedy circuit. Stand-up comedy hadn't just been a stepping stone for Williams's TV and movie career; it was a necessary part of his existence. He did it because he had to. For all his acting achievements and awards, Robin was first and foremost a stand-up comedian. He needed the immediacy of onstage creativity and audience reaction. He was in the comedians' category of 'They do it because they must'. Eddie and I went back onstage together and tried to remain respectful, without being po-faced.

From the first series of *Mork & Mindy*, I was obsessed with Robin Williams, seeking out whatever scraps I could find about him, at a time when entire back-catalogues were not instantaneously accessible via the Internet. Most of my teenage spare time was spent idling in record shops, avoiding confrontations and broken hearts by excessive browsing. One afternoon in the HMV Oxford Street basement I heard over the speakers a Robin Williams routine that I hadn't heard before. My heart skipped a beat and my pupils dilated, and I rushed to the checkout. 'What is this?'

'Oh, it's the soundtrack to a new film with Robin Williams called *Good Morning, Vietnam*.'

It sounded like the greatest film ever made: Robin Williams

as a rebellious riffing DJ during the Vietnam War. I had to see it *now*. Unfortunately in the 1980s there was a huge gap between US and UK cinema releases. The soundtrack was readily available to us snaggle-toothed Englanders, but the film wasn't due out for another six months. This was an unbearable situation. I was a teenager and I would not take 'No' for an answer, despite the fact that 'No' was an inescapable reality.

When we are grown-up and grey, it can be difficult to recall how fanatical our teenage brains were, how desperate our need for our favourite things, and how delirious our delight when we got to them. I took to memorizing the *Good Morning, Vietnam* soundtrack and imagining the rest of the film, over and over again.

In the summer of 1988 I went to America. I would see the Grand Canyon, the Twin Towers, the Golden Gate Bridge and Monument Valley, but to hell with all that architecture and geology – I wanted to see *Good Morning, Vietnam*. Infuriatingly, at each city we got to, the letters of *Good Morning, Vietnam* were being taken down from cinema awnings and being replaced with *Arthur 2: On the Rocks*. After two months of doomed endeavour, I finally caught up with the film on its final showing in a sinister side-street cinema in Portland, Oregon. I loved it. I sat in the splintered seat and mouthed along to the routines that I knew by heart. And all of that teen obsession surged back, when I heard about Robin Williams's death – an adulation that had been watered down by ageing and other preoccupations.

The suicide of a comedian carries with it a mythic narrative, an expectation of inevitability, despite the fact that very few comedians do take their own lives.

A couple of months before the Edinburgh Fringe, I had been touring Australia alone. I had a little grey dog over my head; not the ominous black one, but one that nevertheless carried with it a fug of unhappiness, for little or no reason. In each city I had someone assigned to me, to ensure I didn't just go wandering off; someone who knew where the theatre was, and pointed me towards the local curiosities and attractions. In Adelaide it was a retired head teacher. We had some long conversations about atheism, murder rates and church architecture, of which Adelaide has rather a lot. Sitting in a hotel bar after the last show, chatting over beer bottles, she turned to me and said, 'You comedians need to do more material on suicide.'

After a show, people frequently like to tell you stories that you could turn into 'one of your routines', but this was a bolder suggestion than usual. I presumed this proposition was inspired by experience, and that turned out to be right. She explained that her daughter had killed herself, and she believed that if suicide could be talked about openly – joked about by comedians onstage – then that might help it become part of normal conversation, rather than being hidden away, something to be ashamed about.

Australian comedian Laura Davis thinks about suicide more than most.

In one of the most striking moments of her debut solo show, *Cake in the Rain*, she talks about the condition. Roughly every twenty-five minutes she thinks about taking her life. For her, this is not a morbid moment, but one that allows her to think positively about why she shouldn't kill herself. Her blog post about the trees of Melbourne and her love of thirty-cent McDonald's soft-serve cones convince her there is a reason to go on. Most people who have suicidal thoughts do not act on them, but how many people realize that such thoughts are quite common?

Laura often has people approach her after a gig. She tells me that it can be awkward and difficult sometimes, but she feels that if she opens herself up to these ideas, it's her responsibility to make sure she handles them safely and correctly. 'Most of the time it's just people who are happy to come up and say, "Oh! Me, too! I thought maybe I was the only one! I feel better now!"' And that is part of the use of the frivolous low art of comedy, as there can be moments where thoughts of 'Me, too' are pragmatically useful.

I wondered how much stand-up had helped with suicide ideation. Before stand-up, Laura said she used to self-harm as an outlet for her feelings. She now feels that stand-up is the socially acceptable form of self-harm, 'forcing my unwilling feet out into those lights, always with a little "fuck you, you're doing it". The most mortifying death onstage, always met with a little bit of giddy glee at my own misfortune.'

Also, she no longer sees a psychiatrist. Laura believes that much of her anxiety came from repressing a strong personality, something she doesn't need to do any more. She doesn't suggest that stand-up is a certifiable replacement for a mental-health professional, but for her it has helped process her hyper-vigilant thoughts, and what once stymied her can now be publicly presented.

The nihilistic philosopher E. M. Cioran wrote, 'The man who has never imagined his own annihilation, who has not anticipated recourse to the rope, the bullet, poison or the sea, is a degraded galley slave or a worm crawling on the cosmic carrion.'[4] He died of natural causes at the age of eighty-four.

I have found out that many people contemplate suicide regularly, but it is a thought experiment, rather than an imminent or likely action. You sit in the bath and think: 'What's the point? How would the world change without me? How much do I want to switch the sensory input off for ever? What would be the most painless way to do it? Urgh, what would people find? Would I leave an embarrassing corpse? Will it look like I died in a masturbation accident? How cross will my wife be, if I bring down the light fitting and the ceiling collapses during the attempt at strangulation?'

My socked feet never get as far as the open window. I don't even get as far as Dorothy Parker's list of the downside of most suicidal aids. Guns, nooses, razors, drugs and rivers all get the knock-back, and so 'you might as well live'. It's just a little existentialism, not a suicidal urge.

The problem with trying to find the humour in suicide is that, understandably, some people just don't think you should. I wrote a short piece about trying to work out how to approach the subject – tactfully, absurdly, stupidly or insightfully? – and a few people just said, 'Back away. Don't do it.' But quite a few more, including people who had lost friends and partners, who had attempted it themselves or who worked in mental health, said: 'Why not try it and see how it goes? It doesn't have to be taboo.'

I was fortunate in having the offer of help from someone who had attempted to kill himself on three occasions. He explained the ludicrousness of it, the strange elements of the mundane. He first decided to kill himself on a Friday, but then took stock and thought, 'Hang on, if I kill myself on Friday, I'll miss the weekend. Better to do it on Sunday.' The whole thing seemed oddly ordinary, for such a final action. He presumed his family would probably miss him for a bit, but not for too long, and then they'd get over it all and move on. The great clown and Beckett actor Max Wall once went to kill himself in his garage. Just as he was about to lose consciousness, a voice came into his head and said, 'Don't be a cunt, Max' and that was the end of that.

My first memories of suicidal thoughts were when I was eight years old. I have always been an over-thinker, though my anxiety was usually hidden by the noise of my appalling hissy-fits and fury. I am of the generation that was told too much by public-information films – the beauty and wonder of fireworks was destroyed by being told that they'd soon rob of you of an eye or finger; playing with a Frisbee was a sure-fire way of being electro-cuted to death; water was to drown in; and polished floors would see you suffering irreparable brain damage after a cracked skull. All of these festered and bred nightmares, on top of my ongoing, non-televised fear of existence. It was the multiple warnings about rabies, just a thin sliver of sea away in France, that terri-fied me most. Perhaps it was these thoughts of slavering dogs and hydrophobic cats that were still playing in the minds of the most fervent Brexit voters.

'Rabies Means Death' was the punchline to a short public-information film in which a foolish woman attempts to smuggle a kitten into the country in her handbag. Her scurrilous trot to the airport was intercut with shots of an African child in agonizing death-throes in a hospital bed, and all voiced by the usually avun-cular Clive Swift, best known as the husband of Hyacinth Bucket in *Keeping Up Appearances*. The more terrifying sister-film to this was narrated by Michael Jayston – Peter Guillam in the TV version of *Tinker, Tailor, Soldier, Spy* and a much-used voiceover artist – adding a commanding-officer urgency both to plague-outbreak warnings and new forms of margarine. A loveable Labrador saunters through the streets, as people turn and run in fear and cat-shows are cancelled.

In one film, a bitten child must have injections in its belly button. The agony of this is renowned. I decided the imminent rabies outbreak was too terrifying to live through, and thought the best thing to do would be to kill myself. I tried this a few times in the local church. What I discovered is that you can't commit suicide by holding your breath. It seems your body is wired to make you breathe again; it doesn't just let you stop as you turn puce. You need to add water, or an illegal carrier bag that doesn't meet the required health-and-safety standards. I never did bother with a river or a plastic sack, so I don't think my heart was really in stopping my heart.

As so often, the take of the counter-cultural king of American stand-up comedy, George Carlin, on killing yourself is far more brazen than many others could ever be. His decades of creating furious and philosophical stand-up specials meant that he could get away with an attitude that could grate, if delivered by most other stand-ups. Looking at his words on a page – without his chutzpah, puckishness and sly menace – some people might take exception to his take.

'Do you realize that right this second, right now, somewhere around the world, some guy is getting ready to kill himself? Isn't that great? D'y'ever stop to think about that kinda shit? I do. It's fun, and it's interesting, and it's true! . . . I just think it's interesting to know that at any moment the odds are good that some guy is dragging a chair across the garage floor, trying to get it right underneath that ceiling beam, don't wanna be too far off-centre. If it's worth doing, it's worth doing right.'[5]

After his suicide flourish, going into the minutiae of debating how to do it, the risk of surviving it and the hole in your head that necessitates buying a hat, the audience applauds and whistles. It takes a great comedian to come up with a really crowd-pleasing routine about killing yourself.

At the end of his routine about suicide, despite his show being titled *Life Is Worth Losing*, George Carlin summed up his need to live: 'Life is full of interesting things, that's why I could never commit suicide. I'm having too much fun keeping an eye on you folks.'

On his 2008 comedy special, *It's Bad for Ya*, seventy-one-year-old Carlin joked, 'You know what I've been doing? Going through my address book and crossing out the dead people. It gives you a feeling of power, of superiority, to have outlasted another old friend.' He commented on the advantages of old age, 'It's a great time of life, you get to take advantage of people, and you're not responsible for anything.'

He died a short while after recording that show.

I started waiting for death at an early age, perhaps as a result of the car accident I was part of, or maybe I was always going to be a morbid little nit.

One day when I was nine I was watching *Blue Peter*. It was 1978 and they were talking about the year 2000. I realized I would be thirty-one then and close to halfway through my life. We must have been studying fractions in school that week because, with a shudder of terror, I also realized I was one-eighth of the way through my life – general averages of life expectancy being taken into account. One-eighth of the way through my life and I had done almost nothing, save for tree-climbing and burying hamsters in the back garden.

I may have forgotten my first thoughts on mortality, as it appears that at around six years old, many children experience their initial glimmers of understanding that life might not be for ever.

Between eight and eleven years old, I expected to die in agony and hydrophobic from rabies, due to an old woman smuggling a kitten in her handbag from Calais.

Between twelve and eighteen years old, I expected to die in a nuclear Armageddon, due to the itchy trigger-finger of a superpower.

Between eighteen and twenty-two years, I imagined AIDS would destroy me, despite my far-from-hectic sexual diary. The lesions I presumed were sarcoma turned out to be stretch marks (they rarely mention that men get them, too). Often the means of my imminent death have been related to the public-information films of the time.

Since then, it has been the usual series of cancers, tumours and early-onset this and that that has sent me running to Google or the doctor.

At the time of writing, I have had a few months without noticing any anomaly that suggests death, which worries me, as I am a believer in dramatic irony. The day when I walk in smiling and declare, 'I've never felt better than I do now' is undoubtedly the day I collapse stone-dead due to an energetic amoeba, thought long eradicated, which has not been seen since John Snow found the London water pump that was felling all who drank from it. I may have put the standard internal human diseases and blemishes of doom on the back-burner, as I have taken a step back to stage two, 'nuclear war (and assorted Armageddon disasters)', since major Western powers were taken over by leaders of frightening ineptitude and chaotic vanity.

Therapist and existential philosopher Irvin Yalom said that we are 'forever shadowed by the knowledge that we will grow, blossom and, inevitably, diminish and die'. For existentialists, it is this knowledge of our imminent death that, consciously or unconsciously, drives every minute of our lives, a theory that I can very much relate to. The answer to the problem, though – for it certainly becomes a problem if you are sitting huddled behind your front door, curtains drawn, chain on the latch, too scared to venture out, for fear of rabid dogs or unsuspectingly fetching a young boy's Frisbee down from an electricity pylon – is to be able to confront and accept this knowledge, much as Kübler-Ross worked her whole life trying to help people come to terms with their imminent death. If we can create a sense of meaning in our lives, a sense of permanence, a sense that we have meant something or created something, then accepting the inevitable end becomes far more achievable.

This would be something I would like to explore with a comedy audience, but I'm unsure whether our personal fear of mortality is the easiest subject for an audience looking for a good night out. 'Who here believes, without any medical evidence whatsoever, that they may well be carrying something that will imminently kill them?' is pretty soul-searching, compared to the usual and perhaps more acceptable 'Where are you from?', 'What do you do?' and 'Is that your girlfriend?'

I have tried, 'Hey, just by show of hands, who here has recently and wrongly imagined they would imminently be dying from cancer?', which didn't go down particularly well.

Once I was at the bar afterwards, though, I had people queuing up to tell me about their hypochondria, or more often women telling me about their boyfriend's duplicity in failing to admit that their lives were an endless round of 'What do you think this bump is?' and 'Has my nipple always been that colour?' Someone approached me to say that he had spent a decade presuming that after every sharing of even the most microscopic fluid sample, he had immediately got full-blown AIDS.

Talking to Dr Ben Goldacre, the hyperkinetic epidemiologist and former GP, I was relieved to hear that doctors are hypochondriacs too, possibly worse than the rest of us. With the knowledge of a whole catalogue of terrible diseases and ways of dying, he is aware of the awful possibility that may lie behind every twinge and murmur, any tremor or swelling. Finding a good hypochondriac doctor to be your own GP may be the best course of action for the medically anxious such as myself, rather than those doctors who sit dismissively as they explain that the lump really is nothing at all – it's just the sort of lump that lumps are at your age. If we knew every lump that lumped was just a lump, then we'd be the doctor.

Comics rarely retire; they may slow down and reduce the number of tour dates, but few give up. George Burns, Bob Hope, Joan

Rivers and Bruce Forsyth all kept going until sickness or death made walking onstage an impossibility.

One-liner king Henny Youngman worked in show business for nearly seventy years, and in his later days he would joke, 'I'm so old that when I order a three-minute egg, they make me pay up front.'

Barry Cryer has only been performing for six decades. 'I'm eighty-one on Wednesday, I don't know how long I've got left – I don't even buy green bananas any more.'

For many performers, who may be tired and sometimes ill offstage, everything seems to ignite under the lights. Ken Dodd was still performing at ninety, and his shows were still longer than those of any other performer. Audience members half his age would find themselves exhausted and having to leave the auditorium long before Ken was thinking of departing; and yet, on arriving at the theatre, the staff often saw a stooped, tired-looking old man.

Billy Connolly is a comedy genius. No one else makes it look so effortless and with such great effect. It is not just funny bones; it is funny skin, muscles, blood, spit and vitreous jelly. He is brimming with charm and overflowing with swearing. He swears with such joy that only the harshest or most dunderheaded prude would take offence.

Connolly is a unifying force in British culture. Cassette tapes of his albums were shared in school yards like contraband, with relentless re-listening to his routines failing to dull them. He is naughty, rude and vital, and yet in recent years he has suffered ill health. He has had surgery for early-stage prostate cancer and has been diagnosed with Parkinson's disease. There was incredulity when this hirsute Puck made his illness public. There may have been fears that his first major tour after this announcement might have seen a human in decline, a giant felled, but his *High Horse Tour* proved to be one of his funniest.

Never shy of discussing reality, Connolly dealt with his health head-on. He told the audience, 'I'm not a well man, and I'll tell you about it, to save you symptom-spotting throughout the show.' One of the most memorable routines takes on death and those who choose brown bread: 'Eat brown bread and you'll live longer . . . aye, for about a fortnight.' He then proceeds to picture the brown-breaders with that extra fortnight of decrepitude and pain. 'Why are you crying, Mr Connolly? Oh yes, because all your friends are dead.' His visions of the end are not cruel; they are delivered with a devious glint that dares us to enjoy life.

I think that when you are young, you imagine there is a mindset of the old, a condition of old-mindedness that goes with the wrinkles and the stoop, just as you imagined there might be some transition from child-mind to adult-mind. You wake up one day and think, 'Ah, my child-mind is gone. I want to smoke a pipe and be considerably duller while waxing a car.' And it doesn't happen when you move into your twenties, just as it doesn't happen after seventy.

When you are young, you see people in their seventies and eighties and imagine they are this thing that is 'an old person', and that an old person has old thoughts and dreams, as if there are triggers in the brain that are set off in your late sixties, and they switch you into something fusty and dull, obsessed with knee ache and butterscotch, looking to the past and ruing the future. It's as if you think the person is readying themselves for switching off, by withdrawing from the intrigues of the universe.

When I first played to an audience with people in their eighties in it, I would think, 'Oh no, they won't like my kind of thing, they'll want something of nostalgia mingled with occasional double-entendres and 1940s attitudes.' That is simple and condescending, and I was wrong; these were vivacious and mischievous people. The respect I should show them was to be as rude and silly and furious as on any other night. If they had wanted the old days, they'd have stayed in and tutted about change during the *Six O'Clock News*.

Connolly eradicates the notion that proximity to death dampens the lust for life or joy, fury and curiosity. His most recent shows are a bold declaration of life. You see a human laugh at sickness and death, and you laugh with it, too. It is a quieter voice, but one that says: *Do not dismiss me just yet; if I fade, I fade kicking. I am still a force. I am here until I am not.*

If life is absurd, then so is death. To know there will one day be a world without you is a strange trait to have evolved. We can spend our whole life worrying so much about death that we forget to live while we're here. Be preposterous, know you are absurd, be a joke that lives on for a while – be a punchline that people want to remember.

Afterword

I hate comedy, I really do. Almost everyone
involved with it. So needy.

Barry Crimmins

Happiness, happiness, the greatest thing that I possess.

Ken Dodd

As I finished this book, two notable comedians died, and
I cannot let their deaths go unmentioned, because both
epitomized something very important about comedy. One
I quoted at the start of this book, and the other I spoke to at
length for the chapter on comic ethics. Both brightly illuminated
what it is to be human, but in very different ways.

Ken Dodd saw comedy as a balm and an escape. His aim was
to delight and make people happy, to help them exercise their
chuckle muscle. He walked onstage in a garish hat and coat,
with his tickling sticks, a huge smile across his face, and then
stayed there entertaining his audience for many hours. He would
frequently still be onstage after the coach parties had left and all

the other comedians in the country were in bed. He still had a tour ahead of him when he died, aged ninety.

Barry Crimmins did not use comedy to help his audience escape, but instead as a vehicle with which to confront them with some of the uglier realities of existence and politics. He would amble onstage, beer in hand, in a grey T-shirt and suit jacket, and then call it as he saw it. He scowled and railed and vented at injustice.

Their childhoods were very different. Ken Dodd described his with great fondness, and said that his father was the funniest man he knew – the inspiration for his life in comedy. Barry Crimmins's childhood was savagely altered when, at the age of four, he was repeatedly raped by an acquaintance of his babysitter.

While Dodd's comedy came from ludicrous delight in a candy-coloured world, Crimmins's comedy was a campaign; he wanted a better world for those who were victimized by it. By the early 1990s, comedian friends were suggesting to Barry that he take a break from playing the clubs, as he seemed angrier than ever. They couldn't understand the root of his fury. At a benefit gig one night, they found out. After viciously dissecting the power system in the USA, he started to talk about what had happened to him as a child.

Dodd's comedy was driven by a relentless silliness. Crimmins was driven by a desire to attack and shame bullies, in whatever form they took. What united them both was that I think comedy was the only way they could make sense of their lives. They also knew that they made other people feel better about themselves. Barry's public disclosure led to people wanting to talk about their own experiences. He would often try and help everyone who came to him, even though it could end up damaging his own health. In the film about him, *Call Me Lucky*, Crimmins described the experience of talking to people about what happened in his childhood. Often they would say, 'Oh my God, are you talking to anyone about this?' and he would reply, 'I thought I was talking to you.'

His battle against the bully was not just onstage, as he took it to all areas of his life. He may not have been hugely famous, but he inspired many people, including me, which is why this book is dedicated to him. He made life bearable for some who could barely carry the burden.

When I began this book I was attempting to give up stand-up. I had sort of lost sight of what it meant to me and why I was doing it, so it felt better to stop doing it at all.

It was a typically ill-thought-out idea of mine to believe that the best way to occupy my time, if I was going to give up stand-up comedy, would be to write a book about stand-up comedy. But it was perhaps the right thing to do as well, because it allowed me to really think about why some people believe it is a good idea to try and make other people laugh for a living, and what the other people get from it, if anything.

Suffice to say, as I finish this book, I am touring a show about love, death, art and physics, and writing two more shows for the imminent Edinburgh Fringe festival. By attempting to stop, I have found out what I am. Not only is there no escape, but I am no longer even looking for a way over the wall. It is futile, and I am glad.

My attempt to give up drinking had a similar arc, and a very similar conclusion. After months of remaining as dry as soot, I fell off the wagon because of an audience and my desire to please them. I was performing a double act about anger, in a sweating red-walled room with Michael Legge, when he snapped during one of my lengthier improvisations. Shouting, 'I can't take you not drinking any longer', he strode to the bar and brought back two cans of Red Stripe. He started supping on his, with cheerfully spiteful eyes. The can sat centre-stage on a stool. I berated Michael. I explained to the audience why I had given up, adding just a little fictional melodrama to make Michael seem a crueller man than he was.

There was a moment of silence.

When the tension felt just taut enough, I grabbed the can, tore it open and messily drank it down in one. In previous months I had found myself at fancy dinners, with fine wines on offer, and had turned each glass down. The humble tin of Red Stripe was my undoing, because there was an audience and I had to do whatever was the most funny or ridiculous thing. Similarly, I went back to stand-up because I realized that it allowed me to interact ridiculously with my existence, to show off and be the fool; and in the end that seemed the best thing to do.

As you may have noticed while reading this book, the only thing comedians take seriously is comedy – everything else is up for grabs. It is a way of giving your life shape and purpose. I think scrutinizing your life to find the punchlines is quite healthy.

Sometimes it may not be easy, but whose life is a walk in the park, apart from park-keepers? And even they have to pick up dog shit and used condoms some days, so even a walk in the park is no walk in the park, if you turn professional. Any problems that I may stub my toe on, as I stumble through life, would not vanish if I stopped doing stand-up. They might become more dilute and blunt, but I don't think the cure for the anxiety of existence is remaining in the quiet of the attic; it didn't do much for the first Mrs Rochester.

From the conversations I have had in bringing this book to fruition, I am also more certain than before that for those who are drawn to watch comedy, it can very often be the best way to deal with life, even if it does increase the sharpness of the highs and lows. It can be an effective way of realizing your fears and foibles. It can be a dime-store therapy session, although the waiting list is shorter and it's usually located near a bar.

It doesn't have to be such a deep connection, of course. All some people want or need is a ninety-minute distraction that makes them feel happier to be alive, and at the end they can giggle off to their pizza and Prosecco. That is pretty useful in itself. For others, though, it creates a connection that lasts much longer than the show. For a few, such as the young woman who realized where her life was going wrong as she watched Grace Petrie sing, it may offer a Damascene moment.

In the week before I wrote this, there were three incidents where momentarily I felt the strength and possibility of this connection. While I was signing books and chatting to the audience, a young woman timidly approached me. She wanted to tell me that this was the first gig she had been to since her husband had died. We spoke a little. I gave her a book. I gave her a hug and then worried all the way back on the train whether that had been the right thing to do.

A few days later, a chipper elderly man came up to me and told me his son had persuaded him to come to the gig, and he was glad that he had. His wife had died recently and it had not been easy, but he was having a lovely time.

The day afterwards, as I sat on the stage, pre-gig, chatting to the front row as I sorted things out, a man approached me to say that he had just been to his mother's funeral. 'So no pressure for you to make me laugh tonight.'

If I hadn't become a comedian, I would quite have liked to be a teacher or a vicar. But the priest role was hindered by my atheism, and the teacher role would have meant too many hours with too little recognition. Also, the advantage of stand-up over priesthood is that I don't have to offer salvation, and the advantage over being a teacher is that I neither have to be right nor constantly meet the deadlines of information delivery, set by charlatan education ministers.

I think the best moment of being a stand-up – or being a human of any hue – is when someone tells you that you made life a little easier; when the stranger comes up to you at the bar and says, 'I have been going through a rough patch, and I came along tonight uncertain what it was going to be, and I don't feel so bad now.'

On the first night of my Edinburgh Fringe return, I went to see Hannah Gadsby's *Nanette*, her swansong show explaining why she was giving up stand-up. It started as stand-up, but it then dug deeper into her life as a young woman and a lesbian, and into the abuse, both verbal and physical, that she has received over the years. She said she was giving up stand-up because she realized it was an abusive relationship. She released the tension of the audience, but the tension was only there because she set it up, she said as she explained the joke. And she revealed that often, when she has turned events of her life into a punchline, she has removed the real horror of the event to make it more palatable.

As the hour continued, the room moved from laughter to tension and uncertainty. How should we react? When I left the room at the end of the show, I didn't know whether to burst into tears or vomit, or just sit in stunned silence. It was one hell of a wake-up call, and a show that has not left me. Everyone I know who saw it was profoundly moved. It was a fierce reminder of what can be done with just a microphone, a pool of light and a passionate and carefully thought-through collection of ideas. It was also a reminder to all of the comedians in the room that comedy can have an intense, and ultimately benevolent, power of connection with another person.

'Only connect' is the oft-repeated quotation from E. M. Forster's *Howards End*. As fleeting as it may be, I feel lucky to have had those moments of audience connection. From my selfish point of view, it gives me a little purpose. It is good to know that I may have some use, beyond occasional punchlines. I have realized that this is why I have become a comedian: to connect with people and then to be accepted, even after behaving like a fool. A cynic (or an analyst!) might say this is a compulsive need for acceptance, a repeated pattern and an ongoing search, but maybe I just like showing off and making people laugh. It makes me feel good.

Notes

Introduction: Shouting at Strangers for Money

1. *Misery Loves Comedy*, directed by Kevin Pollak

1 Tell Me About Your Childhood

1. https://www.theguardian.com/culture/2017/sep/10/eddie-izzard-trying-to-get-mother-back-victoria-and-abdul
2. https://www.theguardian.com/culture/2017/aug/04/paul-chowdhry-people-write-this-abuse-to-me-and-ive-just-got-to-take-it
3. *The Comic Inquisition* by John Hind, p.102
4. *Tears of a Clown* documentary for BBC Radio 4, written and presented by the author
5. http://www.wow247.co.uk/2016/02/22/mark-steel-interview-adoption-is-comedy-nature-or-nurture/
6. *A Man Without a Country* by Kurt Vonnegut
7. *The Bitter Buddha*, 2012
8. Jerry Seinfeld, Netflix special, 2017
9. *Ex Machina*, 2015
10. http://www.bbc.co.uk/news/blogs-ouch-28564818
11. http://www.learningdisabilitytoday.co.uk/comedian-with-aspergers-syndrome-to-perform-show-at-edinburgh-festival

2 The Brain, Hardware and Chemistry

1. *When Henry Met Karl*, BBC documentary
2. http://blogs.scientificamerican.com/beautiful-minds/the-real-neuroscience-of-creativity/

3 Talking About Myself Behind My Back

1. https://www.theguardian.com/society/2014/jan/16/successful-comedians-display-symptoms-psychosis-study-says
2. http://www.mirror.co.uk/tv/tv-news/barry-humphries-alter-ego-dame-8521875
3. http://www.phon.ucl.ac.uk/project/audhall/
4. https://www.theatlantic.com/technology/archive/2014/12/what-its-like-to-hallucinate-voices/383607/

4 Daydreaming for a Purpose

1. Bram Gieben, *The Skinny*; http://www.theskinny.co.uk/music/interviews/choose-your-reality-alan-moore-unearthed

5 Is There a Real You?

1. *Counsels and Maxims* by Arthur Schopenhauer, vol. 2, chapter 23
2. https://aras.org/concordance/content/persona-and-anima
3. *The Shadow* by Christopher Perry, Society of Analytical Psychology
4. *The Middle Passage: From Misery to Meaning in Middle Life* by James Hollis (1993), p.94; https://appliedjung.com/the-middle-passage/

6 Getting to Know Your Inner Fraud

1. 'Feeling like a Fraud or an Impostor' by Peter Michaelson, 19 December 2016; http://www.whywesuffer.com/feeling-like-a-fraud-or-an-imposter/
2. 'From Spoofer to Movie Star' by Tina Fey, *The Independent*, 19 March 2010

7 Anxiety and the 'Imp of the Mind'

1. 'On Lying in Bed' from *Tremendous Trifles* by G. K. Chesterton
2. https://www.theguardian.com/stage/2017/may/02/i-was-dehumanised-lemn-sissay-on-hearing-his-harrowing-abuse-report-live-on-stage

8 Morals and Temptations

1. *Reflections on the Human Condition* by Eric Hoffer
2. 'Joan Rivers: The Lost Rolling Stone Interview', by Andy Greene, *Rolling Stone*, 4 September 2014; https://www.rollingstone.com/tv/features/joan-rivers-the-lost-rolling-stone-interview-20140904
3. *Guardian*, 24 February 2017
4. *Daily Telegraph*, 15 March 2018
5. *Guardian*, 5 June 2005
6. https://www.theguardian.com/commentisfree/2016/feb/17/when-i-first-heard-tim-minchins-song-about-cardinal-pell-i-laughed-then-i-started-crying

9 Death, Where Is Thy Punchline?

1. https://www.theguardian.com/stage/2016/jun/26/david-baddiel-my-family-observer-interview

2. https://www.theguardian.com/lifeandstyle/2011/oct/29/jason-cook-comedy-father
3. Kate Kellaway, *Guardian*, 22 January 2012
4. *A Short History of Decay* by E. M. Cioran
5. *Life is Worth Losing* by George Carlin, HBO Special